Regions of Refuge

GONZALO AGUIRRE BELTRAN

The Society for Applied Anthropology Monograph Series
MONOGRAPH NUMBER 12

Society for Applied Anthropology
Publishers of
Human Organization and
SfAA Monograph Series

This Monograph is Number 12 of a series published by the Society for Applied Anthropology, 1703 New Hampshire Avenue, N.W.,
Washington, DC 20009

CONTENTS

EDITOR'S PREFACE

The Society for Applied Anthropology is pleased to publish the first English translation of *Regions of Refuge*. Dr. Aguirre Beltran, author of this book, is a towering figure in Mexican anthropology and has had a profound impact on Mexican social policy. *Regions of Refuge* is a classic work in the history of anthropology.

Regions of Refuge offers a comprehensive theory of social change, explaining why certain areas of a developing country are changing slower than others. Aguirre Beltran's explanation relies on all the eclectic tools of the anthropologist. At times he is a demographer, ecologist, economist, physical anthropologist, political scientist and historian. He constructs an explanatory model of an underdeveloped region (Chiapas), thereby permitting other anthropologists to test their hypotheses and theories of underdevelopment. This book is also an introduction to the anthropology of Latin America. Perhaps most important, it takes a deliberately applied stance on what should be changed. Its perspective makes it a valuable comparative work to similar studies in other underdeveloped regions of the world.

Many scholars have aided in the preparation of this work. Dr. Nancy Modiano deserves our deepest appreciation for authenticating its final translation into English. Earlier translations were done under the direction of Dr. Johannes Wilbert of the Latin American Center at the University of California, Los Angeles. Additional translation assistance came from Dr. Peter Furst, now at SUNY-Albany. Drs. Theodore Downing, Richard A. Thompson, and James Officer of the University of Arizona reviewed the translated manuscript and made valuable editorial suggestions. Dr. Thomas Weaver of the University of Arizona and Barbara J. Walker of the University of Colorado have contributed immeasurably to the final version of the manuscript.

Deward E. Walker, Jr., Professor
Department of Anthropology
University of Colorado
Boulder, Colorado

INTRODUCTION

ROBERT C. HUNT

IT IS a great pleasure and honor for me to be asked to write an introduction to the English translation of *Regiones de Refugio*. I think the book is a very important one, and I have often assigned the book to my classes. This has been hampered by the frequent inability to obtain copies, and by its being in Spanish. I feel that the book is of relevance to more than Latin America, and this translation should afford the opportunity to achieve the distribution I believe the book deserves.

The major concern of this book is the evolution of regional society in Mestizo America. Beltrán has brilliantly and insightfully put together one ideal model of what regional social structure is, and how it is related to twentieth century pressure for modernization. He has woven together a coherent picture using the ideas of historians, economists, political scientists, and anthropologists with relevance and discrimination.

In Mestizo America one of the results of colonialism is a dual economy with a national sector dominated by the market and a local sector composed of isolated, closed corporate communities, often vastly different in culture, which are not dominated by the national money market system.

The local sectors are organized as refuge regions, which are areas isolated both physically and socially from the mainstream of the national society, containing fairly closed communities of peasants, most of whom can be described as Indians, having special relations with the exterior and whose internal characteristics differ markedly from those of other segments of the nation.

This regional, colonial situation, with its element of great rank difference between the two social segments, is dominated by what Beltrán calls the dominical process (*proceso dominical*). The dominical process, as defined by Beltrán, is the domination by a more technically and economically developed center of a less-developed periphery. This he sees as a causal feature in retarding the evolution of the Indian communities. He points out that there can be both internal and external resistance to cultural change; and in most past considerations of the stability of the hinterland, the operation of the dominical process has been ignored. Historically, the process has involved a metropolitan center that organized colonies for the benefit of the mother country by restricting the colonial manufacturing and industry and by depending on cheap labor to extract raw materials.

In order to comprehend events in these refuge regions, it is necessary to take into account three sectors in the population: the Indians, the local Mestizos or Ladinos (nationals resident in refuge regions), and the modernized nationals, including agents of national bureaucracies. Beltrán discusses the mutual relevance of these three, especially with respect to economic development. He sees the dominical process as inhibiting the evolution (modernization or economic development) of the village. He presents a framework for understanding this process, in the course of which he considers a few remedies to the problem. This study, therefore, represents a big step forward in our thinking about social structures in which the closed corporate community of typical anthropological interest forms only a small part.

A major rationale for the original subjugation of the native was race, and, in effect, a caste system based on phenotype was instituted and is still partially maintained, with the "Whites" in the metropolitan region and the natives in the hinterland. Despite great diversity among the natives, a dual society with a dominant and a subordinant group emerged from the early colonial system.

A question of major importance to anthropology raised by this book, is the nature and utility of the various interpretations of the regional structure (dual, multiple, plural, or internal colonialism). There has been considerable discussion in the literature concerning what kind of society Mestizo America is, especially where the position of the Indian in the hinterland is concerned. Anthropologists have seen refuge regions as caste organized; as a multiple society with plural cultures; as a quasi-caste, which is fitted as an enclave into the nationally defined class system; or as a class in a closed and tight mobility situation, with the Indians as a rural proletariat. Essentially, the argument revolves around two basic positions, one of which stresses the differences and the lack of articulation between the groups involved, while the other stresses similarities and integration. The arguments have not as yet been presented in such a way that the differences between them can be clearly resolved, and the disputes are probably not as important as the heated arguments might seem to indicate.

There is so much that we do not yet know that it is not possible to choose among them. First, the purposes for presenting such an analysis are not in all cases clear. For some, the basic goal is to foster the rapid integration of the Indians (the backward rural peoples) into the national system. Others have not committed themselves to this nor to any other visible purpose. Second, a codification (not to say clarification) of the variables within each model, and of the scope of each model, has to be worked out before any really meaningful comparison (and therefore decision about comparative validity) can be made. Some models stress economics, some values, others politics; some look out at the world from the Indian village, others stand in the Capitol and look out to the countryside; some stress pattern stability, others change; and some stress degree of integration of the various groups or categories, while others stress lack of integration.

Beltrán's position and his motivations are unusually clear in this regard. His major goal is to foster the integration of the Indian into the nation, and his book is directed to bureaucrats and politicians as much as to social scientists. To this end, he arrives at the surprising conclusion (at least to the Mesoamerican anthropologist) that refuge regions have a dual, not a plural social structure. Beltrán does not deny that there is great diversity between the Indian (and other) hinterland pueblos. But from the point of view of an economic system, there is great similarity among the systematic relationships of the nationals, the Ladinos, and the various Indian pueblos, and it is these similarities that he wishes to stress. And here his purpose is paramount, for any consideration of rapid evolution in these hinterlands must take into account the economic and political structures that the regional Ladinos control. From this point of view, then, it is perfectly sensible, and indeed probably valid, to analyze these hinterlands in terms of a dual structure. Other analyses are possible, but their utility will be a function of the purposes of the analyst. Judging the comparative utility, then, must await statements of purpose.

It is fairly obvious where we go from here as scientists. We need empirical studies of two sorts: areal and diachronic. One of these lies in our detailed understanding of the variety of responses to the general system in a given region. Mestizos who dominate the regional social structure should no longer be ignored and the symbiosis between Indians and local Mestizos should be looked at carefully. Having studied members of small communities in the past is no justification for so confining future efforts. The field worker will have to get data on the regional operation of national and international commodity markets. Interdisciplinary cooperation with economists, sociologists, and historians is certainly indicated, not only in field research but in graduate training. We have long talked about the necessity of expanding the focus of our research interests to wider forms of sociocultural integration. It is time we produced research results as well as pious programmatic statements. This is not to deny the need for, or to play down, the study of the internal structure of Indian communities. Here, too, the need is great and continuing. But we are, relatively speaking, much farther along with these studies than we are with some of the others.

The need for historical studies of regional social structure is also acute. If we take for granted that a major anthropological concern in Mestizo America is the evolution of the social structure in which the Indian is embedded (the most modern phase of which is discussed as modernization and economic development), then the need for historical studies of these phenomena becomes clear. It is possible, at least in many areas of Mesoamerica, to obtain good data on many realms of life back to the middle of the sixteenth century. These data have either been ignored or handled in only the most cursory fashion. No study of the evolutionary development of these refuge regions will be reasonable without a generous dose of history. I would further argue that it is the responsibility of the anthropologist to do this work, and not that of of the historian. Few historians will be willing to devote any significant amount of work to such backward areas of the world. But more importantly, the anthropologist knows with much greater precision what kinds of questions he wants answers to. We are arguing in effect that it is not only possible, but highly desirable, for anthropologists to work in a context of great time depth. We should, wherever possible, adopt the position that our job is to analyze social structures in time, and for the kind of time I am talking about, real history is essential. But further, this is historical research that the anthropologist not only can, but should, do himself. Synchronic comparisons are perhaps unavoidable given the paucity of historical data in the world. But where the data exist and are readily available both physically and linguistically, the anthropologist should seriously consider diachronic study.

Aguirre Beltrán has shown in this book that he can unite broad-ranging and perceptive reading with extensive practical experience with a change-oriented bureaucracy concerned with the problems of refuge regions, to produce a sensitive and profound model of the world he has been coping with. It is often said that science and technology flourish and respond especially in times of great crisis for the society. One wonders about the extent to which that is true for social science. If this book is representative, then one is tempted to conclude that the impact of practical problems can be salutary indeed.

AUTHOR'S INTRODUCTION

ECONOMIC DEVELOPMENT has been a source of continuing concern for economists during the present century, both for its theoretical aspects and its practical implications. Much evidence has been accumulated to substantiate the various interpretations proposed by scholars to explain the phenomenon of industrialization; all for the purpose of making more accurate predictions. In the European countries that suffered major devastation during the last war, a critical situation existed which was ultimately alleviated through procedures currently used by Western economic theorists. The resurgence of postwar Europe was based on the rational application of orthodox economic concepts which, during the preceding century, had been derived from the Industrial Revolution.

The establishment of the United Nations and the ideological movement which called attention to the fate of the underdeveloped countries which constitute the Third World led to the belief that the Western model of development was a good example to follow. The very low levels of revenues in Third World countries could be raised by retracing the steps of European countries several decades earlier. The first attempts of those who followed this route made it clear that the Western model would not serve everywhere. Economic historians showed that the transition by Europeans to an industrialized economy had occurred under special conditions which could be recreated only with great difficulty. The population explosion in Third World countries introduced a variable which had carried little weight at the time when Western countries began industrializing; the demographic variable totally changed the terms of the equation.

It was then noted that this disadvantage could be partially offset by the vast store of techniques and skills discovered in European countries, which were put freely at the disposal of the underdeveloped countries. The technologically advanced countries attained these techniques and knowledge through centuries of sustained effort; considerable energy had been required to test and retest them. Today the benefits of these techniques and skills are shown through their successful application. There is no need to prove them. They are ready for immediate utilization by the peoples who arrived late at the banquet of progress.

Thus stated, the problem was reduced to offering backward countries the techniques and skills which would allow them to establish the bases for growth and development. Acting on such assumptions, some colonial powers implemented welfare and improvement programs aimed at modernizing the economy of the populations under their control. Modern forms of education, health, transportation, credit, organization, and discipline were put at the disposal of the natives, so that they could begin the adventure of their own development. Unfortunately such programs failed. The people under control took no interest in the innovations proposed, preferring to continue their precarious existence with the protection of traditional wisdom and customs.

The colonial experience made clear the need for ensuring the active participation of the population in all improvement programs, participation which is difficult to obtain with peoples undergoing the destructive effects of domination. Incentives that lead to creativity and to the efforts required for development are found only in a favorable environment, an environment which allows expectations of well-being that the colonial situation does not offer. The roles of master and subordinate established by the social structure place the foreign population on top and the native population at the lowest level of the hierarchy. The existence of such roles is not conducive to securing the necessary cooperation between government and people. Without such cooperation, the success of any development program is ephemeral.

Resistance by the native population against the improvement programs implemented by colonial policy forced the recognition of the existence of a dual social structure, resulting directly from the process of domination. In a single country, living side by side, were two societies founded on different principles and economic practices: (1) the modern society, culturally and industrially complex, represented by the foreign metropolitan population and its descendents, who constituted the governing elite; (2) the traditional or archaic society, represented by the indigenous peoples, who formed the dominated mass. Between the two societies was such a large social and cultural void that the forces necessary to bridge it would have cost more than the metropolis was ever disposed to spend.

The concepts and methods of the industrial economy, based on capitalist principles, were inapplicable in traditional societies lacking a market economy; they could not regulate all the ingredients of production, including land and labor. The latter two, in indigenous communities, are not considered merchandise and therefore are not subject to the rules of price formation nor to the integrative principles of marketing. Forms of work cooperation are based on reciprocity and redistribution, integrative principles which appear deceptively favorable as a basis for building modern cooperatives, but which actually run counter to the norms on which modern capitalism is based.

Proof of the existence of a dual structure in colonial countries led economic planners to follow the line of least resistance, that is, to concern themselves with the growth of the society's modern sector, leaving the traditional or archaic sector to resolve its own problems. Obviously planners preferred to busy themselves with solving those problems with which they were familiar, using the concepts and practices of Western economic theory which they felt themselves especially able to handle. They left out of their development plans the preindustrial sectors whose economic behavior, guided by little understood principles, was unpredictable and inexplicable in terms of the concepts evolved by Western science.

As an unavoidable consequence, economic planners increased the gap separating the society's modern and archaic sectors without obtaining the harmonious growth which could serve as a basis for sustained development. The broadening of the ecomonic, social, and cultural distance dividing the two sectors made the false and untenable nature of the colonial situation more obvious, and led to conflicts which world opinion demanded be solved.

The situation thus described is not limited to colonial nations. It includes many of the independent countries that underwent the colonial experience in the past and today make up the Third World. These countries also suffer the incongruities of a dual society and even more than colonial countries urgently need the theory and methods especially designed to resolve their problems. Today such theory and methods can be found in the conceptual complex called community development.

Development economists like to maintain that Western theory has general application, whatever the phenomena analyzed, and that there is no need for an economic theory especially designed for underdeveloped countries. They are not right. We have noted how economic planners, faced with the problems of a dual society, leave the preindustrial sectors to their own fate in order to dedicate all their efforts and resources to development of the country's modern sectors. The preindustrial sectors are composed especially of the rural population with traditional culture, among whom are found the increasingly impoverished and exploited Indians.

The conflict emerging from the confrontation between the opposing sectors of the dual society necessitates a body of theory to deal with the different phases observed in the process. These phases are unique for each developing country. Whatever phase of the conflict is visible in a given country differs from that of other countries because the variables which make up the economic structures also differ. This forces each country to seek its own concepts and methods which, while they produce economic improvement, support the integration of the modern and traditional sectors of the society. The consolidation of the country as a nation, that is, its passage from foreign dependence to creativity and development, rests upon this.

Among the Latin American countries with dual social structures, Mexico was the first to undertake a social revolution that created the incentives and motives indispensable for formulating theories and practices for the development of the traditional population. These ideas and patterns of action were born individually rather than as a unified system; they emerged here and there, wherever governmental activity experimented with new forms of dealing with people and their long-standing problems. The first attempt at the conceptualization and application of a theory of community development was carried out during the initial years of the revolutionary movement. It took place in an Indian community, the site of an old civilization; this community's improvement and integration into the national society were attempted through what was called integral action, taking into consideration the biological, psychological, social, economic, and cultural totality of the region.

A second great impulse came from the creation of a teaching system aimed at bringing literacy to a rural, preliterate population. Common teaching methods were adapted to the rural milieu; then a type of teacher evolved specifically intended for this situation. This was a teacher with little technical capacity, but with sufficient initiative to promote development in the community in which he exercised his manifold functions. These included, beyond teaching people to read, agricultural improvement, economic organization, public health, recreation, and above all, the reinterpretation of modern ideas in the traditional molds so that the change from the old to the new could be achieved without the serious disorganization of personality and structure that lead to anomie. The theory and practice of Indian education paralleled the concepts and practices of rural education.

A third important contribution was made by the agrarian reform which put land that the farmers had cultivated into their own hands, using a concept of property new to the Western world, and termed the *ejido.*[1] Land, previously concentrated in a few hands, was distributed, granting status in the society to the dispossessed farmers as well as giving them a share in the exercise of the power previously retained by the great landowners. The extension of credit to farmers introduced a powerful force for renewal into communities with subsistence economies; their reorganization into cooperatives made it possible to attempt new structural arrangements, a step forward in the integration of those populations into the national society.

In addition, public health authorities introduced the ideas and practices of scientific medicine, in contrast to traditional methods, into the rural setting. The purposes of the latter are not limited only to resolve anxieties resulting from illness, but also to function as highly esteemed means of social control which precludes the substitution of one type of medicine for the other. This occurs despite the advantages of scientific medicine in the restoration of biological health. The close connection between medicine and other important aspects of culture makes it obvious that implementation of unilateral programs in Indian communities is ineffective. It is practically impossible to abstract one aspect of the culture from its social context. For health programs to be successful, it is necessary that they be included within wider programs of development.

A combination of programs implemented unilaterally within a single body of coherent and integrated action was attempted by applied anthropology, which provisionally took charge of regional populations. Later it became the cardinal thesis of the cultural missions, which consisted of teams of professionals acting in conjunction in the communities where they worked. These cultural missions initially operated in rural areas, both Indian and non-Indian. The strength of the thesis on which they were based made possible their establishment in the urban milieu of the big cities which, acting as magnets for the rural population, receive large contingents of migrants from the traditional sector of society.

The Mexican experience in community development—derived from both unilateral implementation of action and from an understanding of the situation as a whole—permitted scientists specializing in the application of the social sciences to formulate a unified body of ideas and practices called integral action, the theory which underlay the agencies for improvement and integration known as "coordinating centers." In terms of conception and mode of operation, the coordinating centers are the Mexican version of community development projects in the underdeveloped regions of a country. We have called these regions regions of refuge because within their bounds the hereditary structure of colonial times and the archaic, clearly preindustrial culture, have found shelter from the forces of modern civilization.

Elsewhere and on other occasions we have fully expounded the theory of the coordinating centers and the bases of community development in the regions of refuge.[2] In our work *El Proceso de Aculturación* (1957) we made a detailed analysis of the doctrine and methods of community development, the philosophy of the programs, the means employed, the ends pursued, and the motivations and incentives that lead to change. In the present work we wish to complement what has been said previously by focusing on the problems of contact and change in a setting other than the purely cultural. Here we shall put the accent decidedly upon social structure and the processes of integration. We shall take advantage of this opportunity to make marginal comments on the Mexican interpretation of community development theory and on the possibility of its generalization to other dual-structured Latin American countries in the process of development.

Experts from the United Nations have given this definition:

> The expression community development has been incorporated into international use to designate those processes by virtue of which the efforts of a population are added to those of their government to improve the economic, social, and cultural conditions of communities, to integrate these into the life of the country and to permit them to fully contribute to national progress. Two essential elements, therefore, enter into this complex of processes: the participation of the population itself in improving its standard of living, depending on its own initiative as much as possible; and the providing of technical and other services so as to stimulate self help and mutual assistance, and to increase their effectiveness.

The definition also proposes two important goals, improvement and integration, and proposes an end to development action, which is to be the moment when a community has achieved the preconditions or prerequisites that will permit it henceforth to contribute fully to the progress of the nation.

The action implemented by the coordinating centers, as well as their doctrine and methods, ends which they seek, and the limits on their implementation, all concur totally with the definition formulated by the specialized agencies of the United Nations. It is nonetheless of interest to note that work in indigenous communities puts a particular emphasis on the attainment of one of the goals mentioned, namely integration. This emphasis in development programs is the result of the existence of a dual structure, a fact which influences the entire situation. Indigenous populations are not merely underdeveloped farmers; they are, essentially, ethnic groups of a different culture which have great internal cohesion and which present great resistance to integration when the dominant sector seeks to preserve the mechanisms of domination that keep the Indians in obviously subordinate positions.

The ethnic heterogeneity of the Latin American countries included in what has been called Mestizo America is incontrovertible. An important part of the national population, the indigenous sector, is made up of a variegated mixture of self-sufficient and self-contained communities, each of which has a different form of speech from that of the neighboring community, whether this is a separate language or simply a dialectical variation. Whatever the form, a language and a community culture different from the national ones represent barriers to integration which can be overcome only by the methods and techniques gradually being evolved by applied anthropology.

The needs of integration have led to the use of change agents known as "cultural promoters." With unforeseen good fortune, the name and function became widespread immediately, through programs similar to those implemented by coordinating centers in the sister countries of Central and South America. These promoters, bilingual Indians from the communities where they work, are trained in professional skills in order to act as auxiliaries to high level technical staffs. Upon their shoulders falls the responsibility for translating proposed innovations in education, health, agriculture, livestock breeding, business organization, legal defense, urbanization, and recreation in terms of the community's cultural values. Internally induced change favors evolution of the culture and the opening of the closed communities, both essential for integration into the national culture and society.

The use of cultural promoters in community development programs, furthermore, establishes a necessary balance which could not be obtained otherwise. The promoter is a person trained in the use and manipulation of two cultures, his own and the national one; nonetheless, his original culture is the indigenous one and he has been conditioned to it by the early process of enculturation. The high level technician, on the contrary, belongs to a highly specialized industrial culture which often abstracts the content of his discipline from its social context and then proceeds to introduce it into the indigenous community. For the promoter, whatever has to do with economics, education, or health is unintelligible outside its context; even economic transactions ruled by integrative marketing principles are conceived by him within a matrix of social relations. Interaction between the specialized function of the technician and the promoter's socialized function establishes equilibrium that favors innovation.

At the regional level, coordination of the many aspects of the overall program helps give unity and social content to simultaneously implemented activities. Coordination at the national level permits, in turn, articulation of regional programs within national development plans, and eases the transfer of responsibility for development when programs located in the regions of refuge have achieved their goals. Then the specialized organisms of public administration take over the educational, health, or economic functions which normally fall to them, and use the normal channels and procedures to strengthen improvement and integration from the points where the community development programs have left them.

We should devote a final paragraph to urban community development simply to inform the reader that in Mexico we still have not constructed a theory and body of practice adapted to our needs, similar to the one formulated here for rural populations. This lack is due, no doubt, to the fact that the problems of urbanization have only recently entered the critical phase; they derive from the recent population explosion in Latin America. Attempts have been made, using the theory of cultural missions or the concepts of rural social welfare, to apply them to the urban situation. However, there is still an undeniable, pressing need for theory and methods especially designed to analyze and resolve the problems of urban poverty belts. Countries moving toward development confront increasing difficulties in regulating the magnetic attraction exerted upon the rural population by industrial growth centers, and they lack a unified and coherent doctrine for offering the migrants living standards—income, housing, education, and health—consistent with the expectations of modern life.

NOTES

1. The *ejido* is a system of communal farmland ownership. There are several different forms of land use (i.e., cooperative, individual) but in all cases the community, rather than the individual, holds ultimate title.

2. See Beltrán (1955, 1963, 1966) for discussions of The Theory of Coordinating Centers.

Chapter 1

THE PROCESS OF DOMINATION

WHEN ANY SCIENTIFIC discipline precisely identifies the phenomena operating within the area of its particular interest, it creates a vocabulary which assigns a special meaning to each term and gives it a function as a fundamental research tool. Not infrequently a single phenomenon, viewed from the conceptual frameworks of related disciplines, is designated differently, showing different focuses or shades of analysis. These designations generally lead to an enrichment of interpretation; less often, they obscure it.

For this reason it is appropriate at the outset to define the meaning we give to words, in order to avoid later confusion. One of the causal factors in the evolution of cultures and of the societies which contain them is represented by the control exercised by technologically and economically more advanced groups over others with less complex forms of life and organization. The play of forces which makes domination possible and the mechanisms put into effect to maintain it are what we call *the process of domination*.

We shall now try to define the effect on and importance to cultural evolution of two well-defined, contradictory categories, namely, (1) forces favoring change, which originate in innovations generated within the group itself through invention and discovery, or outside the group, through cultural borrowing; and (2) forces opposing change, which arise from resistance within the group itself, resulting from cultural conditioning, or outside the group as a consequence of outside control, authority, subjection, and domination. With these clarifications, we can attempt to examine the process of domination and its implications, using well defined terms.

CULTURAL CHANGE. One of the few constants in human existence is cultural change. No living culture is static, however great its isolation, however scant its population, however simple its technology. Cultural changes may be so slow as to be miniscule, giving the illusion of stagnation even when seen from an historical perspective; nonetheless, from one generation to another every culture does evolve and a scrupulous study of its rules of conduct always shows many modifications which are not apparent to the naïve. The simplest and most conservative cultures of the continent, appearing to exist unaltered since the discovery of America, are typified by the life styles of the jungle Indians who roam the hostile tropics. Ethnographic research, nevertheless, has shown a considerable amount of cultural borrowing, which continually modifies many different aspects of those cultures.[1]

In contrast, other cultures change rapidly and are modified from one generation to the next to such an extent that adaptation to what is new requires a psychological attitude receptive to change. Modern culture in highly developed countries is an example of accelerated change. It should be noted, however, that change does not encompass all the aspects of a culture; rather it is often limited to such aspects as technology, with inventions and discoveries constantly tending to perfect the culture's equipment for dealing with environmental forces. In other aspects, such as social and political organization, ideology and ethics, changes are lamentably slow.

The speed with which cultural change takes place has taken on an unusual importance in our time, because of the great distance separating the technological and economic development of highly industrialized countries from that of colonial or semicolonial peoples. In a world made continually smaller by the growth and speed of communications, differences in development generate maladjustment and provoke imbalances in human life of such magnitude that they cannot be ignored. Under the weight of such pressures and responsibilities, social scientists have felt obliged to examine with all haste those forces which advance and those which hinder development. The study of cultural change has thus become one of the most important and practical tasks of anthropology.[2]

Observation has been made of preliterate peoples before their culture attained its present state of technical development, and human societies have been discovered, such as those in America, which had remained isolated during a considerable part of their evolution, and which nonetheless, produced extremely elaborate life styles. Their achievements in the sciences, in the arts, and in political and social organization, merit their being called high cultures—such as the Maya, the Toltec, the Inca, and others. It was thought for a time that in the growth and fulfillment of human groups, internally generated change was the most important factor in cultural evolution. The evolutionists of the past century used, in fact, the principle of the psychic unity of man to explain both the similarity of beliefs and institutions among different peoples, and the differences between peoples, as distinct stages of culture through which less advanced societies had to pass in order to reach the highest level of civilization.

INVENTION AND DISCOVERY. Many criticisms can be made of the evolutionist theory of the last century, but it is undeniable that its formulation clarified the continuity of culture, the constancy of change, and the existence of internal mechanisms for development. Basically those mechanisms emerged from the process of invention so deeply rooted in human nature. Anthropology understands invention as not only the deliberate creation of a radically new device, machine, or some other object of material culture, but also as new concepts, ideas, or schemes of social, political, or religious organization, and the new economic systems that play such an important role in historical development. The process of invention acts upon the entire culture and not only upon its visible elements.[3]

Once the fundamental methods have been developed, any human society may begin producing an incessant flow of inventions that make the culture increasingly complex. For the most part, however, inventions do not produce dramatic changes in the life of a people; cultural evolution is based on small daily changes, the result of many individual contributions. By distinguishing between great and small changes we can better understand the role of invention in cultural development; sometimes it produces a basic innovation and other times simple changes in the details of accepted practices. The sum total of these large and small changes gives the process of invention its dimension. It allows one to see, in the totality of any culture, the importance of internally generated changes as compared to changes acquired through borrowing.

From time to time people find themselves subjected to violent fluctuations resulting in sudden cultural changes. This phenomenon comes about when a severe disorganization brings with it a nativist, restorative movement as a heroic remedy. Wallace calls it the process of revitalization and says it is created through the deliberate and organized attempts by members of an ethnic group to construct a more satisfactory culture through rapid acceptance of multiple innovations. Generally, rapid fruition of inventions comes about when the group finds itself in an obvious position of subordination and inferiority with respect to a dominant society. When the messianic movement endangers the position of superiority established by the elite, physical coercion halts or slows the pace of innovation (Wallace 1963: 143-56).

But even without the unexpected assistance of the revitalization process, the process of invention, with its cumulative character, explains how tribal peoples with a rudimentary economy—among them the Mesoamericans—could achieve surprisingly high levels of culture in a relatively short period of time. These levels were attained when a system of counting, based on a positional ordering of values which involved the concept and use of the mathematical quantity zero, was created, advancing Mesoamerica a thousand years to the level of Hindu civilization, and two thousand years ahead of mathematics in Western Europe with its more highly developed technology and economy.[4]

There is no doubt that, in order to achieve such notable advances, the Mesoamerican peoples did not rely exclusively on their own inventive faculty; rather, in their evolution towards more complex cultural forms they exchanged discoveries and inventions, borrowing many cultural elements. The explosive rise of the Aztec people, whom the Europeans found as the dominant group in Mesoamerica at the time of conquest, cannot be understood otherwise. In the period of a few centuries, these people moved from the simple organization of a seminomadic tribe to become the nucleus of a powerful confederation, possessing a culture that was extremely elaborate and efficient in many respects. The surprising rise of the Aztec people can only be explained on the basis of their borrowing of cultural elements from the peoples who preceded them in the hegemony and with whom they were in contact. The rise of the Inca people was similar. Lévi-Strauss states that in both cases there was a brief coalition of very different cultures, some of which were very old and themselves heterogeneous.[5] In effect, despite its enormous importance, the process of invention alone is not sufficient to explain the evolution of a culture.

CULTURAL BORROWING. Borrowing between culturally related peoples is never as obvious as that which takes place between peoples whose life styles differ considerably. At its inception, the study of the transmission of elements from one culture to another was largely limited to tracing the diffusion of traits or combinations of traits among neighboring tribes with simple cultures who occupied clearly defined geographical areas. The purpose of the research was to reconstruct the cultural history of peoples who lacked written history and thus could not rely on any documentation other than that supplied by observation of their ways of life.

It was soon seen that analysis of the process of cultural transmission through diffusion among neighboring tribes was less important than studies of the mechanisms by which Western culture, technically and economically more developed, transmitted its own cultural elements to peoples of simpler cultures and in turn received foreign cultural elements. This process of reciprocal modification of cultural patterns was called acculturation.

Elsewhere (Beltrán 1957) we defined acculturation as the process of change which emerges from contact between groups with different cultures and is characterized by the continuous conflict between opposing life styles tending toward total identity with each other. This is seen, objectively, at various levels of opposition. The study of contact between Western European culture as represented by the Spanish, and American indigenous cultures as represented by the Aztec, allows comparison of the past with the present, the compulsive or voluntary character of the borrowing, group or individual participation in the interchange, the continuity or intermittence of contacts, and the deliberate inducement of change or its spontaneous occurrence. These opposing forces gave rise to what we could well call the Mexican version of western culture and, by extension, the Indo-Ladino version which is present at various levels of contradiction in the Mesoamerican countries.

This is not the moment to list the characteristics of the different aspects of Indo-Ladino culture in Mestizo America,[6] but it is indeed suitable to note that the process of acculturation continues to work vigorously in favor of the continuity of the groups which are direct descendents of the original populations that made contact: Indians and Ladinos. This trend continues despite the fact that biological mixing and the fusion of conflicting cultures gave birth to a majority population of mixed ancestry and to a culture which, based on the interpenetration of its antagonistic elements and the reinterpretation of its opposing elements, has evolved into a new culture, different from the ones from which it arose. The distinctive profile and character of Indo-Ladino culture was caused by the process of acculturation, and was reinforced by invention.

CULTURAL STABILITY. In spite of 450 years of contact, the persistence of representatives of the original antagonistic groups is one of the significant features of Mestizo America, as well as one of the most powerful motivations for governmental action to integrate them into national societies forged by historical development. However, such persistence is also an objective manifestation of the forces opposing invention, acculturation, and consequently, cultural evolution. These forces are composed of the mechanisms for stability and continuity, without which invention and acculturation would lack meaning.

The economic development of European and North American cultures and the colonial domination that they held over underdeveloped peoples until a few years ago favored coerced or spontaneous acceptance of the life styles of industrial culture and particularly of its technological products. Colonial and semicolonial peoples never accepted such cultural traits uncritically, even when the new was obviously superior to the old. They responded to innovation on the basis of traditional experience, accepting that which could be reinterpreted and integrated into their own cultural patterns, and rejecting that which they took to be inoperative or dangerous to the stability and continuity of their way of life.

Their selective acceptance of cultural traits made preliterate peoples appear hostile and impervious to change, and their position of exploitation and submission was rationalized and ascribed to their stubborn traditionalism. In reality, stabilizing forces are not only generated by the culture under siege but also, and to a large degree, by the dominating culture. In effect, two categories of opposing forces enter into play: (1) those from within the culture, represented by the process of enculturation, and (2) those exercised from without the consequences of the process of domination.

Herskovits defines enculturation as the process by which the individual assimilates the traditions of his group and conducts himself in conformity with them (1945:491). He distinguishes two contrasting stages: one in childhood and one at the adult level. During the first, the person is conditioned by the basic patterns of his culture. He learns to handle the symbols of the language, accepted forms of behavior, recognized values, and the institutions to which he should adapt. All this he assimilates subconsciously, so that adhesion to his own group's life ways is firmly and solidly established. During the second stage, enculturation operates at a conscious level. What is offered to an individual may be accepted or rejected; he selects critically among the alternatives presented.

The first conditioning level of enculturation produces the mechanisms that give each culture its stability. This level spares the culture from disorganization even in periods of violently rapid change. The second or conscious level of enculturation opens the doors to change and reconditioning. This latter aspect of enculturation, balancing the first, prevents a people from being impervious to evolution, however simple and isolated they may appear. Resistance to change, however, cannot be explained by internally generated forces if these are not reinforced from without. External pressures are brought into play by the process of domination; its modes of action will be the object of careful analysis and clarification.

COLONIALISM. The processes of invention and acculturation and their opposites, those of enculturation and domination, have not been studied to the same degree. While the first three phenomena inspired numerous examinations and ample studies, the domination process has merited scant consideration or has been completely avoided in anthropological research. The reason for this is in part that cultural anthropology channels its interests toward the interpretation of cultural, rather than social phenomena, and the domination process focuses on the latter.

When confronting the problems of ethnic minorities and the nature of interracial relations, North American anthropologists have reverted to an analysis of the domination process from the angle of prejudice, of rivalries, and hatred among groups. They believed the process originated in multiple causes, adding economic and social factors to those of fear, aggression, and sexual conflicts. These studies, while stimulating and illustrative, abstract the psychological, educational, economic, or legal aspects of the process, and thus give a partial picture of the problem. Had they considered it in its entirety, they would have been forced to attack the political implications, and in doing so they would have entered into an arena in which scientists feel particularly uncomfortable.

This explains why those same anthropologists in their ethnographic descriptions of Indian communities, limit their discussions of the political aspects of the cultures under examination to regional problems. They handle the subject with kid gloves. It is obvious, therefore, that when they study communities subjected to colonial domination they avoid references to the phenomenon of domination and as far as possible, extrapolate the communities from their broader context and present them as isolated entities. This focus is comfortable because it avoids conflicts with colonial powers but at the same time it abstracts a fundamental part of reality.

In Europe, especially in countries with a long colonial history or in those now engaged in imperialism, the position of anthropologists is particularly delicate, since the neutrality of their scientific role is in constant conflict with their loyalties as citizens of a metropolis;[7] in those countries anthropology is inevitably tied to the colonial administration.[8]

Of course, there are exceptions to the rule; many of them arose during the ominous years of the struggle against Nazism. Some anthropologists have made unbiased analyses of the process of domination in cases where its operating mechanisms are obvious, such as in colonial countries and in the problems of minorities. In the majority of Latin American countries the colonial experience came to an end after the early years of the nineteenth century. Legal termination of foreign domination, however, did not dissolve the contradictions resulting from three centuries of conditioning and a situation of super- vs. subordination. The social structure of those countries is completely saturated with the remains of the colonial past; this explains the present underdevelopment of their populations. A brief reference to that history is necessary in order to see the process in its global context.

The cardinal feature of the colonization of America is the fact that its implementation and development were made according to the needs of the mother country and not to those of the Indian population. The structure of subordinate ethnic groups was violently changed in order that they serve as *instruments* of the metropolis.[9] The Indian elite was forced to collaborate and the mechanisms that were used to force recruitment of manual labor and the consequent migratory movements were developed in response to the needs of the metropolitan economy. As an inevitable result of this policy, some ethnic groups adapted to colonial life as serfs, while others, living far from the centers of exploitation in regions made hostile by climate or topography, where movements of men and goods were most difficult, resisted.

Colonized peoples have a dual history, their own and that of European domination, and this duality influenced the way in which colonialism developed.[10] The dominant group was composed of various agents–administrators, settlers, and missionaries–who brought different orientations to their respective activities. Some put major emphasis on political, others on economic, and the last on ideological domination, but all cooperated in establishing a sovereignty that lasted for centuries. The process of domination thus established gradually created operating mechanisms, perfecting them so as to reinforce sovereignty without resorting to physical coercion except in unusual cases.

METHODS OF DOMINATION. The methods to be analyzed in the contemporary colonial context are the same as those operative in the past, with variations caused by time, place, and the prevailing state of technical progress (Kennedy 1945). They are as follows:

First, *racial segregation* sanctioned by law, which erects a barrier–commonly called a color bar–aimed at separating foreigners from natives and mixed peoples. The total social, economic, and political structure of the colonial system is based on this mechanism. It leads to the creation of a dual society, cut horizontally by skin color, which places the dominant group in the upper stratum and the subject masses in the lower one. Due to segregation, colonial society is a society of castes, with vertical movement impeded from caste to caste. Often the castes are separated spatially, the dominant group in the seignorial city, and the natives in the hinterland. Relations between the groups are oriented by constellations of superiority-inferiority or super- and subordination. The people of these groups are not judged on the basis of individual value or skill, but as undifferentiated members of aggregations above or below the color bar.

Furnivall (1939:446) maintains that the typical characteristic of the colonial situation is the existence of a plural society. In a certain sense every society is plural, given that it contains dissimilar elements with divergent interests (Gould & Kolb 1964). Furnivall, however, referred to societies with diverse social groups which, although forming a political unit, live side by side without mixing. In these societies reaction to exploitation takes the form of an exacerbated nationalism which forces a confrontation between the groups, thus aggravating the instability of the entire society. According to Furnivall, this obliges an outside force–a colonial power–to become the agent capable of giving cohesion and unity to the plural society. In Mestizo America there are no such plural societies.

Instead, there are diverse cultural groups, ethnic groups which do not speak the same language, and which have differing forms of livelihood, dress, housing, gods, and traditions. But this diversity or cultural pluralism does not necessarily imply the existence of plural societies. The only kind of society established is a stratified one, composed of the dominant group of metropolitan origin, and the dominated or colonized group. Balandier notes correctly that in the colonial situation the phenomenon of pluralism is not important; what is essential is the racial basis for the division of groups, their fundamental heterogeneity, the antagonistic relations, and the obligation to coexist within the limits of a single political framework, which is to say that the important factor is the process of domination.[11]

Segregation is rooted in a preconception which no longer serves as a basis for action—however, for reasons other than that it lacks a scientific foundation. That preconception is the innate superiority of the White over the Indian.[12] This basic principle of colonial ideology, sometimes phrased in religious terms, sometimes in economic or cultural terms, has been the basis for domination from the beginning of European expansion until recently. Decolonization, provoked by the last world war, placed colonial powers in the uncomfortable position of being unable to continue justifying themselves along racial lines. Belief in the innate inferiority of races of color, nevertheless, is a prejudice that is far from eradicated.

Secondly, *political control* is retained by the dominant group, which leaves the masses without participation in government. Administration of the colony is directed from the mother country; the foreign group, representing the metropolis, occupies and profits from key positions. Even when in some colonies or regions within colonies, the natives maintain a separate political apparatus and appear to constitute a small local aristocracy forming an indirect government, this apparatus is only a facade.[13] Direct or indirect control of the country in terms of internal as well as external relations denotes an administrative system encrusted on the very heart of the colonized group; that is, the establishment of a relationship of dominance and submission.

Political domination accompanies the cultural domination that oppresses native cultures and retards their development. Political control entails a doctrine or policy that may be oriented towards incorporating indigenous people into the colonial culture to function as proletarians in a class society, or it may be aimed at leaving them in the underdevelopment of their autochthonous state—in an apparent posture of respect for subordinate cultures—enabling them to coexist in a caste society.

Political subjugation is rationalized by the theory that the natives are incapable of governing themselves and would fall into the hands of dictators if self-determination were permitted. But nothing is done to train them in political action and when agitators appear they are incarcerated. Such policies entail an increase in political rights for the dominant group, at the cost of the prerogatives that the natives should enjoy.

Thirdly, *economic dependence* reduces the indigenous population to the condition of a useful instrument. The colonial area is exploited as the hinterland of the metropolis for the production of primary materials; these are exported for processing to the mother or to other Western countries. The dependent areas are relegated to a nonindustrial economy where agricultural or mining activities predominate. Industrialization is reserved for Europe. The natives have no participation in the direction or ownership of large-scale exploitative enterprises, nor in importation. They can work only in subsistence activities or as untrained salaried workers in foreign-owned businesses.

Colonial populations are typically agricultural; when they enter the urban sector they do so as unskilled laborers or servants. There is an enormous discrepancy between the salaries of White and native residents. There does not exist, as in the metropolis, a middle or intermediate class between the elite and the masses. The occupational barriers exist at the caste level and there is no economic ladder for the natives. The earnings of foreigners are based fundamentally on cheap Indian labor.

In the colonial area technical facilities are mediocre; roads and other means of communication, built with forced labor, are aimed at serving the interests of foreign companies and merchants.[14] Taxes force the native to seek hard cash, putting him at the mercy of the monopolizers of his products. The recruitment of manual labor for haciendas and plantations fixes salaries and working conditions and sets a pattern for circulation of men and merchandise, giving every advantage to the colonial exploiters. To these factors is added the expropriation of agrarian property and the formation of a landowning bourgeoisie in whose hands the greater portion of good, arable land is concentrated. Administrative action is directed toward building the infrastructure for an exploited colony.

Economic subordination is supported by the rationalization that the natives are incompetent to run the system of production and distribution even in their own house. Boeke (1953:4) even maintained the existence of a dual economy with different systems for natives and Europeans; the traditional Indian subsistence economy, and the modern economy of colonialists.[15] He hypothesized as drastic a difference between the two economic systems as that which supposedly exists, according to Lévy-Bruhl (1928, 1930, 1935, 1938, 1945, 1947), between the mental functions of primitive peoples and Europeans, between a logical and prelogical mentality. While it is true that a modern economy is superimposed on a subsistence system, and a dual economy thus exists, the two are not different in nature, only in orientation. The operation of the process of domination, however, prevents unification of the two. Natives behave rationally in their commercial transactions as well as in all other areas of their economy. If their goals differ from those of the dominant group, this indicates that they can be reoriented through technical and economic education.

Fourthly, *unequal treatment* grants varying kinds of services to the populations involved. For obvious reasons, the problems of health and sanitation cannot be abstracted from the total society; therefore the native population is the object of coercive preventive measures for the protection of the dominant group settled within its territory. On the other hand, education is deliberately withheld from the masses, since an increase in knowledge is a powerful force, seriously affecting the colonial structure based on relationships of domination and subordination. Formal education is incompatible with a rigid caste system. It is not strange, therefore, that the struggle between missionaries and settlers—the former propagating evangelization, the latter defending ignorance—ends with the settlers' triumph. Unequal treatment is not limited to education; it encompasses all spheres of life, including justice and law, and it is justified by the danger to the colony if the natives rebel.

Fifthly, *social distance* is maintained, and limits contact between the groups to stereotyped situations and norms of behavior (De la Fuente 1964a:265). Colonization is static; it evolves from the lesser to the greater. At its inception, racial mixing is tolerated and the products of such mixing generally enter the dominant group. When the colony is secure, mixed-bloods are forcibly rejected and enlarge the colonized group. Once the colonial system is solidly established, the groups become mutually exclusive and endogamous. The superior caste creates privileged associations for recreation, friendship, and religion which the natives may not approach. When natives and Whites find themselves in situations where contact is unavoidable, for example in small, isolated towns, rules of etiquette are jealously adhered to, formalizing the relationships and symbolizing the social distance between the groups. This distance varies as to quantity and quality, according to the characteristics of the colonizers. In America the Portuguese and Spaniards had less interest in social distance than did the British and Dutch; nevertheless, the general pattern is maintained as a mechanism of domination.

Sixth, *missionary action* consolidates armed conquest by circulating an ideology whose goals, located in the afterlife, promote conformity and make subordination and abuse tolerable.[16] The purpose of evangelization, of course, is not to serve as a means of domination; on the contrary, it seeks to attain ecumenical equality without distinctions of race or color and struggles to achieve this goal. But in the colonial setting it is inevitably converted into an instrument of imperialism.[17] The fact that missionaries enter into open conflict with governors and merchants, for whom political control and economic dependence are the specific ends of colonization, is not the point. In the fight between utopia and reality, the missionaries finally lose, and against the express will and expectations of its agents, missionary activity is exploited to extend political control and economic exploitation.

Evangelization is a paradoxical force, ambivalent in nature; it both unites and divides.[18] It acts upon ethnic groups as an aggressive force, disintegrating tribal organization, weakening family solidarity, and disturbing kinship structures. In addition, it demands loyalty to the faith it imposes which is greater than the loyalty owed to tradition. The colonial system takes advantage of the revolutionary value of missionary action to attain its own ends; the anomie produced in the early stages of Christianization is exploited by administrators to establish an imperialist structure on those ruins. Religious motivation, seeking to extend the light of the Christian faith to the pagans of the world, justified the discovery and conquest of America; this same motivation, when used to rationalize the impurity of a native religion, justifies its destruction and replacement.

The mechanisms of domination analyzed thus far clearly bring to light the operating modes of outside forces opposing normal cultural evolution and progress. Colonial society, composed of two conflicting social orders, is purposely structured so that an elite, conditioned by the feudal spirit, may maintain underdeveloped indigenous populations in subordination. It oppresses them and prevents them from attaining the free fulfillment of their cultural patterns, norms of social organization, economic behavior, and political and religious associations. In order to justify this repressive conduct, colonial society elaborates upon an ideology, motivated by racial preconceptions, which stamps the entire situation with demonstrable falsity.

MINORITY GROUPS. The mechanisms of the process of domination are also found in situations other than the colonial. In Latin America, now politically independent, not all human groups participate equally in wealth, prestige, and power. There are groups in the national society which belong to the working class and, whipped by poverty, do not enjoy the benefits reserved for the middle and upper classes. The peasants and urban squatters living in the poverty belts surrounding the great cities enjoy very low levels of health, nutrition, housing, and education. These groups often suffer the ridicule and sneers of their social superiors because of their ignorance and rusticity. They are subject to exploitation, but they are integral members of the majority group; they speak the national language, show no notable differences in physical makeup and dress, and, of greatest importance, feel themselves to be part of the national society; their loyalties, rights, and duties derive from this membership.

In the heart of the Mestizo American countries of Latin America there are other groups which do not feel that they belong to the great national society. They are distinguished from the rest of society by their dress, which accents their physical characteristics; by their aboriginal language which separates them from general communication; by their culture, which differs in many respects from Western culture; and by their direct descent from the native ethnic groups who were defeated in the conquest and subjected to foreign domination. These groups are known generically as Indians and, although they comprise a respectable number and in some cases more than 50% of the total population of a country, sociologically they are minority groups.

Ethnic minorities, like colonized peoples, experience the effects of the process of domination, but with an extremely important difference: they are entitled to the benefits of a legally recognized citizenship which is sanctioned by the national society. At the national level there are no serious obstacles to a member of an ethnic minority becoming integrated into the majority, as long as he so desires. At the regional or local level, however, the mechanisms of domination prevent equality, block mobility, promote group isolation, and maintain the colonial status quo, preserving anachronistic caste relationships within the heart of the class society.

Since the problem of ethnic minorities is located at the regional level, we must analyze it there in order to avoid serious conceptual errors. Considered sociologically, the terms minority, minority group, or ethnic group imply possession of certain incapacities and dysfunctional characteristics which are more important than the mere numbers of members. A minority group is inherently different and *does not belong* to the dominant regional society; for this reason it is consciously or unconsciously excluded from full participation in cultural life.[19] Thus separated, the ethnic group is the object of different and unequal treatment.

The important characteristics defining the *status* of the minority are: (1) The lack of power, evident in prejudice, discrimination and segregation as promoted by the regional majority (Wagley & Harris 1958). The majority is such not by virtue of numbers, which are generally small, but because of the economic, political, and social power which it exercises. (2) The lack of power is related to the characteristics that the majority considers to be undesirable, such as physical appearance, language, religion, and other aspects of the different, minority culture. (3) Conspicuousness of incapacitating characteristics and the loss of power which follows, lead to the development of attitudes and forms of conduct among ethnic groups which create self-conscious social units. A people cannot be discriminated against for a long time, says Wirth, without generating a sense of isolation and persecution and without acquiring the idea that it is more different from others than it really is (Wirth 1945:348).

The undesirable characteristics and social incapacity operate within a global society in which men are considered potentially equal and where a national creed guarantees them equality of rights and opportunities. Contrary to the attitude held by the regional society, the national society encourages ethnic groups to arise and claim their rights. When minorities have a low technological culture incompatible with modern life, the national society promulgates protective laws which unsuccessfully try to prevent interference by the regional society with the goods and persons belonging to the subordinate group. Regional interests, in conflict with national ones, determine the status of minorities and consequently the degree to which loss of power and incapacitating characteristics interfere with cultural evolution.

In Latin America spatial segregation based on prejudice confines ethnic groups with a tropical jungle culture to reservations that are set aside by law. The status of these primitive groups does not extend to the ethnic groups with an agrarian culture, known generically as Indians. These latter enjoy citizenship, though neither authentic nor full, which places them on a plane of legal equality with the national society; nevertheless, in the regional setting they are segregated—and segregate themselves—in regions of refuge which operate, in fact, as reservations.

In these areas the groups which are sociological minorities, the Indians, reinforce the ties which identify and heighten the characteristics which distinguish them. In addition, in these regions the sociological majority, composed of Ladinos—national residents—acts as an external force on the ethnic group. In practice, the incapacities increase heterogeneity, block social and cultural change, promote the ignorance which raises communication barriers and propagate the stigmatization of Indians as inferior beings, so as to justify exploitation of the group as well as of its resources (Allport 1963).

In the ethnically mixed situation of the refuges the mechanisms of domination generate external forces that join with internal ones in restraining the rate of social and cultural change. These mechanisms function to maintain the inherited status quo, the caste structure, in colonies of exploitation—in order to obstruct the emergence of class societies which represent a step forward in the evolution of humanity.

NOTES

1. Linton (1944:325) affirms that "there probably does not exist a society today that owes more than 10% of its total elements to inventions made by members of its own society."

2. Herskovits considers that: "Despite these difficulties, the need to press toward an understanding of the process of cultural change is at the present time of particular urgency. The question can advantageously be reexamined in the light of concepts currently held by students of culture, while from a wider point of view, it is imperative that the deepest probing be brought to bear on it because consciousness of changing conditions is abroad in the world as perhaps never before in the experience of mankind. What occasions change and what discourages it; the scope of change, whether extensive or minute, and its rate; selectivity in the acceptance of changes in prospect—these are all matters to which must be brought the finest perceptions of the range of cultures and the fullest historical study if situations which many regard as already beyond control are to be shaped to the well-being of mankind" (1945: 170).

3. Barnett, the anthropologist who has written the most complete work on the subject states: "An innovation is here defined as any thought, behavior, or thing that is new because it is qualitatively different from existing forms. Strictly speaking, every innovation is an idea, or a constellation of ideas; but some innovations by their nature must remain mental organizations only, whereas others may be given overt and tangible expression. 'Innovation' is therefore a comprehensive term covering all kinds of mental constructs, whether they can be given sensible representation or not. A novelty is understood in the same way; hence, 'innovation' and 'novelty' are hereafter used synonymously, the choice of one term over the other being dictated solely by lexical propriety. To a limited extent 'invention' is also used as a synonym for 'innovation.' There would be no objection to a consistent equation of these two terms were it not that popular usage puts a more restricted meaning upon invention than is intended for the word innovation. For most people an invention is a thing, and the label seems inappropriate when applied to novel behavior patterns, theories, and social relations. While maintaining that there is no psychological distinction between the conception of a new object and a new act or theory, the present study retains the conventional implications of the term 'invention.' When it is used it means simply a technological innovation, a new thing. Custom has also governed the use of the term 'discovery.' It is fruitless to try to establish a rigorous and meaningful distinction between 'discovery' and 'invention,' and nothing is to be gained by redefining the two words. On the contrary, communication is facilitated by conforming to ordinary usage. Beyond this purpose no significance should be attached to the differential employment of 'invention' and 'discovery.' Both are names for innovations."

4. Morely states: "at a certain point during the IV or III Century, B.C. the Maya priests, for the first time in human history, conceived . . . the use of the mathematical quantity of zero; a portentuous development in abstract thinking" (1947:306).

5. Lévi-Strauss (1958:106) nevertheless, advises: "on the other hand, the social organization of the Aztecs and the Incas, has come down to us through the descriptions of the conquerers who were enamored of their discovery and who ascribed to it a systematic character it probably did not possess.... From the pre-eminent position temporarily occupied by one tribe among so many others, we cannot conclude that that tribe's particular customs were observed throughout the whole region. . . . even if its dignitaries had an interest in giving that impression, especially to the European newcomers."

6. Gillin includes in what he calls Mestizo America: the 13 mainland republics which are predominantly Mestizo, both racially and culturally. They are Mexico, Guatemala, Honduras, El Salvador, Nicaragua, Panama, Colombia, Venezuela, Ecuador, Peru, Bolivia, Chile, and Paraguay. All of them still have Indian minorities; all of them were originally colonized by Spain, and Spanish is the official language" (1949:158).

7. Malinowsky (1945:17) advises: "As regards the possibility of practical applications, the conception of culture change as the impact of Western civilization and the reaction thereto of indigenous cultures is the only fruitful approach. We must treat the plans, intentions, and interests of White contact agents as something which can only be realized through cooperation with the African; or which fails because of real conflict of interests, faulty planning, misunderstanding, or lack of a common ground for effective joint work. Here the anthropologist can act as adviser only if he realizes clearly that at times there is a possibility of effective coöperation; that there are definite conditions under which this is possible, while in certain cases an inevitable clash must result."

8. Evans-Pritchard says: "Since social anthropologists mostly study primitive societies, the information they collect and the conclusions they come to obviously have some bearing on problems of the administration and education of primitive peoples. It will at once be acknowledged that if it is the policy of a colonial government to administer a people through their chiefs it is useful to know who are the chiefs and what are their functions and authority and privileges and obligations. Also, if it is intended to administer people according to their own laws and customs one has first to discover what these are. It is evident also that if it is intended to change a people's economy, for example to alter their system of land tenure, to encourage them to grow export crops, or to institute markets and a money economy, it is of some advantage to be able to estimate, at any rate roughly, what social effects these changes are likely to bring about.... It is evident also that if a missionary wishes to convert a native people to Christianity some knowledge of their own religious beliefs and practices is required.... The value of social anthropology to administration has been generally recognized from the beginning of the century and both the Colonial Office and colonial governments have shown an increasing interest in anthropological teaching and research.... Many anthropologists have for a long time spoken about applied anthropology much as one speaks about applied medicine or engineering.... Such anthropologists have constantly stressed the application of their findings to affairs, the emphasis in England being on colonial problems, and in America on political and industrial problems. Its more cautious advocates have,... held that there can only be applied social anthropology when the science of man is much more advanced than it is today" (Evans-Pritchard 1962:109).

9. Palerm (1952:20) states: "The Conquest was accomplished by a type of pact between the aboriginal upper class and the Spaniards. In reality, the conquerors constituted—we are speaking especially of the XVI Century—not the only group dominating the socially undifferentiated Indians, but rather the highest level of a pyramid. The welfare of the Indian nobles, as well as their positions of political authority, were partially respected."

10. Balandier (1963:7) states: "The historian reminds us that colonial societies are the products of a double history. In the case of Africa, one, particularly African—'These societies, so stable and unmoveable in appearance, are all or almost all, the end product of a combination of different peoples which history squashed, mixed and imposed'—has placed homogeneous social structures face to face; the other, largely conditioned by European domination, put radically heterogeneous social forms into contact. A concrete study of these societies cannot be done without *situating* them in relation to this double history."

11. Balandier (1963:15) adds: "In a work dedicated to the colonies, E. A. Walcker calls attention to the fact that they constitute plural societies. He notes that the colony—a global society—is generally composed of a varying number of groups more or less aware of their existence, frequently opposing one another on the basis of skin color, and that try to live by standards of behavior which differ within each of the political sectors. Walcker continues: these groups, which speak different languages, eat different foods, frequently engage in different occupations assigned by law or custom, wear different clothing... inhabit different types of houses, follow different traditions, worship different gods, possess different ideas about good and evil..." "What is interesting," concludes Balandier, "is not the mention of pluralism, but the indication of its specific traits."

12. Boas states: "It is easy to show that racism has no scientific standing. It is based fundamentally on two misconceptions: The one, the confusion of heredity in a family and heredity in a population; the other, the unproved assumption that the differences in culture which we observe among peoples of different types are primarily due to biological causes" (Boas 1946:30). Boas himself (1964) devotes Chapter 13 of his book to the study of the racial problem in modern society.

13. Mair (1962:263) reports that, "Where colonial governments found a state organization in existence, there was no difficulty in identifying men who exercised authority and could be required, as the condition of retaining it, to exercise it on behalf of the new ruler."

14. Hammond points out how, even in those cases where colonial policy constructs works of infrastructure, such as irrigation projects, their utilization fails because they lack significance for the natives, "they are required to follow the instructions of the European agronomists or be penalized" (1959:256).

15. Beals (1965:2) summarizes the discussion that was stirred by Boeke's theory as follows: "Many of the western contacts and concomitant changes had a clearly economic character . . . the control of those activities should be left in Dutch hands, reserving the rural and traditional activities to the Indians, that is, the lowest level of the labor force."

16. Houtart in regard to Spanish colonialism, explains: "One of the bases for political control by the crown, which gave rise to a profound confusion between the temporal and spiritual domains, was the regime of patronage conceded in the Bull of Pope Alexander II. Under this, the king controlled, through the Council of the Indies, the administration of the Church; it named the ecclesiastical offices, set the limits of the dioceses, and collected the tithes. All religious organization was put under temporal control and the clergy was turned into a group of government functionaries and collaborators since it had to depend on the Crown for its income. This regime of patronage had as its gravest consequence the irremediable binding of evangelicism to the crown" (1964:19).

17. Las Casas (1822) had been, without doubt, the most tenacious opponent of Spanish colonialism. The expulsion of the Jesuits from the American dominions in the last third of the eighteenth century was the most dramatic expression of the conflict between colonialism and evangelism. Piddington writes, "the missionaries have been constant in their defense of the rights of the natives against the economic depradations and at times against the administrative actions of the highest levels . . . they fought individually and through their organizations to change the tide of European imperialism and in many cases they were successful in mitigating its worse effects" (1957:678).

18. Nida (1954) devotes his entire work to educating the missionaries on the dangers of indiscriminate evangelical action. Hunter states "That Christianity is in some measure a disintegrating force in the tribal community cannot be denied. It tends to weaken the ancestor cult which makes for family solidarity. In congregations new social groups are formed which may conflict with existing kinship groups. Converts are taught that loyalty to their faith must take precedence over loyalty to their chief. Christians are forbidden to share in certain traditional observations which make for tribal solidarity. But at the same time Christian influences assist adaptation to the new conditions produced by economic contacts with Europeans" (Hunter 1964: 355).

19. Balandier referring to the colonial situation, tells us that, "political domination is accompanied by cultural domination . . . and the result is that the European cultures oppress the sources of native culture" (1963:13).

Chapter 2

ENEMY ECOLOGY

COMMUNITY DEVELOPMENT programs in Latin American countries show similar as well as disparate characteristics which originate in the particulars of the respective sociocultural environments. In many countries, especially those of Mestizo America, such programs are implemented in a setting where populations with differing cultures but living in the same territory interact. Dependency relationships exist among these groups, tying them to a common destiny and shaping generally well-structured sociogeographical units.

The Ladino population shares the life styles of the modern Latin American culture and forms the dominant sector of the equation. The indigenous groups—remnants of the ancient inhabitants of America—retain their old values, customs, and behavior norms, little modified by invention and acculturation, and appear to be the most backward section of the national population. Thus they are subject to subjugation and exploitation by the technically and economically more developed groups.

The regions where the colonial situation persists are regions of refuge and exhibit particular characteristics. Of these, ecological aspects will be explored first in the following paragraphs.

THE HOSTILE LANDSCAPE. Latin American geographers call that part of a countryside which has not been disturbed by human activity *climax zones*; today it is difficult to find such areas. Since that distant time when America was first populated, men have settled throughout the mainland and outlying islands, occupied deserts and swamps, jungles and forests, savannas and highlands, ravines and mountains; nothing has escaped their inquisitive search. As their technology developed, they increasingly changed the land. The scope of man-made alterations increased however, when Europeans discovered the New World and began modifying the habitat, using much more efficient cultural and technical instruments.

These changes reached such a point that today the greater part of the land in the economically advanced regions is taken up by large cities, complicated road systems, man-made lakes, and geometric, cultivated fields. There are, however, other regions where man's works are not so apparent; there the land, altered many centuries ago, has returned to a state very similar to the primeval because its utilization by human groups is so rudimentary that the very essence of the climax zone is barely disturbed.[1] In those regions of refuge man is so immersed in his natural environment that it is difficult to separate him from it.

The landscape varies substantially. It changes with altitude, latitude, and other determinants such as vegetation and typography which define the kinds of environment to which man must adapt. Regions of refuge are located in areas that are particularly hostile or inaccessible to human movement, where exploitation of available resources necessitates the investment of considerable effort even for modern technology, and where this effort is not recompensed proportionately. Thus they are kept in reserve by industrial society for future use as long as the need for their resources is not sufficiently great to warrant their exploitation.[2] There are three basic types of environments that are inhospitable or difficult to penetrate: deserts, tropical jungles, and mountain ranges. Each one offers opportunities or barriers which should be considered.

In Mestizo America the desert environment is represented by the arid lands of northern

Mexico—lands extending the length of the Pacific coast from Peru to the middle of Chile—and those of Patagonia. Rain is absent or very scarce. The temperature, high during hours of strong sunlight, changes dramatically at sundown, causing daily variations exceeding the annual mean variation. Vegetation consists of plants which store water, long-rooted perennials which bloom with rainfall, and annuals that lie dormant during droughts and grow and mature rapidly with any precipitation. In the desert water comes from wells which are irregularly distributed throughout the territory, or from outside sources, currents that enter the thirsty land and wander toward, but seldom reach, the sea.

This environment offers few opportunities for human life; regardless of the growing development of motorized means of communication the desert is still an insurmountable barrier for all practical purposes.[3] Regions of refuge in the desert support only hunters and gatherers who live in small bands or are in the process of becoming extinct. But they do not offer equal shelter to agricultural communities taking advantage of the water found in the occasional rivers that originate elsewhere, since their right to this water is disputed by the dominant Ladino population.

Tropical jungles present a second adverse environment which, until very recently, was openly hostile. The Orinoco-Amazon basin, with a type of jungle that extends along the Caribbean coast and the Gulf of Mexico, is the most extensive area of tropical land in the world. Geographers distinguish between rain forests and semideciduous jungle, using quantitative rather than qualitative criteria to differentiate them. In both environments hundreds of plant species grow in close proximity. Giant and medium size trees form an immense roof for shrub vegetation and shade the soil, which receives only those rays of light that filter through the foliage. Rain is continual and torrential except during the ill-defined dry season; temperature is uniformly high and humidity extreme throughout the year.

Despite the fact that man's primeval ancestors originated in tropical regions, and that the oldest American civilizations flowered in jungles and swamps, a large portion of these lands has reverted to virgin conditions.[4] For the hunter and gatherer the tropics offer few opportunities; movement in the jungle is laborious and often small gullies formed by heavy rains are the only means of communication, when their navigation is possible at all. Animal life is sparse on the ground but birds and aboreal mammals abound in the jungle roof. Various species of trees bear fruit during the course of the annual cycle but neither animal nor plant life are plentiful enough to sustain high density populations at reasonable levels.

Agricultural peoples with a simple technology find in the tropics only the insecurities of itinerant agriculture. They use swidden methods and must constantly maintain the exhausting effort of felling trees and keeping the earth free from the jungle's encroachment.[5] It is true that in some tropical areas with good soil, intensive agriculture provides the possibility of sustaining a large population. However, here the complex of tropical life is circumscribed by the specific environment of the Americas and it seems clear that the opportunities offered by it are considerably fewer than the obstacles it poses.

The dense, heavy, primeval jungle of the Orinoco-Amazon basin was an impassable barrier for our aboriginal ancestors and continues to be so for modern man. Only small agricultural communities with primitive cultures manage to establish themselves firmly in this inhospitable habitat and to survive the threat of total extinction or a problematical integration into the civilized world. For American jungle populations, the barriers raised by the tropical environment form the largest region of refuge in the world. In Mesoamerica, however, the construction of dams and other infrastructure facilities in the watershed facing the Caribbean and the Gulf of Mexico is causing the disappearance, little by little, of the old refuges.

THE MOUNTAINOUS ENVIRONMENT. The third environment which we have classified as hostile is that of inaccessible mountain ranges, where difficulties lie in the very remoteness and rugged nature of the territory more than in anything else. Altitude is an effective substitute for latitude in determining climate. Thus, throughout intertropical America high mountains modify the environment found along the Tropics of Cancer and Capricorn and the Equator. A scale of environments is produced in accordance with altitude above sea level. This includes tropical jungles at the lowest level, temperate zones at the intermediate, and at the highest, forests of conifers bordering the snow line. Of course this vertical zoning is not regular; the influence of local factors is great and increases the extreme variety found throughout the area.

At low altitudes the mountainous environment offers excellent opportunities for human life. In Mesoamerica as well as in South America, the mountain ranges contain plains, mesas, valleys, and gentle slopes which provide areas with moderate temperatures and well-distributed rainfall, suitable for the development of intensive agriculture. These richly endowed intermontane areas were chosen by culturally and economically more advanced populations for their habitat. In the same mountainous countryside there are also snow covered peaks, rocky summits, steep cliffs, ravines and gorges, ridges, and craggy heights, which form small valleys, little mesas and narrow pockets containing bits of poor quality land. These areas of rugged countryside, isolated from transportation routes by physical barriers, with a harsh landscape and scanty agricultural yields, constitute regions of refuge. They are not immense areas like the Amazon basin, nor limited reservations for the protection of small groups, as are the deserts; they are compendia of small or medium sized territorial units, distributed throughout the continental mountain range. They contain the greater part of the indigenous population of the Americas.[6]

In the competition for territorial occupation and resources, populations with different cultures tend to settle in places that can supply the means for them to live and perpetuate themselves in accordance with their technology. In the struggle for occupation of the habitat, groups with less developed cultures remain in regions that are marginal because of climate or topography where it is only possible to maintain life at a subsistence level. Considered ecologically, these are regions where plant and animal species, including man, are protected from competition by physical barriers.[7] These less favored regions are refuges because their marginal situation and isolation protect them from the aggression of more technologically advanced groups. One could say that to a certain degree the Indians were pushed into them by European expansion, but it would be more correct historically to state that in those regions the older, established populations simply survived. Because of hostile typography and the particular characteristics of colonial exploitation, such populations were saved from extinction and thus could preserve their life styles to a greater or lesser degree, with modifications produced by acculturation.

As a consequence of the foregoing, in the refuges not only do human groups with simple cultures survive as objective examples of archaic life styles, but so do plant and animal species that disappeared long ago in the more favored regions. In the same way, other mineral and energy resources, especially hydraulic ones, remain untapped until the more advanced groups achieve an industrial culture that encourages their use. As in the case of man, the archaic fauna and copious plant varieties extant in these regions are not the result of a persecution that drove plants and animals from their former habitat to areas of shelter. The ones already there survived, protected by physical barriers. As noted, the concept of the region of refuge never implies protection of men, animals or plants from beyond their territorial limits. It is the shelter of those already within its limits, those in possession of the area.

Vavilov (1951) supports the theory that the highlands gave rise to agriculture in America. In this environment he finds optimum conditions for a diversity of plant species and subspecies. He believes that the isolation and marginality of the regions of refuge, the small intermontane valleys, favored preservation of the physiological types that have disappeared from more accessive areas. A superficial glance at the effects of the ecological disturbances produced by European colonization and colonialism helps considerably in understanding the important function of regions of refuge as areas where individuals, associations, and cultural forms which otherwise would have inevitably disappeared, were conserved. Destruction of the Indies began shortly after their discovery; the sedentary agricultural population was decimated by contact. In one or two generations war, subjugation, and epidemics from Western Europe wiped out the Indians living along the tropical coasts. Livestock, introduced by the Spaniards, contributed to the depopulation, invading the cultivated fields of the Indians who had survived the initial collapse. In temperate areas the rainy foothills and great valleys of the highlands were occupied by foreign settlers who possessed far more advanced knowledge and techniques than those of the natives.

Sauer (1956) estimates that the progressive and rapidly cumulative effects of European exploitation became truly malignant at the end of the colonial era and the beginning of the Independence period as a direct result of forces set loose by the Industrial Revolution.[8] The former way of life, based on surpluses produced by the use of resources, was replaced by the exploitation of a territory's productive capacity to obtain profit. Excessive waste led to the extinction of forms and species that indigenous farmers had laboriously developed; commercialization of agriculture meant that only a small fraction of the domesticated species and varieties was intensively exploited. Thus the broad range of genes found in noncommercial plant and animal life was lost, drastically reducing the results of biological evolution. Another consequence of unbridled exploitation was the limitation of useful species when previously existing ecological combinations were replaced by others of short lived commercial value. A final effect was the loss of soil when steeply sloping lands, susceptible to erosion, were cultivated using highly effective tools incorrectly, or when intense, unrestricted, and depleting use was made of the fertile topsoil to obtain lucrative harvests.[9]

To a great extent, the regions of refuge escaped this destruction. However, biologists, concerned with reproduction of plant varieties endowed with strong powers of survival or adaptability, search the refuges for such domestic plants with diminishing success. Some regions of refuge—especially those whose marginality and isolation have disappeared because of technical progress and thus no longer qualify as such—have undergone the disruption of industrialization without profiting from its organizational effects. The thin, poor soil of those regions shows severe erosion. The forced commercial harvests which they have produced have destroyed the primary as well as the secondary vegetation and soil coverage to such a point that in large areas the earth consists of desolate and sterile subsoil. Other regions of refuge, still providing shelter, have preserved the remaining forms of human life and a diversity of plant and animal species within their borders without causing serious changes in the habitat. Of course, isolation and marginality play an important role in maintaining these shelters and are their defining features. But none of them would persist if their inhabitants trusted in the passive hope that such factors would always work in their favor. It should not be forgotten that the regions of refuge offer shelter to the adapted group and its members, never to the outsider. Active defense of the condition of shelter is the sine qua non of its existence. This function is performed through the mechanism of territoriality, whose mode of operation we shall now examine in detail.

TERRITORIALITY. The tendency among anthropologists is to explain man's problems in cultural terms, among sociologists to interpret them structurally, and among economists to view them from the reference points of their particular discipline. Certainly the answers supplied by man's culture, his social structure, or his economy to the questions of modern life are mutually consistent and, more often than not, form integrated theories which satisfactorily answer our questions. Because of their accuracy and persuasiveness, these theories have been so diffused and widely accepted that social scientists today are increasingly inclined to disdain explanations based on biological causality, viewing them as worthless in comparison with the importance and authority of the former.

However, while man has transcended nature, he cannot escape its inexorable laws nor free himself from its organic bonds through the cultural systems that are the patrimony of the human race. Malinowski rightly based his functional theory of culture on the organism's basic needs, and noted how the processes of reproduction, metabolism, growth, and the achievement of comfort and security, among others, take place within cultural settings which respond to instincts and which, in turn, condition them (Malinowski 1944). One of those fundamental needs is expressed through the mechanism of territoriality, which was classified by biologists only a few years ago. Its value is not limited to explaining the conduct of lower animals; it also illuminates certain human attitudes during the early periods of historical evolution as well as in recent stages, attitudes which apparently are the residues of biologically imposed behavior.

In 1920 Howard released his observations of the habits of a certain species of songbird. He confirmed that the comings and goings of each pair that had formed a nest were generally restricted to a limited radius and that the male actively defended his territory against the intrusion of other males of the same species. When the males arrived in the spring, each marked off his territory. One of the most important functions of the birds' song seemed to be that of proclaiming territorial possession, warning that the area had been found vacant. Similar territorial behavior was discovered later in other species of birds. It could then be asserted that a territory commonly served as a field for mating, nesting, and feeding, and that it could be occupied by individuals, families, or flocks of birds. Members of the last nest close to each other so that proximity allows the nests to be defended against more powerful foreign attackers (Bates 1962).

The essence of territoriality is that whoever proclaims it is constantly ready to defend the area against intruders, particularly if they are of the same species, and that an individual within his own territory behaves in an aggressive, fearless way, which is very different from the conduct observed when he is away from it. One consequence of this behavior is the spacing of the population in such a fashion that territorial availability becomes the limiting factor in setting the maximum size of that population in any given place.[10] When the mechanism of territoriality was studied in social mammals it could be shown, as well, that when a particular species occupies a specific area, excess members are expelled. Forced to become marauders, they are easy prey for predators.

Knowledge of the mechanism of territoriality was increased by careful studies by Carpenter (1958) in a community of howler monkeys on a small island near Panama. The population was divided into clans of varying sizes, each of which had a carefully delimited territory. The extent of the territory varied in accordance with the size of the clan and the nature of the forest habitat. In the center of the territory were trees in which the monkeys slept and around these was their feeding area. The outlying sections were seldom frequented; neighboring clans always avoided them since there was inevitably a fierce battle when members of the two clans met at the frontier. In this particular case only howler monkeys were involved.

The concept of territoriality developed by biologists brought important changes to the widely accepted idea that population size was determined by the availability of food. It had already been noted that, due to unknown circumstances, wild species multiplied until a balance between births and deaths was reached, but this equilibrium clearly was not achieved through the mechanism of hunger. For the hare to survive, nourishment must be adequate to develop strong muscles. Life depends on speed, which is lost if he multiplies to such a point that adequate food cannot be obtained. It is obvious that all animals in the natural environment maintain the vigor necessary for survival; otherwise, the species would become extinct (Sauvy 1963). Then what is it that happens? The concept of territoriality as instinctive behavior provides the answer. Defense of the territory by its occupants maintains subsistence at an adequate level. Expulsion of excess members from the population aids in this purpose, but in addition, the territory is always larger than that which is strictly necessary to maintain the optimum number of inhabitants. In reality, this mechanism serves to assure that a species does not live at the limit of the food supply.

Heidiger advanced research on territorial behavior when he described the methods used by various vertebrates to precisely mark off and recognize their particular areas. He described four procedures: optical, acoustical, olfactory, and a combination of these. The first, apparently the most primitive, predominates among lower vertebrates, fishes, reptiles, and paradoxically, among men; it makes use of signs which are left or placed in the territory and which serve to delimit it. The acoustical method plays an important role among birds, in the same way that the olfactory method is characteristic of prosimians. Some species have glands whose strongly scented secretions are used to mark off their area of control, while others simply use excretions such as urine and feces. The latter procedure seems to be identified especially with nocturnal primates. Diurnal primates prefer the acoustical method which is much more practical and effective in the dense forest than the olfactory and optical methods (Heidiger 1961).

The importance of the above observations lies in the fact that they indicate the existence of different and very exact mechanisms for territorial demarcation. Everything points to the supposition that the earth's surface is a complex system of mosaics composed of clearly delimited territories, the abodes of the individuals or groups possessing and defending them against neighbors of the same species. The integrated territorial mosaic is the primary possession of every animal species. In some species, territorial possession is temporary and limited to the mating season. Others appear to have no clear territorial relationship, or may manifest strange distortions in terms of space and time. Nevertheless, in all classes of vertebrates there are examples of enduring territorial ownership and evidence of defense by its occupants, as well as proof that such territory has a definite size and specific internal structure.

THE ROLE OF PROPERTY. Study of the territoriality mechanism in human groups is difficult due to the enormous problems involved in separating cultural from purely biological factors. Ethnographic descriptions of the very simple organization of certain human groups such as the Semang of the Malay Peninsula (Forde 1953), show them to have a life style that is very close to nature. The Semang form into small bands of 20 to 30 persons, usually an extended family, each of which claims possession of a correspondingly small territory, wherein grow trees whose fruit is especially prized. The band's exclusive enjoyment of these trees is recognized by neighbors, while the gathering of roots or hunting in another's territory is permitted. In this case apparently possession of the trees rather than of the land defines territoriality. Among the Bushmen of the Kalahari desert, territoriality works to guarantee possession of watering places. Thus, even in periods of intense drought the small groups never cross into neighboring territories without the consent of the rightful owners, whom they recognize as having exclusive use of the puddles whose water they solicit (Shapera 1951).

Other primitive peoples known generically as Chichimecs, lived in the semiarid regions of northern Mexico and the southern United States. All of them disappeared after contact with Western culture, since it is very difficult for bands living at such a precarious level to survive for long after their habitat is disturbed. These bands also possessed territories in which they hunted small game and gathered forest products, and they fiercely resisted intrusion by individuals from neighboring bands who sought to contest their ownership. Some of these bands changed their economic systems from collecting to producing foodstuffs and created an agrarian culture through domestication of plants and animals. Thus they established a relationship which was less dependent upon what the habitat offered, and were able to increase their numbers and the size of their territory.

At different times in their historical evolution, Mesoamerican agricultural peoples achieved cultures with very elaborate ceremonial structures and great richness in terms of the monumental character of their buildings. But all maintained a very strong relationship between the members of the group and the cultivated land as the basis of their social organization. This relationship is called the *calpulli* and in anthropological terms it should be translated as the territorial clan.[11] It was in response to the basic need manifested through the mechanism of territoriality that Mesoamerican Indians created the cultural complex called the *calpulli*.

The corporate group's relationship to the territory includes both rational and emotional ties. The community claims recognition of its possession of the land because it obtains its means of subsistence from it, and also because the mystical nature with which it endows its habitat requires that the group perform a series of traditionally established reciprocal acts which constitute a sacrificial complex. Places considered sacred, where mythical ancestors or gods live, are as important or more so than cultivated lands. The two together form the community's patrimony and recognition of this patrimony by neighboring peoples defines the group's right of ownership. By emphasizing defense of the area delimited by the group, the mechanism of territoriality offers a biological basis for the concept of land ownership.

In a magnificent essay on nature and the function of property, Hallowell along with others, denied the significance of analogies between biological and social types of ownership.[12] They argued that in human societies the correlative obligations conceded by others are the basis of ownership. This right to property is not only recognized but sanctioned socially. As noted, the opposition of some sociologists and cultural anthropologists, who deny that the right of land ownership derives from a remote organic need, is reduced to problems of conceptualization. Western jurists, conditioned by Roman law, encounter these same problems when they come into contact with the exotic characteristics of ownership in non-Western law. Since the latter do not correspond to the patterns to which they are accustomed, their interpretations give rise to contradicting criteria. Some maintain that ownership could not be established before the production of economic surpluses which came with the birth of agriculture, while others give an evolutionist connotation to the terms "possession" and "ownership," maintaining that the latter pertains to civilization while the former characterizes the early periods of humanity. Whatever position is adopted, the importance of the concept, considered biologically or socially, is obvious.

But the problem goes even further. The concept of territoriality is pregnant in its implications. The more it is used as a tool for analysis, the more satisfactorily can the biological bases of certain forms of human behavior be explained, behavior such as feuds between neighboring communities. Hostile behavior, as stated above, serves to safeguard territories and populations, but when the groups experience demographic pressure, its principal function is to disperse surplus members into the conflict filled borders of the territory, exposing this surplus to destruction. As one might suppose, hostility among neighbors increases in direct proportion to the increase in population density, since the latter frequently coincides with unwanted and surreptitious incursions. Recognition of their rights to a demarcated territory authorizes peoples whose land has been invaded to destroy the invaders. However, feelings of loyalty to the members of one's own group who have been cut down by the other group, oblige one to take reprisals and thus to begin a feud with the neighbors.

If things proceeded in this way and if a loose rein were given to the aggression engendered by the mechanisms of territoriality, conflicts between communities would end only with the annihilation of the weakest, but this does not always happen. The problem is resolved through an ingenious means, most clearly known among Mesoamerican communities as the *flower war*, a kind of warfare which is still practiced, secretly or in a disguised form, in the regions of refuge. This is expiatory combat, conducted according to institutionalized rules which prevent the destruction of the weaker group (Hoebel 1961:553). Not only are feuds not avoided, they are actually encouraged; but, at the same time, aggression is channeled so that the harm done is never irreparable.

Territorial aggression has been identified furthermore, as one of the causes that favors the development of a group's specific cultural forms; and, even more successfully, acts against change in traditional behavior patterns. In the regions of refuge this often implies cultural pluralism. Each group remains faithful to the beliefs and customs inherited from its ancestors and maintains them without substantial change. Groups maintain dialectal variations or separate languages which hinder communication among them, and deny membership in the community to those who were not born within it (Coon and Hunt 1963:27). All of this differs from what happens in ecologically and culturally more favored regions, where industrial civilization encourages acceptance of innovations at the same time that it represses all provocations against outsiders.

Another aspect of the mechanisms of territoriality has to do with the mobility of the corporate group. All characteristics of territoriality seem aimed at keeping the population within the limits of a given area. Territorial defense, hostility against intruders, group authority, and resource allocation are all factors which tend to keep members rooted in their own territory. These same factors which cause cultural stability also cause migratory movements to be infrequent. This rule is based on cases which are generally observed, but there are exceptions.

Using this theorum, Keith postulated that the major racial stocks developed directly from primeval man whose fossil remains have been discovered in the same areas occupied by those stocks today (Keith 1931). The immobilizing effects of territoriality would explain the astonishing similarity of the Java Man to the present day Australian, or of the Peking Man to today's Mongolian. The similarities, expounded by Weidenreich (1946: 84)[13] are undeniable; but this somehow suggests that primeval man did not enjoy spatial mobility, whereas from the viewpoint of organic evolution, all evidence points to the existence of Pleistocene migratory currents which facilitated the crossbreeding of different human races from a very early time.

Although relatively recent, the populating of America demonstrates the migratory capability of early man. However, such movement requires considerable time. It cannot be denied that territoriality, considered from the medium or short-range view, favors demographic stability. Human migrations such as we know in the world today are innovations commonly motivated by economic development. In the regions of refuge, in existence since the colonial era, Indian and Ladino populations are still subject to the extraordinary force of territorial imperatives. Consequently they remain stationary and maintain their original genetic makeup without major alterations.

REGIONALITY. Man's interaction with his physical environment, the influence of territoriality on land demarcation, and the many forces put into play by the colonial experience, all explain the protective nature of the organization of the native communities that survived colonization and independence. As one result of this historical process, preservation of archaic life styles was always accompanied by retention of the territory which the communities had occupied before the Spanish conquest. The area, as delimited in ancient times, was the basis for the communes or Indian republics; today it provides township boundaries.[14] Land ownership in some cases remained in the hands of the ethnic group; in others it was transferred to the Ladino aristocracy in the regional center. But in either case, the native residents have always claimed and defended their right to use the resources within their municipal boundaries. The unit composed of a number of these indigenous communities, organized around a seignorial city, is a region of refuge.

Considered ecologically, some characteristics of the region of refuge should be noted. First, it is a natural area because geographically it is rather uniform in terms of geologic composition and in the particulars of soil, climate, vegetation, and animal life. This statement is invalid, however, if we conceive of it as a precisely characterized area and different from the surrounding territory.[15] Mountains continue or gradually disappear within neighboring regions; boundaries are indicated occasionally by important geographic features, but these are never precise.[16] As with territoriality, the central portion of the region of refuge defines its physiognomy; the features of marginal zones are not important. In any case, as has been pointed out numerous times, the region of refuge is particularly inhospitable. The rugged typography, the difficulties of movement, the traditional life styles and the tense interethnic relations based on Ladino dominance of the Indian, are all factors that generate antipathy (Diegues 1952).

The region of refuge is also a habitat in dynamic equilibrium; its environment has not been altered by technology to the point of endangering natural resources. The nature of the landscape is largely determined by the population's level of knowledge and technical skills. Resources have different meanings to the groups living there. Potentialities are absolute, but their realization is determined by social needs and by the nature of the instruments and ideas used to exploit them. Devastation of forests for profit or extensive cultivation of primary materials or commercial export crops commonly takes place when development begins. In the mountains, the ecological balance barely disturbs the milieu.

It is fair to say that science and technology are not destructive per se; on the contrary, as the cultural heritage grows, more and more of the environment becomes useful and significant. As Mumford maintains, the natural conditions of a region are augmented rather than nullified by the use of ideas and skills. For the indigenous hunter the forest is only a place to hunt; for modern man it is also a source of wood, protection against soil erosion, a place for recreation, and a field for scientific observation. The principal problem of human settlement is that of adapting the environment to its many and newer needs without irreparably disturbing the balance of nature (Mumford 1932:313).

One more characteristic concerns demographic structure; it consists of hamlets, a few towns and a city, all united into a living community. City-dwelling Ladinos occupy the most important niche; they form the dominant group and consequently control the composition and functioning of the community (Huntington 1962). The Indians, concentrated in towns or dispersed in hamlets, find themselves in situations of rivalry and discrimination. Gathered into hostile communities, they live in dependence and subordination to the city, which maintains law and order and uses physical coercion, a component of the domination process. The city, being the most important apparatus of the living community, gives the region its particular nature and character (Hawley 1962:266).

In Europe, a long process led to the concentration of peasants into small villages, which later formed the basis for urban life with the construction of cities. Finally, the city best situated within the communication network, with a large area of cultivable land and a water supply or some similar advantage, emerged as the regional capital. This process was not repeated in the settlement of Mestizo America (Dickenson 1961). The community nucleus created by the Spaniards had the characteristics of a city from the moment of its founding (Quintero 1964:117). In many cases these settlements did not prosper and, lacking economic and other conditions necessary for their survival, were soon abandoned. But in other cases, regional cities were founded as royal cities, located in jurisdictions which were inaccessible and endowed with a large Indian tribute paying population. The stated purpose of a royal city was to exercise domination over the region and its inhabitants. Regardless of its size and however few its inhabitants, it was supported by the subjugation of the indigenous communities which it governed. It did not limit its jurisdiction to the municipal territory but, through the *alcalde mayor*, extended its authority to neighboring towns, communes, or Indian republics.

The regional city, as the home of the Ladino population in Indian territory, plays a dominant role in the colonial situation as *chef-lieu* of the geographical area where it acts as a powerful integrating factor.[17] Viewed ecologically the region of refuge is an area of hostile territory with a homogeneous environment which is redefined by human settlement, by domestication of plants and animals and by the introduction of new species, and is occupied by a biological community with a Ladino city in the dominant position. It exercises control over the land, energy, and movements of the subordinate Indian population, and does so at the level permitted by their lack of technology.

NOTES

1. Sahlins (1964:144) observes: "Advanced cultures are distinguished by superior means of coping with the world. The improvements in productive technology that have occurred through prehistory and history, especially the several revolutions from the development of agriculture to the development of nuclear power, are the best known, but they are not alone. There have been very important improvements in the technology of mobilization, that is, in means for delivery of power, goods, persons, and messages. These particularly give advantage in intercultural relations, making it increasingly possible to base an advance on the exploitation of surrounding societies through trade, conquest, or colonial rule."

2. Wolf in describing the relations characteristic of corporate rural communities, states: "The first of these is location on *marginal land*. Needs within the larger society which might compel the absorption and exploitation of this land are weak or absent, and the existing level of technology and transportation may make such absorption difficult. In other words, the amount of energy required to destroy the existing structure of the corporate community and to reorganize it at present outweighs the capacity of the larger society" (1955:457).

3. Birket-Smith (1960:128) reports that since Herodotus there have been dramatic descriptions of the difficulties of the desert habitat with its lack of shelter from the sun, its high temperatures, sandstorms, and sparse and irregular rainfall that kills the inhabitants from thirst or drowns them in sudden floods. Nonetheless man has created various techniques to use even the desert habitat for agriculture. Dobyns (1951) refers to the practices of the desert dwellers of Sonora, who channel flood waters into depressions or *bolsas* constructed with earthen walls. They wait for the stored water to saturate the earth and when they are sure of sufficient moisture they prepare and sow the land. Through this ingenious method a good, heavy shower can suffice, even during a prolonged drought, for a profitable harvest for the *bolseros*.

4. Bates (1952:71) states: "For America there is no argument about the tropical origin of civilization. Indeed, the local civilizations failed ever to spread far outside of the tropics, and no high level of culture was achieved in the north until European man turned up bringing Western European culture with him. I might note in passing that even this Western European culture, for a long time, did better in the tropics than outside on the American continents. The Spaniards were little interested in anything north of Mexico and the West Indies, and when the English and others took to colonizing the higher latitudes (from lack of alternative) their 'success' from the point of view of the development of 'high' or complex culture was not immediate."

5. Gourou states: "The tropical soils are poorer and more fragile than the soils of temperate regions. Their exploitation requires great precaution if one wants to avoid their impoverishment and destruction. These conditions give tropical agriculture a precarious character not present in temperate zone agriculture; so long as they are not dry regions where erosion awaits fallow land . . . tropical soils impose severe conditions on agriculture. Man has to be talented if he wants to save his land. In all the hot humid regions the farmer has found the same solutions to the problems posed

by the soil. The universals of space are perenially repeated in time; the Europeans in Brazil used the same procedures as the Indians, the Negroes, the Indonesians, or the Melanesians. The aim is to produce carbohydrates, the basic human food, through itinerant harvests. The technique is everywhere the same: alternating slash-and-burn with long fallow periods; in short, it is enough to recall the terms *ray* from ancient Indochina, *caingin* from the Philippines, *milpa* and *coamil* from Mexico, and *conueo* from Venezuela, all names for this technique" (Gourou 1953:15 and 29).

6. The special conditions of the Andean countries, such as the considerably higher altitude of inhabited areas than those of other countries of the continent and the cold temperature of the Pacific caused by the Humboldt Current, change the South American situation to such a point that a precise evaluation of it is necessary. Three main areas stand out in those countries: the Coast, the Andes, and the Amazon. The first is a desert habitat interrupted occasionally by alluvial fans formed by rivers descending to the sea. The coastal valleys are occupied by culturally and economically developed populations that displaced the original Indians during the early colonial period. The industrial cities and most numerous population groups are located in those valleys. The Amazon region has already been discussed.

The Andes are of greatest interest. They are formed by a great wall that runs parallel to the Pacific Ocean and rises to more than 6,000 meters above sea level. In its rough typography many different natural regions are found. Pulgar Vidal (1939) reduced these to eight in his geography of Peru. Residents of the place more commonly refer to the following four: the *yunga*, the *queshua*, the *puna* and the *cordillera*.

The *yunga* comprises the hot Andean slopes, both the humid eastern and the dry western ones, ranging from 500 to 2,500 meters above sea level. It is made up of narrow valleys and gorges formed at the juncture of Andean mountain spurs. The latter form occasional small terraces where the Indians live. The insect that carries *verruga*, a serious infectious disease, flourishes in the *yunga*.

The *queshua* extends from 2,500 to 3,500 meters above sea level. At the end of the *yunga*, the gorges turn into valleys that form, from Ecuador to Bolivia, longitudinal belts or amphitheaters of terraced hills with rivers running through the lowest level. It is the agricultural region par excellence of the inter-Andean range. Its climate is temperate with regular rainfall throughout the summer, from December to March. Corn is the basic crop and the Eucalyptus tree, introduced at the end of the last century, is the most important source of wood and fuel in places where vegetation is particularly sparse.

The *puna* rises from 3,500 to 4,500 meters above sea level; in Ecuador it is called the *páramo*. It occupies the mountain skirts and gently sloping spurs separating the fertile valleys of the inter-Andean range. In the highlands of Peru it forms part of the great altiplano where large bodies of water are also found, among them the largest high altitude lake in the world, Lake Titicaca. The region is cold and windy; in some places the cutting wind makes it so inhospitable that it is called *puna brava*. The plains descending gently from the mountain peaks are more hospitable; they are densely populated around Lake Titicaca and are called pampas. The *puna* is the region of *soroche* or mountain sickness, the most obvious manifestation of a brutal climate. It is a treeless land covered with varying kinds of long grasses. Among these the type known as *ichu* is prevalent and is used as fodder as well as for constructing roofs of dwellings. Around the lakes and *bofedales* grows a reed, the *totora*, which is highly important in the Indian economy from Ecuador to Bolivia. In the pampas the bitter potato is cultivated, from which *chuño, quinoa* and *cañiqua* are produced. In addition to animals introduced by the Europeans, flocks of American *auquénidos*—the llama, alpaca, vicuña and guanaco—graze the sparse vegetation of the *puna* and are protected from extinction in the regions of refuge.

Above the *puna*, mosses and lichen constitute the *cordillera's* thin vegetation until it disappears at the lower limit of the glaciers. The highest range of the Andes, that facing the Amazon, stores a large quantity of solid water in the form of snow and is called the *cordillera blanca*. The one facing the Pacific and its coastal desert is usually empty of glaciers and is called the *cordillera negra*.

7. Chapple and Coon (1953:93) add: "Barriers, when effective, create what is known as refuge areas. A refuge area is a region in which animal and vegetable species, and man as well, are protected by barriers from competition, and in which change comes less rapidly than in regions of greater circulation."

8. Sauer (1963:147) states: "In the late eighteenth century the progressively and rapidly cumulative destructive effects of European exploitation become marked. They are indeed an important and integral part of the industrial and commercial revolution. In the space of a century and a half—only two full lifetimes—more damage has been done to the productive capacity of the world than in all of human history preceding."

9. Sauer states: "The Spaniards passed in a few years from the trading and looting of metals to successful prospecting, at which they became so adept that it is still said that the good mines of today are the *antiguas* of colonial working. When mines were abandoned, it was less often due to the working-out of the ore bodies than to inability to cope with water in shafts and to the exhaustion of the necessary fuel and timber. A good illustration has been worked out for Parral in Mexico (West 1949). Zacatecas, today in the midst of a high sparse grassland, was in colonial times

a woodland of oak and pine and, at lower levels, of mesquite. About Andean mines the scant wood was soon exhausted, necessitating recourse to cutting mats of tola health and even the clumps of coarse ichu (stipa) grass. Quite commonly the old mining reales of North and South America are surrounded by a broad zone of reduced and impoverished vegetation. The effects were increased by the concentration of pack and work animals in the mines, with resultant overpasturing. Similar attrition took place about towns and cities, through timber-cutting, charcoal and lime-burning, and overpasturing."

10. Bartholomew and Birdsell (1962:24) add: "Thus territoriality is one of the primary factors which determine the density of population. It organizes a local population into a well-spaced array that allows adequate living conditions for all successful individuals. It limits the breeding population which can exist in suitable habitats and thus helps to prevent increase beyond the long-term carrying capacity of the range. This dispersive effect of territoriality can hardly help but be an important causal factor both in migration and in the spread of genes through a population."

11. Thompson (1937:60) states: "The land, basis of Mexican civilization, was divided between three categories of owners. The first, and most important, was the *calpulli*, or geographical clan of which there were twenty in Mexico City at the time of the fall of the Aztec regime."

12. Hallowel (1955:248) states: "Discussions of property among animals have centered around such phenomena as food-storing, the defense of the nest, prey, territorial domain, etc. There will be no need either to review the reported facts here, or to question them in any way. The problem at issue is the interpretation of their significance. To put the matter baldly, neither the de facto control exercised by animals over certain objects, nor the aggressive defense of them, is itself evidence that property as an institution exists among them. The question is: In what sense are such phenomena comparable with the society recognized and sanctioned rights in valuable objects that characterize property in human societies? The ambiguity in the use of the term property is no doubt partly responsible for the reputed human analogies found in animals." [Footnote indicated in original omitted here.]

13. Nesturj (1965:73) denies Weidenreich's hypothesis regarding the existence of several centers where different races formed.

14. Tax was the first to state: "That the Indians today who speak dialects of one language (such as Quiché or Cakchiquel) are not in any sense organized as a social group is evident from even a cursory study of Guatemala. . . . Nor is it clear that such linguistic terms as Quiché represent political or cultural groups that existed at the time of the Conquest. . . . The linguistic terms cannot be used unquestioningly, therefore to describe ethnic groups. . . .

Fortunately toward this end it is possible to isolate—quickly and certainly—groups of people who do represent without question, social and cultural units; and it is possible to name and define their type of organization and to describe their respective cultures. The people of Guatemala live in municipios which are territorial administrative divisions commonly recognized in all governmental matters, but which are also—as it happens—the basic ethnic divisions and cultural groups into which the country is divided" (Tax 1937:424).

15. Sauer (1963:363) warns: "In all regional studies—and we equate regional geography and historical geography—a serious problem is in the definition of the term 'area.' There has been so much inconclusive discussion of the term 'region' or 'area' that apparently no one definition suffices.

Most commonly the attempt has been to proceed from the 'natural area.' Yet it is hard to know what constitutes a natural area, unless it be an island, for climates, land forms, and soil provinces are likely to diverge widely. Hence the preference for the study of islands and areas that simulate insular conditions in their sharpness of outline."

Watson (1957:472) prefers the use of the concept *functional region*. "This is an area, dominated by a particular community of interest and activity, which functions in a characteristic way. As Stevens points out, a geographical region is the result of a synthesis of environmental and human factors. These factors are actually two aspects of the same thing. The geographer focuses attention on the synthesis in space—on the region; the sociologist on the synthesis in life—on the community. Since the community is a vital entity, it is dynamic, and has certain functions. Social geography studies the community in the region, and finds function and form more or less fused together in what he has come to call the functional region."

16. Núñez del Prado informs us that on occasions the vertical topography of Peru delimits precise levels on the mountainside. He states: "There are three altitude bands in what we might call the working area of Q'ero. On the first, at 4,000 to 4,500 meters despite its being a residential zone, the population is distributed among eleven sites along the snow line. . . . Q'ero is located in the second band, at more than 3,300 meters, where 53 varieties of edible potatoes and 15 of *chuno*, or 68 varieties in all are grown, as are 8 of *coas*, 8 of *ollucos*, and 3 of *añu*; in addition sheep, vacunos, horses, and some pigs and chickens are raised. . . . All the families of Q'ero have a house in the town or between one and 3 homes of relatives, which frequently serve as way stations en route to the third level, located between 1,800 and

2,000 meters, where the woods are found. . . . The altitude, climate, topography, and natural resources are all completely different at the 3 levels, each about 60 kilometers wide" (Núñez del Parado 1946:278).

Murra (1959:400) notes that the principal function of the *mitmaq* or Inca colonizers, "was the expansion of the area of corn cultivation. Bernabé Cobo tells us that when the population was located too high in the *puna* they were provided with corn growing lands at the coast or in the *montaña*. In such cases the mountain terrains were supplemented by contrasting lands."

17. Aguirre Beltrán (1953a) analyzed the Indo-Ladino structure of the Tzeltal-Tzotzil region, noting for the first time the importance of Ciudad Las Casas as the metropolis or regional *chef-lieu*. In *Programes de Salud en la Situación Intercultural* (1955) he formulated the theory of regional integration of the ruling center and satellite communities of the hinterland, and further developed that theory in *El Proceso de Aculturación* (1957).

Chapter 3

PROBLEMS OF POPULATION

The Demographic Cycle

IN CLASSIC GREEK usage, the term colony denoted simply a territory populated by emigrants of the mother country. The colonization of the New World by Ladinos or Iberian Latins differed because it entailed the establishment of dominant groups in an area already occupied by large masses of conquered peoples. The colonial situation disappeared at the national level a century and a half ago in all the important countries of the Americas; however, in some of the underdeveloped ones, it persists on the regional level, a bit of historical residue.

In these regions, which we have called regions of refuge, it is easy to see a structure of domination with a surprising number of archaic elements that are totally extinct in culturally and economically more advanced regions. Ladinos and subordinate Indians live together, the former as a dominant elite, the latter gathered into satellite communities around the Ladino center. Together they live as a dual population, segregated from each other, neighbors divided by a mutual barrier of prejudice and racial preconceptions.

Indians and Ladinos differ as to genetic makeup and phenotype; initially they were each part of very distinct racial groups and to a great extent they maintain the differences. Contrary to what happens on the national level, where mixture and acculturation form new physical types and modes of conduct, in the regions of refuge racial and social segregation endure. When the Europeans settled in the newly won land they created an ethnic stratification which placed them in the dominant position; their successors maintain this position by means of endogamy, which functions with great efficiency.

Biological and cultural mixing is very limited and remnants of hereditary differences not obliterated by time because of the inertia of the genetic stock are evident.[1] The Indians do not form a homogeneous population, but rather isolated communities that vary in terms of individual gene frequency. Isolation results from the obstacles forming the boundaries of the region, but within its borders the separation of communities is a function of their occupying different habitats in the same geographical framework.[2]

Loyalty to the group, marital restrictions, contact taboos, dialect or language variations, and tribal membership are all barriers added by men and are as powerful as those raised by nature. Prevailing conditions slow the genetic flow between the ethnic units, for the barriers of segregation and isolation function with great vigor. Nevertheless, the demographic complex and the conduct to which it gives rise are clearly the same in both populations, Indian and Ladino, since both are characterized by underdevelopment. Thus we may treat the two as if they constituted a single unit.

During the total course of their development, human groups pass through a series of changes determined by modifications in the relationship between births and deaths. This series is called the demographic cycle; for Blacker (1947) it is composed of five evolutionary phases. In the first, the high stationary phase, the birth and death rates are equally high. The unstable equilibrium achieved in this way is broken in times of peace and abundance, or by famine, war or epidemics which favor sudden increases or decreases, respectively, in the population. Survival, as noted, depends on considerable use of the generative force, as a high number of births must be maintained to compensate for numerous or unforeseen deaths.[3]

In the second or early expansive phase, better social organization reduces mortality, while births remain high. In the third phase—late expansive—the birth rate falls, but so does mortality, so that the population increase is still significant. In the following, late stationary phase, stability is again attained as births and deaths balance at very low rates. At this time net population increase is zero; there is no tendency either toward increase or decrease in the population, and contrary to what happens in the first phase, there are no violent fluctuations. The last phase, that of decline, is largely hypothetical; it has been manifested only in some European countries during the 1930s when, for a while, deaths superseded births (Barnett 1950).

If we accept the fact that during the years there have been variations in the demographic behavior of national populations so that phases or steps can be outlined which show distinct levels of evolution or kinds of behavior, then the regions of refuge would be placed in the first phase, similar to the long periods before the Industrial Revolution, when time seemed to pass slowly.[4] In fact, in these regions population problems are characterized by their timelessness. Compared with the problems of the culturally more advanced groups, it is easy to see differences originating from the fact that they are removed from the pressures of time.

These problems are similar to the ones which confronted today's prosperous nations long before their takeoff toward sustained growth; extreme cases can be compared to the problems of prehistoric peoples as brought to light by recent paleodemography. Regions of refuge are characterized by a demographic lag, by the evolutionary distance separating them from industrialized regions, and by the formation through tradition of antieconomical patterns of mortality, nutritional balance, life expectancy, births, population density, and growth.

THE MORTALITY RATE: One of the most instructive characteristics of the demographic complex is the mortality rate, or the relationship between the number of deaths per year and the number of inhabitants (reduced generally to 1,000) counted midway through the same year. In the regions of refuge the mortality rate is very high and oscillates between 35 and 40 per every 1,000 inhabitants. High mortality is due to the lack of effective means for preventing accidents and illness. Magical medicine, used by the Indians, functions as a means of social control, among other things, rather than as an instrument for lowering the continually high death rates; it is aimed at maintaining cohesion and survival of the community as a group rather than at effectively controlling suffering or for continuing individual life.

This undesirable situation is made obvious by the high gross or general mortality rate and is aggravated dramatically when specific rates are considered, rates such as infant mortality, which reaches figures of 250 deaths of infants under one year of age for each 1,000 born alive. In certain cases it reaches the incredible level of 800 per 1,000.[5] High infant mortality is a corollary of the prevalence of infectious diseases, which are endemic or spread by epidemics and which diminish the population and maintain an unstable equilibrium between health and illness.

The absence of effective means for controlling contagious disease has been a common experience in man's history, particularly during the Middle Ages, when he suffered calamitous epidemics and plagues and triumphed over them only with great difficulty. The simple fact that in the regions of refuge infectious diseases persist, is an unmistakable sign of the demographic lag. This is reinforced by the persistence of archaic illnesses which have disappeared among industrialized peoples; the mere detection of these is a sure sign of poor health.

NUTRITIONAL BALANCE. As important as mortality, nutritional imbalance or hunger has been considered a basic element in demographic behavior. The notable increase in communications as the world grows smaller and information and access become easier, has reduced the magnitude of this misfortune in countries where a prolonged drought, a devastating flood, or some other unforeseen catastrophe has lowered the availability of foodstuffs to alarming levels.

However, in underdeveloped countries, the regions of refuge remain exposed to hunger, isolated from the outside world, with a traditional structure of domination that hinders the effective implementation of generally accepted human rights. There, the old scourge of mankind periodically appears. In spite of the above, hunger, however notorious, is not the most destructive factor; rather, it is malnutrition, which insidiously decreases man's capacity to maintain health and prevent illness.

By modern standards the nutrition of the inhabitants of the regions of refuge is poor in terms of quantity as well as quality. The average diet is far below 2,200 calories, a sum considered insufficient for sustained well-being by nutritionists. The consumption of animal proteins necessary for growth is low; fewer than 30 grams of protein are eaten daily.[6] The amount of minerals and vitamins included in the diet is not only low but incomplete, causing frequent deficiency diseases which decrease the vigor of the population.

Although the above figures describing the nutritional balance in the regions of refuge are true, they may be incorrectly interpreted. In the Western world and particularly among neo-Malthusians there is a clear tendency to exaggerate certain principles, awakening anxieties upon which birth control policies may be based. However, these factors should be studied in the proper context, so that the conclusions drawn from them have scientific value. It seems obvious that surviving human groups—including the most primitive—have been able to continue because during the course of their development they have overcome the obstacles posed by hunger and sickness. In the animal world the balance between birth and death is much higher than the level of malnutrition. In the cultural world created by man, nutritional balance invariably has been attained by all populations that have managed to survive. There is no other way to explain the minimal organic vigor implied by the successful response to the challenge of nature and life in society (Sauvy 1953:22).

If we take the above into account, we can easily understand how, in terms of nutritional balance, the important factor is not deficiencies in the quantity and quality of nutriments in the regions of refuge. This balance appears inadequate because of different nutritional patterns, manifested in eating behaviors which, because of their strangeness, are thought to be irrational. These regions undergo years of scarcity and years of abundance, periods of want or of plenty, which are ruled by meteorological accidents or by the dictates of the ritual calendar. During the uncontrolled license of the fiestas, excessive food, including animal proteins, is consumed, and alcoholic beverages are consumed without moderation. These protein-rich foods are generally considered taboo as a direct result of the prohibition set upon beef and pork by colonial legislation. This dissipation is followed by a monotonous diet lacking in all luxuries, a forced fast between intervals of gluttony. This nutritional rhythm, in which periods of abstinence predominate, contributes to the conviction that there is permanent malnutrition. What is really seen is a different nutritional pattern, with behavior far removed from our own.[7] Rather than implying in some way a defense of the Indian model and the consequent disapproval of the Western, we wish to make clear the diversity between the models. In fact, the excellence of the latter over the former seems proven by the greater protection afforded by a continually balanced diet.

LIFE EXPECTANCY. As an inevitable result of high mortality and the inadequate nutritional pattern, life expectancy at birth is low. Even when reliable statistics are lacking, samples taken in the regions of refuge show that life expectancy at birth varies between 30 and 40 years. The demographic behavior of these regions parallels that of archaic peoples, whose average life expectancy has been shown to be near to or less than that cited above.[8]

Men and women who have barely transcended the conditions of animal life do not long outlive the end of their reproductive cycles. Because of this fact, the male assumes the obligations of an adult at an early age and achieves the rank of elder before facing and overcoming the crisis of middle age. Although the attainment of maturity is cause for respect and veneration in agrarian cultures and children are the best insurance for their parents' old age, only rarely do the latter enjoy the benefits of such security or of the esteem which the young are obliged to show them. Generally people die in the full vigor of their working years.

Women have no better luck; a higher proportion die and do so earlier than men.[9] In addition to the exhausting agricultural labor which is their duty, they tend flocks, make clothing, ceramics, and household tools, tend to the continuous domestic activities, raise children, and run the risks attendant upon their upbringing. In the rough environment of a simple culture, there are few instruments at hand to guarantee the life of a woman in labor and these are useless in case of complicated births or virulent puperal fever. It was with reason that Mesoamerican peoples considered childbirth to be valiant combat and bestowed upon women who died as a result of it the eternal, divine status of *cihuateteo*, goddess of women.

FERTILITY RATES. Adverse forces, tending to diminish or annihilate human groups, are in constant conflict with the opposing forces of fertility and survival; extinction, stagnation, or the explosive growth of populations all depend upon their balance or imbalance. In the regions of refuge, where there is strong competition for land and technology is primitive, an effective method of survival is the incorporation of inhabitants into rigid structures which maintain group cohesion through adherence to traditional life styles as well as through promotion of an ethnocentric loyalty which hinders acceptance of anything foreign.[10]

All of the above is achieved through endogamy, which, as it regulates relations between the sexes, prevents marriages with nonmembers of the group. In this way a kinship system takes shape in which descendance is traced from a common ancestor, binding all members of the community with real or imagined blood ties, and giving each individual an ascribed status and defined participation in the allocation of resources.

The emphasis placed on descent from a common ancestor, although rooted in the elemental biological necessities of the family, makes endogamy an autonomous institution, a carrier of values with greater power over personal relations than that exercised by the nuclear family. As its numbers and land increase, the closed community becomes oriented toward increasing its prestige and perpetuating its power; it confers and controls the means of subsistence and the destiny of its members. Thus the kinship system provides the fabric for the social structure for the peoples of the regions of refuge.

With its closed membership, effective authority, and continuity through successive generations, endogamy allows organization of economic activities and a feeling of unity based on the group's common origin. It evokes an emotional response in its members, who consider the community as the source of life and the vehicle of their immortality. Through such ingenious means it provides powerful motivation for a high fertility rate, which indeed is one of its specific functions. High birth rates—in the area of 40 per 1,000—have been statistically verified for populations living in regions of refuge.

High birth rates are found among both Indians and Ladinos, that is, in both component groups of the intercultural situation. Among the former, however, it would appear that internalization of reproductive patterns is very strong. Anxiety to reproduce, manifested in the desire to produce numerous children is reinforced by supernatural or social sanctions which reward individuals who conform to the established norms and threaten those who do not.

Among the Indians, the child confers adult status upon the parents. As long as a young couple remain childless their own status as children is retained and consequently they are not considered full members of the community. Adult status permits them to aspire to a cargo in the group's government. The rules governing matrimony—fully explained elsewhere (Beltran 1955:77-82; Beltran and Arciniega 1954: 179-81)—contribute to exhaustive use of the sexual cycle and oblige early childbearing. They prohibit bachelorhood as well as permanent widowhood. Sterility in both men and women is considered disgraceful; abortion and infanticide are punished; nursing and maternal care are highly valued; as is the satisfactory education of the child. At a very early age the latter contributes to the family income by becoming a productive member.

Among Ladinos, the endogamous circles are smaller—they do not form a community based on kinship—but one none the less vigorous. Marriages between neighboring families sometimes border on incest and numerous children are as welcomed by those high in the class structure as by those at the bottom. Generally, families average six children, corresponding to a birth rate of close to 40 per 1,000. However, belonging as they do to a relatively open society, these urban nuclei are more exposed to outside influences than are the Indians.

DENSITY. Population distribution in the regions of refuge, and more importantly, the relation between the number of inhabitants and the land—that is, population density—are determined by the resources of the environment and by the technology employed to exploit them.[11] This density varies considerably from one region to another. In the tropical jungles population density is extremely low, as it is in the wooded zones of the high mountains, on the semiarid steppes and great plains. On the other hand, in the intermontane valleys, both along the humid lake shores and where irrigation is lacking, the population clusters into relatively compact conglomerates and reaches high densities. In regions of refuge where the population is scattered, the density is less than one inhabitant per square kilometer; in areas where the Indians are concentrated, population density rises to more than 50 inhabitants per square kilometer.

As we have said, variations in the man-land relationship seen in the regions of refuge are determined by the nature of the useable resources. The comparative study of population density would be of little profit if it did not take this into account. To this end, demographers have refined their procedures by putting density into terms of area of cultivable land, not gross area. Since climate, soil, and other conditions vary in the different zones of a country, equivalents for variable resources were also created. In this way they came to the conclusion that the regions of refuge with high adjusted densities present problems of demographic pressure; on the other hand, those with low density suffer the effects of underpopulation.

The theory of demographic pressure has always been expounded in highly suggestive terms as an imminent danger necessitating prompt and energetic action. In reality we cannot speak of overpopulation based on gross or adjusted density, because those phrases stand for concepts of the satisfactions which man extracts from his habitat (Clark 1955). That is, the simple man-land relationship lacks meaning when one forgets that the most important factor it scores is the state of scientific knowledge possessed by a people and the level to which their technology has advanced. Given that the level of science and technology permits the entire and fruitful use of available resources, it could and in fact does happen that a peasant community with swidden agriculture requires a larger cultivable area than a horticultural community with irrigation. If both occupied territory of an equal area, the first group, with low population density, would experience demographic pressure while the second, with high density, would not.

From this frame of reference, it is easy to prove that all regions of refuge are inherently characterized by the existence of permanent demographic pressure and that this pressure has been present since the regions came into existence. The concentration of community lands in the hands of *hacendados* and plantation owners reduced the Indians' cultivable land, and they were forced to retreat to the safety of those regions which were least desired by the Ladino settlers. Contacts between carriers of Western culture and natives did not involve any important transfer of knowledge or techniques that might have facilitated the exploitation of those regions. Since then, numerous Indian groups have survived in their redoubts, using swidden technology in a limited area. Difficulties in defending the areas have caused them to shrink continually, pushed in by frontier landlords of the dominant Ladino group. The constant size of the population in the regions of refuge caused by a balance between deaths and births, the need imposed by swidden agriculture to maintain a large area of land fallow for many years, and the dispersion in tenancy and land use resulting from that system, all serve to mask population pressures to such a point that they are often thought to be nonexistent.

DEMOGRAPHIC GROWTH. Population does not constitute an independent variable in the complex mass of problems raised by a society's development; on the contrary, it is an endogenous variable understandable only in relation to the social structure, technological level, economic system, and other variables that determine the progress or backwardness of a human group. In the regions of refuge these variables produce forces both favoring and opposing growth, which conflict with one another and achieve dynamic equilibrium, thus stamping the demographic process with particular antieconomic characteristics.

In fact, the gross and infant mortality rates remain high and limit the gains from high fertility rates, causing an unproductive use of the generative force. The average of six children born to a family, commonly observed in Indian and tribal populations, does not indicate real population increase since mortality diminishes the number to two surviving children. In such conditions, growth rates are mere replacement rates, and the waste of the generative force is evident. In order to achieve cultural continuity and social survival, the group uses considerable biological force; it wastes human life thoughtlessly. With some truth, Sauvy asserts:

> In primitive societies and among little developed peoples, richer in men than in goods, objects are looked after and repaired with infinite care, but men are not. It is more economical to create them anew. In developed populations, man acquires value; contrarily, objects are discarded after little use because it is less costly to make them anew and men, rarer and more precious, become the object of attentive care (1963:329).

The natural growth of a population is measured by the difference between births and deaths; its social growth, by the favorable balance of immigration over emigration. In the regions of refuge natural increase offers the only possibility of growth. The clannish or closed nature of the human groups represses social mobility and in practical terms, nullifies it. Groups from outside the community, even Indians of the same area with the same culture, language, and status, are rarely admitted to full membership in the endogamous circle. Thus renovation of the population's genetic structure is hindered, and variations as to physical types are few. But above all, contact with outsiders and their life styles is avoided.

These characteristics make growth slow and uneven; the mechanisms regulating it resemble closely those governing the biotic equilibrium in animal societies, where hunger and sickness determine demographic stability. The population in the region of refuge does not grow, or does so slowly. In the course of history, when adverse forces have acquired greater weight it has been pushed to the brink of extinction only to surge forth immediately with an unexpected increase in births and thus produce, finally, merely a frustrated flowering. With such an uncertain rhythm, it is obvious that population growth is antieconomical.

EXPLOSIVE CHANGE. The deplorable picture outlined above describes the situation which prevailed in the regions of refuge from their inception until a few years ago, before the end of the last world war. Since then the situation has taken an unexpected turn which has especially affected the mortality rate, both generally and for infants. This rate, which had remained consistently high for centuries, suddenly began to drop, decreasing by at least half. At the same time the birth rate remained high or even rose, and the resulting breach between the two rates increased daily. The traditional stagnation ended abruptly; the difference between births and deaths and the growth in life expectancy increased continuously. When the regions of refuge burst suddenly into the expansive phase of their demographic evolution, they did so without maintaining a parallel rhythm of change in the other dependent variables.[12]

The decline in mortality and its consequences took place among present-day developed peoples more than 100 years ago, when they began the takeoff towards new economic forms. Births fell subsequently, when these groups firmly adopted values which led to rapid modernization and urbanization. The declines in both deaths and births that began not long ago were slow moving tendencies which provoked no serious disturbances. They accompanied the improvement in the tenor of life brought about by economic development and contributed to its realization. There was no demographic explosion; there was a consistently maintained population increase. Thus, the changes were not the same as those presently confronting the regions of refuge which face problems demanding different explanations and solutions.

Basically, two types of factors mediate in the decline of mortality: (1) those depending on consumption levels and directly connected with the economic variable, and (2) those derived from improvement in scientific knowledge, related only indirectly to per capita income. In the demographic history of developed countries, an increase in consumption levels brought about a decline in death rates, while in the developing countries of today—especially in their regions of refuge—the decline in mortality has been caused by improvement in scientific knowledge, enabling public health authorities to successfully implement programs for erradication of the long-time scourges of humanity—endemic and epidemic diseases.[13]

The discovery of antibiotics and certain insecticides such as DDT, and their easy availability at low cost, have permitted campaigns against malaria, venereal diseases, and typhus, among others, and have lowered death rates sharply. Certainly many of these campaigns did not reach the more remote regions of refuge and when they did reach them, did not include the entire population. In the Indo-Ladino binomial, the Ladinos were generally protected while the Indians were not. Cities and Ladino settlements benefitted from the campaigns, while the Indians rejected them although some were forced to accept them through coercion. Nonetheless, it cannot be doubted that preventive measures among Ladinos as well as among the Indians residing in contact with them, and the general health improvement of the developed regions surrounding the regions of refuge, were all positive influences in improving the sanitary situation in those regions. The decline in deaths in them is a fact, although the statistics leave much to be desired.

THE BIRTH LAG. The spectacular decline in death rates in the regions of refuge gave the demographers of poverty the hope that a similar decline in birth rates would occur shortly; models of the developed countries were used and it was thought that demographic history could repeat itself.[14] Things did not happen as expected because the causes of the decreases in the two cases were different. In the industrial countries the decline began during the first half of the last century and slowly reached its climax during the 1930s. It is generally accepted that the decline in both deaths and births was caused by improvements in economic and social conditions. The agricultural and industrial revolutions produced higher per capita income, better housing, more clothing and, in the long run, more humane treatment for the peasant and the worker. Prosperity brought with it an abundant and balanced diet, expansion of education and the right to good health; that is, a rise in standards of living. In the regions of refuge the decline in the death rate was caused by progress in the physical and biological sciences originating in the culturally and economically more developed areas. A decline in the birth rate has not yet appeared.

The sensitivity of the death rate to public health programs can be explained not only by the considerable effectiveness of modern medicine but also by the fact that both conservation of health and the struggle against death are welcomed by all peoples of the world, including those isolated in the regions of refuge. The response in terms of the birth rate has not been the same. A reduction in births is a serious matter which damages highly esteemed social values linked to the group's survival, and to its power, prestige, and well-being. The combination of elements which modified the goals and social structures of the industrialized regions, and which are necessary to obtain the active compliance of a population in producing fewer children, did not appear in the regions of refuge concurrently with the sharp fall in mortality. The change in social goals and structures is a slow process, effected by such factors as urbanization, economic modernization, social mobility, change in the status of women, secularization of customs, and concomitant loss in religious belief, and fear of supernatural sanctions.[15]

In the developed regions this process began when the decline in mortality appeared and took almost a century to be completed. The difference between birth and death rates was never great. There was a sustained population increase which seemed to stop momentarily in the 1930s, when the breach between births and deaths was closed. In the regions of refuge, on the other hand, the decline in births is considerably behind the decline in deaths. This lag has increased as the two demographic forces move in opposite directions: births upward and deaths downward. The gap between the two tendencies grows continuously and will continue to do so while births remain high, that is, as long as the population experiences none of the stimuli dependent upon improvement in economic and social conditions. An exact knowledge of the nature of those stimuli and of the ways in which they operate is important because it explains the nature of one of the basic components of the demographic process, fertility.

The biological capacity to reproduce is known as fecundity; the actual exercise of fecundity is called fertility. In human groups the two terms are not equivalent because cultural conditioning alters the simple biological situation. Differences in birth rates between regions or between classes in the same region are not caused by the greater or smaller reproductive capacity of men and women, but rather by the different uses to which they put that capacity.[16] The above definitions embody the belief that fecundity, as a biological function, does not vary or varies within very narrow limits throughout the human race, while fertility, a function of the social structure, is and may be modified by very different motivations.

SOCIOECONOMIC MOTIVATION. The demographic behavior of societies with a subsistence economy is often described as irrational by writers who view it superficially. The enormous burden which those societies place on the woman seems to be irrational in any light: they force her to bear children from a very early age until the termination of her active sexual cycle; she is also obliged to nurse her children for a prolonged period regardless of the other tasks placed upon her by the division of labor. However, when demographers analyze the various religious, social and economic motivations supporting the traditional norms, they produce perfectly rational explanations for such behavior. Continuing this research, they also provide satisfactory explanations for the rational motivations leading those peoples to limit fertility when takeoff toward sustained development occurs.

In the course of the present analysis we have made frequent reference to such explanations, without noting that they are not all of equal significance. In many cases they represent complementary or competing theories at different levels of abstraction; in others, they are partial or incomplete explanations of the forces that determine the demographic situation. In various essays, demographers have tried to construct general frameworks which include the different theories in a unified and integrated conceptual system. Thus a system has emerged, composed of theories which differ from each other in terms of the emphasis placed upon cultural, structural, or economic factors, but which coincide in their basic premises. Leibenstein (1963) authored the most recent formulation of an integral system of ideas, focusing upon population problems from the angle and in the language of economics. His framework allows a coherent explanation of the demographic phenomenon as it is expressed in the regions of refuge undergoing change.

According to Leibenstein, human groups regulate their demographic behavior as if they were roughly estimating the desired number of births. Such estimates take into account the increase in satisfaction over expenditures resulting from the births of additional children. Benefits arise from considering the child: (1) as a consumer good or source of pleasure for the parents; (2) as an agent of production who in due time will contribute to the family budget; (3) as a potential source of security for his kin, especially in their old age. Costs include direct or conventional expenses imposed by the maintenance and raising of the child and the indirect or incidental costs represented by lost wages during the gestation and nursing periods owing to the mother's incapacity to move or work. The relationship of profits and costs to the factors of economic growth is so close that the two analyses should be made together. These economic factors are: (1) increase in income, (2) greater survival, and (3) changes in occupational distribution. We shall look at each of them in turn.

The effect of income upon consumption satisfaction does not appear significant, since it is difficult to predict whether parents experience greater or less pleasure from an additional child when their income rises or falls. On the other hand, the relationship between the value of a child as contributor to the family income and variations in per capita income is clear. To the degree that income increases, there is less need to use children as sources of income. The rise in living standards, on the other hand, means that training and formation of the child takes longer and that, therefore, a shorter time is available in which to use him as an agent of production. A similar tendency is observed in regard to the child's usefulness as a factor of potential security. When income increases, the ability of parents to insure and provide for their own old age also increases and the need for children as a source of security declines. In regard to costs, the effect of income is obvious.[17] The conventional costs of supporting a child increase to the degree that per capita income increases, as rearing and formation of the child depend upon the social position of the parents. Indirect costs behave similarly. Opportunities for mothers to be employed in productive activities grow as income rises, and therefore the costs of losing such opportunities also increase.

The effect of survival upon costs and benefits is, of course, important, but it is not proportional, as in the case of income. Initially the decline in mortality rates is inexpensive; however, the costs of additional improvements increase in direct proportion to the increase in life expectancy. Similarly, increased survival theoretically makes benefits rise since each birth entails more prospective years of life and therefore, presumably, more years of satisfaction and a greater value placed on children as productive agents, and sources of security for the mature years. But these benefits are proportional to increased survival only to the point at which their effect begins to decline as a motivating force for additional children. Survival does not apply only to infants but also to older age groups and a decline in mortality among persons who have come of age indicates a lower value placed upon children as a source of family income and security in old age.

The basic effect of occupational distribution is to increase direct and indirect costs. To the extent that the tenor of life improves, specialization and economic and social mobility increase. The environment thus created requires more costly training for children and an increasing abandonment of family obligations by the parents in order to take advantage of new social and economic opportunities. Increased specialization, produced by the growth in per capita production, entails a combination of social and economic circumstances in which the costs of opportunity for a large family rise rapidly. In the last half of the nineteenth century, Arsène Dumont (1890:106) called this kind of cost *social capillarity*, and noted that during the period when family size declined, new attitudes toward social mobility developed which lead to a rise of parents' position or in that of their children on the hierarchical scale.[18]

STAGNATION AND CHANGE. Having discussed the basic premises of our analysis of demographic forces, let us consider their possible use in interpreting the situation of the regions of refuge during stages of stagnation and change. During times of stagnation, examination of benefits and costs indicates that they create motivations for high fertility rates. Since mortality rates are high, a considerable number of conceptions is required to create enough children for at least two of them to survive and replace the parents. In an agricultural environment, the benefits ascribed to those two children are high while direct and indirect costs are always low. Survival is certainly given highest priority in societies where life is lived on a subsistence level. Despite the fact that the birth rate is high, the number of newborns who survive is barely sufficient to replace and perpetuate the family and lineage. With such high mortality, all motivation leads to maximum fertility. Potential parents know that opportunities for survival are few and that only with the maximum number of births can they be reasonably sure of having children who will outlive them.

In the stage of change, the salient characteristic of demographic behavior in the regions of refuge is a sharp fall in mortality and a continued high birth rate. This lag in fertility, which begins when the birth rate does not reflect the decline in mortality, should be attributed to two complementary factors. Leibenstein (1963:166) calls the first factor retardation in realization; this refers to the fact that time and patience are required for a change in the conditions which enable a similar decline in births to take place. The impact of an improvement in survival possibilities is not felt immediately. The decrease in mortality, if it takes place quickly, gives little opportunity for the creation of new responses with which to confront realistically the new situation; the people, conditioned to traditional responses, react in accordance with their internalized behavior which maximizes anxiety regarding reproduction. The more gradual the process of change, the weaker is the impact upon the human group and the greater the time available to adapt to the new situation. These facts justify a certain retardation in the decline in fertility.

The other factor explaining this retardation is the increase in survival, which initially raises benefits and lowers costs. Increased income permits the parents the satisfaction of a greater number of children. Given the fact that initially the mortality rate drops more rapidly in the lower age groups than in the higher ones, the benefits accruing from children as agents of production and security also increase. The costs of support decline because of the effect of increased survival; although the gross annual cost of support increases, the net cost falls because the initial decline in mortality reduces drastically the proportion of those who die in their productive years. Consequently, motivations for a reduction in fertility do not develop in the early stages of economic improvement.

The forces generated by economic growth make the benefits derived from additional children as sources of pleasure or agents of production and security, progressively less important, while costs of support and upbringing increase. The growing rise in income produces changes in social structure and organization which are of great importance in the gradual disappearance of those benefits. Urbanization, as a concomitant of the increase in income; time, as children remain for increasingly long periods in school; and systems of insurance against unemployment, illness and old age; reduce the role of children to providing pleasure only. Indirect costs, arising from the opportunities for remunerative work which open for women, and from the increased needs derived from greater mobility, continually increase to the degree that income grows. When the critical takeoff point is reached in economic growth, the balance changes and the new trend is toward creation of motivation for a decline in fertility.

The relation between a decline in fertility and economic growth is obvious; to produce the former it is necessary that the latter reach a critical level. Ethnographic research has not yet discovered a single agrarian society with a subsistence economy showing a tendency towards decreased fertility. This only takes place when the structure of the society changes. The practical implications of an analysis of the problem of birth rates, as well as other factors facing the regions of refuge, are truly stimulating, and they will be considered in the appropriate place.

NOTES

1. Dobzhansky states: "An endless and notoriously inconclusive discussion of the 'race problem' has been going on for many years in the biological, anthropological, and sociological literature. Stripped of unnecessary verbiage, the question is this: is a 'race' a concrete entity existing in nature, or is it merely an abstraction with a very limited usefulness. To a geneticist it seems clear enough that all the lucubrations on the 'race problem' fail to take into account that a race is not a static entity but a process. Race formation begins when the frequency of a certain gene or genes becomes slightly different in one part of a population from what it is in other parts. If the differentiation is allowed to proceed unimpeded, most or all of the individuals of one race may come to possess certain genes which those of the other race do not. Finally, mechanisms preventing the interbreeding of races may develop, splitting what used to be a single collective genotype into two or more separate ones. When such mechanisms have developed and the prevention of interbreeding is more or less complete, we are dealing with separate species. A race becomes more and more of a 'concrete entity' as this process goes on; what is essential about races is not their state of being but that of becoming. But when the separation of races is complete, we are dealing with races no longer, for what have emerged are separate species" (1941:62).

2. Monge (1962) is perhaps the one who has most vigorously reiterated the anatomical, physiological, and even genetic diversity resulting from the vertical nature of the Andean habitat. He has even asserted that the Andean man, who lives between 2,000 and 5,000 meters, belongs to a climatic or physiological variant of the human race, with different biological characteristics from those of man at sea level. The Conference of Anthropological Sciences held under his leadership in Lima in 1951 devoted much of its time to the study of man in his ecological relationship to the Andes. Hurtado (1951) described significant differences in the height, weight, chest measurement, and cardiovascular system, in hematology and in acid balance observed at varying altitudes. Of course the differences include both Indians and *mistis*, both highland inhabitants.

3. Coon and Hunt state: "In the European colonial regions, the natives, without exception, continued to represent Phase I of the population trend for some time after the arrival of the whites (for example in the Union of South Africa, New Zealand, and the United States). The first contact most primitive tribes had with Europeans led at first to a sharp drop in population. The factors here are a high mortality rate–through the introduction of diseases, through brutal decimation, and through the natives' being driven into poverty-stricken and retreat areas–as well as a falling birth rate. Such a drop is caused by, among other things, venereal disease, enlisting the male population as migrant laborers, as well as mental depression brought on by the dissolution of the tribal order and ethnically ingrained systems of values. As a result, a number of smaller primitive groups died out (Tasmanian, some American Indian and Melanesian tribes); others, however, survived the adaption crisis and returned to the group of stationary populations or even became growing populations by adopting certain elements of the colonialists' culture, thus causing their mortality rate to drop. This holds true for numerous Melanesian groups, for the Maori in New Zealand, and for North American Indians (1963:51).

4. See Shannon (1957) Introduction to Part III, "The demographic characteristics of undeveloped areas."

5. Pressat (1961). The countries with the highest levels of sanitation are close to rates of 20 per 1,000, beyond which it is difficult to go, due to the intervention of constitutional and hereditary factors which are very difficult to separate.

6. Josué de Castro (1964:112) attributes the high birth rate in underdeveloped countries to protein deficiencies. His argument goes as follows: "In regard to sexual behavior, it has been proven that chronic hunger–specific or latent–acts quite differently than acute hunger. People suffering from chronic malnutrition, after lowering their sexual drives, demonstrate heightened drives and a clear increase in fertility. This intensification of the reproductive capacity among peoples suffering from chronic hunger is explained by means of a complex mechanism which includes both psychological and physiological factors. Psychologically, chronic hunger heightens the sexual drive as a means of emotional compensation. All physiologists recognize that under normal conditions there is some competition among the instincts of nutrition and reproduction; whenever one is antenuated the other increases." Josué presents experiments in laboratory animals and then creates a graph in which he correlates protein ingestion and birth rates in developed, developing, and underdeveloped countries. There one sees that the highest birth rates correspond to the lowest rates of protein consumption. Nevertheless, Josué makes no distinction between fertility and fecundity; that is, between reproductive capacity and the exercise of that capacity where nonbiological motivations intervene.

Coontz (1960:50) in his study of population theories, dedicates a paragraph to an analysis of previous analyses based on diet, which originated with Doubleday's work. According to him, "the great general law that appears to really regulate increase, or decrease of life, as much vegetable as animal is this: . . . the intensity of each state." Regarding the protein theory, Coontz says, "Of course, it is up to the biologists and physiologists to determine if diet regulates human fertility . . . Shall we infer that the consumption of proteins in that country has been less in the present period than in the worst years of the depression?"

7. See Aguirre Beltrán (1955), Chapter III "Culture and Nutrition." Barriga et al. (1965) deal with the fundamental importance of nutrition in cultural change.

8. Coon and Hunt state: "According to paleodemographic research, the mortality trend has shown a constantly downward tendency ever since the dawn of history. In the Paleolithic Age, few people lived beyond their fiftieth birthday. In the Neolithic Age and in the Bronze Age, on the other hand, people died at an older age and there is proof that some lived beyond 60 years of age. In later epochs, the proportion of older people in the population continued to grow, but by no means regularly and not to the same degree in all areas. Where infant and child mortality can be established (late Iron Age in Sweden, early Middle Ages in Hungary), it is not substantially above Phase I of modern European times in the case of sedentary populations. In most prehistoric populations, female mortality is higher than male mortality. The fact that life span extends far beyond the sexually and reproductively active years is a specifically human phenomenon and represents a result of advancing civilization" (1963:47).

9. Wrong (1957:57) states: "In almost all populations life expectancy for women is greater than that for men. The female may or may not be weaker than the male, but she does manage to live longer. There are more widows than widowers throughout the world, and the tendency of males to marry younger females in most societies increases the probability of their wives surviving them. Various factors enter into this sexual difference. Men's work is generally more tiring and more dangerous, exposing them to greater risk of death. Women run the risk of dying in childbirth, and in those countries where modern medical attention is rare the mortality rates are higher for women than for men during the child bearing years. But in the developed countries—by eliminating puperal fever—even during the child bearing years women have lower mortality rates than men. Therefore women's greater longevity is clearer in the more advanced countries."

10. Lorimer states: "Corporate clans and lineages (with closed membership, a system of authority, and continuity through successive generations) are widely prevalent among the dominant tribal societies in areas of intense competition for resources among tribal societies. They are a common, though not universal, characteristic of such situations. These forms of social organization are not found with equal frequency among people with more primitive techniques in regions of refuge. And they are not found, at least with the same force, in well-established agrarian civilizations.

Corporate kinship groups, according to the thesis defined in the previous chapter, also tend to induce strong motivation for high fertility. Under normal conditions the level of fertility characteristic of societies with such groups is likely to be well above that required for mere replacement of population, bringing increase of population. Under the conditions of intertribal competition for resources, increase of population in any society does not necessarily depress its level of subsistence. It may, on the contrary, increase its power to retain its present resources or to enlarge these resources through the occupation of adjacent lands" (1954:92).

11. Loyo (1943:50) states: "The influence of population density over public works, communication, public services, public safety, social discipline, public health, the growing needs of backward groups and the processes of imitation and invention, have been studied rather carefully in some countries for some historical periods. The density necessary to accelerate progress for some groups varies, as is obvious according to the geographic, cultural, etc., obstacles that have to be overcome. Population increase varies in its importance, according to the nature of the people, their historical evolution, and their current situation. Population increase, by itself, has little effect."

12. Taeuber (1965:44) states with alarm: "Perhaps the greatest social and political process of our times is the development of aspirations among the ordinary peoples of Latin America, Asia, and Africa. The corollary of aspirations in a milieu of population growth, precarious economic advance, and rigidity in social structures is frustration."

13. Davis (1963:211) states: "In today's underdeveloped countries, on the other hand, the spectacular declines of mortality are being made by importing the latest medical discoveries from the most industrialized countries, usually with the help of medical personnel and funds from the latter nations. Modern techniques, applied on a mass basis under government sponsorship, have achieved almost miraculous results in the control of infectious diseases and other ailments among backward peoples. These results do not depend on economic development within the areas in question, because funds and personnel can be brought in from outside. They do not depend on scientific discoveries within the areas in question, because the research is done in the laboratories of America, Australia and Europe. This is why the extremely fast drop in the death rate in the world's backward areas is occurring at a more primitive stage of economic development than it did in the Western industrial nations. As noted above, the most rapid death rate declines in the latter countries came after 1900, a time when these countries were already industrialized and when their birth rates had already started down. In the backward lands today, death rates are being brought down at a faster clip among

peoples who in some cases are scarcely removed from savagery and in other cases are overwhelmingly agrarian."

14. Kuznets (1955:954) explains: "This suggests an important contrast between the currently underdeveloped countries and the situation of the developed countries as it was just before the introduction of the major technological changes that ushered in the modern industrial system—the system whose adoption constitutes much of the content of modern economic development. At that time, mid or late 18th century, many of the developed countries of today were already advanced economically—by contemporary standards; had already experienced fairly sustained growth over the earlier centuries, and enjoyed political independence in doing so; and were direct participants in and beneficiaries of the extension of knowledge and changes in attitudes that constituted the three revolutions mentioned. In contrast, most underdeveloped countries of today are inheritors of much older civilizations which, however economically superior in the distant past, include strongly entrenched elements that constitute serious obstacles to the adoption of the modern industrial system. They face the problems of development after decades, if not centuries, of political subjection which, granted some beneficial effects, left a heritage against which the newly established independent regimes must struggle. Thus, they must approach the task of utilizing the available potential of economic knowledge not from the position of near leadership and at the end of a cumulative process of preceding growth and learning carried on under conditions of political independence; but from the position of laggards by a long distance and after a period in which internal organization was distorted either by political subjection or by co-existence with the aggressive leaders of the economic civilization of the West."

15. Cipolla (1964:104) states: "The three basic types of economic organization, hunting, agriculture and industry, are accompanied by three corresponding scales of economic and demographic levels by which society acts . . . the range of a society from one type of organization to another implies that there will also be some drastic cultural and social changes . . . when industrialization occurs gradually, these socio-cultural changes occur simultaneously with the economic ones and equilibrium is maintained. Nevertheless, when industrialization increases artificially, as is happening in many backward regions now, the socio-cultural sector can be far more resistant to change than the economic structure."

16. Carr-Saunders studies the influence of birth control over the fertility rate (1939:101).

17. Spengler (1964:813) tells us, however: "The circumstances which underlie the connections between income and fertility are not well known. In fact, the information available about the social-psychological processes which connect change in income with the responses of the individual experiencing this income change is very slight."

18. Gonnard (1945:335) explains Dumont's ideas. For him, "The limited resources the individual possesses may be put to various uses: consumption for personal pleasure, reproductive or industrial consumption, sterile consumption, and consumption for raising a new generation. . . . The individual aspires to raise himself up—to educate himself—his education demands the consumption of greater resources. The more he spends to advance himself, the less will be left for the care of his children, and even less if he tries to advance each of them . . . Generally speaking, civilization tends to increase the role of this drive of man to improve himself and to sacrifice an increasingly greater part of his resources to do so. Civilization implies the creation of new necessities, new pleasures, new activities, all of which permit and require an increase in personal expenses, be they for pleasure or for advancement. The social structure includes more and more levels as civilization becomes more refined. *Capilarity* becomes more important; it produces the effect of increasing pressure on the liquid skin and the lengthening of the tube in which the liquid rises. Less of the family wealth is left to the children and (at the same time) a greater portion of it is needed for each child, as it becomes more and more expensive to instruct and care for them."

Chapter 4

HUMAN MOBILITY

Change of Residence

OUR EXAMINATION of population problems would be incomplete were we to limit the analysis to factors of fertility and mortality without taking into account migration, that is, change of residence by persons from one area, region, or country to another. Migration is an important component of demographic change and, together with fertility and mortality, shapes the mechanisms which cause human groups to increase or decline. Migration is part of the general process of movement of both goods and persons; however, it has peculiar characteristics which limit the range of phenomena that it influences. We maintain that migration is a change of residence, but a change that entails a readjustment of the migrants' affiliations. They break loyalties, obligations, and duties to their community of origin in order to acquire membership in the new one.

In the regions of refuge, Indian communities generally have an exogamous kinship structure which expels women from their *calpul*, barrio, or moiety to that of the husband. In accordance with marriage rules, women who marry change residence permanently and break their original affiliations; despite this, the movement of wives brought about by exogamy does not constitute a true migration. The selective movement of one of the sexes is compensated by the fact that a *calpul*, barrio, or moiety receives as many women as leave it. The rupture in affiliation comes about through institutionalized channels and does not entail the breaking of community unity but, on the contrary, strengthens it.[1] To speak of true migration it is necessary that the persons involved in the process cross the border which defines them as people. In the regions of refuge this is represented by the territorial frontiers separating one community from another. The change in residence and affiliation from one's original community to an outside one defines migration.

The transfer of laborers recruited for work away from the community does not satisfy the requisites of true migration either. Commonly, so-called migrant laborers are contracted for seasonal work by plantation owners who need abundant manual labor in the critical periods of the agricultural cycle. Once these periods are over, the hired workers return to their places of origin, to await further calls; the Indian community acts as a reservoir of readily available manual labor. For the most part the transactions take place through special control processes which leave the prospective employee no alternative but a forced transfer to the plantation, with no insurance as to salary, the nature of his work or unexpected contingencies which might arise in a strange environment. When the worker returns to his community, liberated from the psychic and physical oppression of outside control, he is reintegrated into his own culture and patterns of economic behavior. His contact with modern patterns in a situation where he is under domination is neither pleasant nor does it serve as an incentive for him to promote modifications in the traditional patterns of his own community. The so-called migrant worker does not break off affiliations with his community of origin; there his family and lineage remain the source of his security and the roots of his survival (Van Hecke 1951:3).

It was thought for some time that work outside the community would be a powerful inducement for cultural change. In fact, one of the rationalizations for the coercive use of indigenous manual labor was that the mobilization of the workers would rebound to their benefit. Coming into contact with modern economic structures in places where community sanctions could not be applied to those who departed from tradition, the migrant—it was said—would easily adopt new techniques which would change his inefficient modes of production.[2] It is undeniable that continuous exposure to the persuasive influence of a foreign culture causes involuntary changes in the culture and personalities of migrant workers, above all in workers from simple subsistence level agrarian societies. What is ignored or not understood in this respect is the immeasurable power of the internal defense mechanisms put into play by communities faced with threats to their stability. These mechanisms force the migrant workers who return to the heart of the family to conform to traditional patterns. It is easily seen that migratory work must rupture the bonds between the migrant and his community—something which never deliberately takes place—if cultural change is to occur.

The types of moves which have been analyzed so far are frequently observed in the regions of refuge. Also observed are other kinds which neither entail (1) crossing of frontiers as in migration; (2) permanent residence in the new community; nor (3) readjustments in affiliation. The dynamics of these moves tend to mask the stagnation and immobility which are the cardinal, prevailing characteristics in these regions and which pertain to both Indian and Ladino communities. As we know, isolation is one factor which works powerfully to impart to the Indian regions their sheltering quality, but this benefit, if it may be called that, imposes an inexorable cost. That cost is measured in the biological, social, economic, and cultural consequences of isolation. Lack of biological exchange causes an absence of mutations in the genetic makeup and the deterioration of possibilities for survival. Lack of social, economic, and cultural communication causes underdevelopment, stagnation, and immobility.

CHANGE OF AFFILIATION. Despite the preponderance of forces safeguarding the stability of the regions of refuge, opposing forces for change, although weak, are always present and preclude the total and catastrophic absence of human mobility. When we examined territoriality we noted that it operates to maintain balance between available resources, techniques of production, and population. Thus, in normal times the population never reaches the point of perennial undernourishment which might force it to live at the limits of the food supply. The high mortality rates in these regions effectively regulate the relationship between resources and population and prevent a disproportionate increase in the latter. The free exercise of the generative force, on the other hand, prevents an absolute decline in population.

When mortality does not balance the birth rate, the biotic balance seeks its level through migration, that is, by the expulsion of surplus inhabitants. In primitive conditions, ostracism is generally equivalent to exposure to rapid death, which only a few escape. Like all biosocial forces, the mechanism of territoriality includes two opposing tendencies: when the biotic balance is achieved through mortality, territoriality operates against human mobility; when equilibrium is maintained through migration, it favors geographic mobility. To be sure, migratory movement takes place in only one direction, that is, from the center outward. This directionality negates the revolutionary consequences of migration and channels both it and mortality toward maintaining the established order.

In the regions of refuge there are often communities with extensive areas that are not always fully occupied. Vacant land sometimes results from bad soil, which prevents profitable harvests unless fertilizers are used, and sometimes from scant rainfall which necessitates irrigation for the land to be productive. Empty lands may be caused by an unhealthy climate where both endemic diseases and epidemics flourish, requiring costly sanitation measures, or they may simply result from a lack of roads which makes them inaccessible. Communities with vacant lands are generally those farthest from the regional center and consequently the ones least desired by Ladinos.

When the mechanisms of territoriality are in operation and surplus inhabitants are exposed to destruction, this does not always produce the intended results. Some of those expelled survive by marauding in the empty lands and manage to establish a means of living there. New migrants increase the number of marauders and through such infiltration sufficient new inhabitants gather to defend themselves against attacks by the people in whose territory they have made their home. Migrants, expelled from their communities of origin, break their former affiliations, but if they achieve the capacity for self-defense as a group, they usually do not seek affiliation with the strangers in whose lands they have settled. Rather they remain apart as a differentiated group, through the years strengthening the characteristics which distinguish them as an ethnic minority. If these minorities establish themselves in territories contiguous to their former community of affiliation they may establish ties with it, thus increasing the size of the original community's territory.

Migration through infiltration takes place every day. Although it is cumulative, the number of migrants at any given time is small and thus the migration is not apparent. Vacant lands in the regions of refuge are technically considered to be reserved for redistribution to the national population. When an attempt is finally made to occupy them they are often taken by infiltration. Occasionally the migrant farmers establish occupation rights and agrarian authorities find themselves forced to give legal sanction to such possession.

The ways in which migration through infiltration occurs depend upon many circumstances, including the technological level of the migrants, their rate of technological change, the amount and quality of available land, and transportation and health conditions. When conditions are particularly inhospitable, migration is small; when they are favorable it assumes considerable proportions because of its cumulative nature. Such large numbers hinder or prevent internal colonization projects, and when these are implemented it is often discovered with surprise that the most fertile, most accessible, best endowed lands have already been occupied. Therefore the cost of colonization increases and its success, which seemed assured when the opening of these lands was planned, is endangered (Forsythe 1942).

In the agricultural lands of the regions of refuge, nativistic or messianic movements cause migrations which are less frequent but broader. They arise when the internal problems and domination within the Indian communities become intolerable. Domination of the Indians by the Ladino city inevitably produces a deterioration in native culture and personality, which results in anomie or disorganization of the established order. Resistance to internally or externally generated change aggravates anomie, which can only be resolved when the pressure of repressed innovations becomes sufficiently strong to force a revolution in prevailing conditions. Reform is made possible by the appearance of a messianic leader who is sensitive to the collective aspirations of the people and capable of catalyzing them into patterns of action which integrate all the energies of the group. Nativist movements sometimes fuse the dissatisfactions of a large number of communities; others include only the members of a single community. Generally, however, they involve small but aggressive specific groups which constitute a minority of the agrarian society of which they are a part.

Insurrection by a nativist or revitalizing messianic movement within an Indian community entails serious danger for the larger, traditionally conservative group as well as for the Ladino city charged with maintaining the colonial order which is challenged. The Ladinos' sense of imminent danger touches off a violent opposition which gathers regional and national forces and hurls them against the rebellion. The dissident group undergoes real or symbolic decapitation of its messianic leader as well as repudiation by the majority of the community. The only alternative for members of the messianic movement is migration, and they move en masse to empty territories outside the original community, breaking their ties in order to establish a new community (Linton 1943). When territoriality leads to migration through infiltration or to messianic migration, it operates as a conservative rather than as a revolutionary force. Migration is aimed at maintaining the traditional order, biotic equilibrium, continuity, and stability of the community culture.

CHANGE OF HABITAT. The Indian community and the region of which it is a part are largely self-sufficient and self-contained. They demand of their members unconditional and unrestricted attachment to traditional patterns of behavior because these have demonstrated their usefulness as instruments for survival. The population extracts a living from local resources with customary practices which create a firm feeling of security in those who follow them. Man is bound to the earth by sacred ties which establish obligations and mutual reciprocities; the earth belongs to man and man belongs to the earth. The relationship between man and the earth is so close that existence apart from it cannot be conceived. Everything tends to immobilize the population in the region of refuge. Inherited patterns of behavior intimately tie the inhabitants to the objects and activities of daily life and produce in them a profound identification with their place of residence (Hawley 1962:335). There is no impetus for individuals, the community, or the regional population to move; as noted, messianic migrations and migration by infiltration are ominous signs of punishment. Stability and communal cohesion annul stimuli to circulation and change.

The immobility in which the regions of refuge remained from their beginnings until recently was broken by forces operating to disturb the established pattern. The general improvement in the state of public health and of the environment caused a sharp decline in mortality and disturbed the biotic equilibrium among natural resources, production techniques, and number of inhabitants. In many communities the breaking up of cultivable land resulted in unproductive minifundia which use a greater work force than was necessary to maintain agricultural production with traditional methods. This disguised underemployment gives rise to the emotive complex in the people known as demographic pressure. Since the once self-sufficient community resists technological change, the only alternative is migration of excess inhabitants, stimulated by demographic pressure. The moral climate prevailing today in these communities discourages continued use of expedients which would lead to messianism or infiltration. Transfer to new lands, acquired with legal titles, has social sanction and viability, however, and the people see no more expeditious road than that which leads back to agriculture.

Opening of virgin lands is done through obsolete techniques inherited by the migrants; they move as a group, following patterns which lend cohesion to the community. This kind of colonization retains much of the danger inherent in migration in the primitive community, that is, as exposure to death. In fact, mobilization does take a high toll in lives, both in the actual transfer and in adaptation to the new habitat. Transfer entails consumption of capital goods in quantities which are not always available. Food reserves must sustain the migrants during the trip, when time and human energy are used to compensate for the lack of access roads and adequate transportation. Transporting tools and other possessions entails additional cost. Food needs persist after the destination has been reached, since the migrants must wait out the long period between sowing and harvesting. In autarkic communities living at subsistence levels, such needs are rarely met. It is to be expected therefore that their migration is accompanied by high mortality rates which increase when the period of adaptation to the new habitat is prolonged. Primitive techniques must be adjusted to meet unknown or unexpected situations. The enormous cost of migration makes the community turn to it as a last resort, when the feeling of overpopulation becomes critical.[3]

There are two kinds of external force causing migratory movements in the regions of refuge: those which force them through coercion and those which induce them by various moral pressures. The former commonly appear with construction, in the community's territory, of industrial works which transform hydraulic energy into electricity. The dams required by such works may affect one or many communities, which are then compelled to abandon their habitat and move to new ones. Because of the Indians' defenselessness, those in charge of the move often do not take into sufficient account the dangers involved, and proceed without taking the necessary precautions for lowering risks. Under such conditions the Indians pay a high price in lives, in frustrated persons who do not adapt, and in communal maladjustments leading to anomie. In many cases the arduous task of remaking community life and rediscovering adequate responses to the new habitat takes a long time.[4]

Migrations originating in external pressures that do not entail physical coercion are usually abortive. The demand for an agrarian reform which breaks up latifundia and gives the peasants the land they cultivate is often diverted by an appeal to the deceptive expedient of internal colonization. In the face of a threatened land redistribution, the landowning aristocracy argues for exploiting tropical lands with sparse populations, fertile soil, and incipient development as opposed to the destruction of the haciendas' wealth. This argument leads to proposals, which the public accepts, for a colonization program administered by various governmental agencies. The model adopted by these agencies, when they begin work in virgin territories, includes commercial agriculture as it developed under European expansion during the golden age of colonization, in the years preceding the first World War. European enterprises went into virgin lands put at their disposal through colonial domination, founding capitalist plantations and mixed exploitative businesses administered by small proprietors, both dedicated to producing crops and primary materials for export. Measured by the returns it produced for European cities, the colonial model offered unsurpassable prospects. However, it was never mentioned that in a great number of cases the virgin lands were usurped from Indian communities, nor that the labor exploited on plantations was that of migrant workers who had been recruited through coercion.[5]

The domination model is a good lure for colonization of virgin lands by groups living where available land is held by large owners. It is easy to create the belief that such a program will not only promote the flowering of virgin lands but also make a major contribution to the country's economic development without the upheavals necessarily produced by agrarian redistribution. Redistribution of men as a substitute for redistribution of land is commonly initiated with a pilot project involving mobilization of one of the peasant communities located in a region of refuge, in the belief that there the feeling of overpopulation is most intense. The enterprise encounters difficulties from the people's resistance to mobilization, the low level of their technology and the absence of capital. What is originally thought to be a good solution for a serious threat becomes an irritation once it is made clear that population redistribution, so popular when the concept of demographic pressure was at its apogee, is less promising than formerly supposed.

If it is pursued, the difficulties of internal colonization grow and the costs and complications of population moves rise and multiply. The fundamental error of such migrations is to consider them independent variables in economic development; in planning them, the nonagricultural factors of the equation which made the success of colonial enterprises feasible are not taken into account.[6] When implemented alone, rural repopulation soon loses its vigor, as it entails a simple change of habitat and never a change of occupation. Such repopulation, as Davis observes (1955:787), tends merely to increase the number of peasants, not to raise their standard of living nor to contribute to the economic progress of the country. Only when technological change is adopted in the Indian communities is the transfer of the population effective. Nevertheless, it should be kept in mind that technological change includes modification of the balance between resources and inhabitants, which results in the relief of demographic pressure and, therefore, of the stimuli to migrate. Further, modern technology increases the use of capital and decreases the use of manual labor; mechanization of the countryside requires fewer people on the land. All this leads to the conclusion that the channeling of excess agrarian populations toward agricultural expansion does not lead to development.

CHANGE IN OCCUPATION. Conditions prevailing in the regions of refuge until the years immediately preceding World War II have changed greatly in their salient aspects, especially regarding population increases. Progress in medicine and public health caused a sharp drop in mortality rates without causing a similar decline in births. Therefore natural population growth has increased unexpectedly, introducing into Indian communities, dominated by the Ladino city, problems of excess manual labor that cannot be absorbed by the customary means of production. Obsolete technology forces the Indian into close dependency upon the resources of the habitat.

Rural overpopulation brings with it disguised underemployment which makes the regions of refuge a reserve of manual labor for exploitation by plantations. The solution offered by seasonal migration is highly unsatisfactory. Through such work migrant workers fulfill some pressing needs—particularly those arising from the economy of prestige—which require unusual expenditures, but they do not solve the problem of earning a living. Migratory work complements and makes underemployment tolerable, but it is not a solution. The worker who leaves the community returns with some capital which allows him to acquire the scarce products denied him by underemployment because it utilizes biotic energy, this advantage is nullified by the inability of customary technology to provide new employment for new generations. Under such circumstances the remaining alternative for these generations is to search for work away from the community. Due to their technological backwardness and to the habits and beliefs of the prospective migrants, the most suitable type of migration is to a new agricultural region. Empty zones existed until very recently, but they are increasingly difficult to find. They are not only scarce, but their location in hostile environments requires a difficult process of adaption.

The economic development of the Mestizo American countries, including programs of modernization, urbanization, and industrialization carried on at a steady rate, offers the most expeditious solution for Indian communities, namely migration to the city. The results of this migration are effective in proportion to the degree by which economic growth supersedes population growth. It is easily seen that migration from the countryside to the city is not only different in kind from those previously analyzed, but also contributes most among them to the country's development because of its economic implications. In effect, rural-urban migration is not a simple change of habitat. The migrant moves from a rural landscape barely modified by man's hand, to a diametrically opposed urban setting where the habitat has been so changed through human activity that it approaches a totally artificial environment.

Furthermore, a change in affiliation does not presuppose serious personality conflicts when the rupture with one agrarian community leads to membership in another of the same or similar technological, economic, and cultural levels. Rural-urban migration, on the other hand, entails a change in livelihood, an important modification in the occupational role of the migrant, as Barcley notes.[7] The peasant stops cultivating the land in order to dedicate himself henceforth to manufacturing or services. He ends his affiliation to a small, self-contained, religiously oriented community in order to enter a large, impersonal, secular society which has extraordinarily complex forms of living and social cohesion. Moving from the countryside to the city entails an occupational change and a psychic trauma, the incisiveness of which increases in proportion to the difference between the cultures involved. The transfer involves many physical and mental changes; it is not the mere passage from one culture to another, but rather from a simple, rustic, preliterate culture to one which is exceptionally complicated. The evolutionary distance which the Indian must travel is truly astonishing. It separates a magico-religious cosmography from the scientific world view that marked the beginning of the atomic age. The chances are great that the Indian will give up his attempt to cross the distance; not all of those who undertake the journey persevere.

Migration is a means of population adjustment and balance whereby persons are redistributed geographically, so as to best contribute through their work to the balanced development of the country. It acts like a syphon, sucking manual labor from depressed areas and emptying it into areas of opportunity (Kant 1965:348). It is well known that the regions of refuge are depressed areas, often situated within large provinces or zones which are in themselves depressed areas. In some cases the depressed area is an entire department or federal unit and the state or departmental capital, regardless of the prestige of its title, is really the *chef-lieu* or center of a region of refuge. In such cases, within the entire area there are no urban centers as important as the regional metropolis, only urban or semiurban secondary centers surrounding it.

In this situation the metropolis and secondary centers are weak focuses of attraction for the rural population. The lack the capacity to absorb the excess population, being, as they are, an integral part of the obsolete structure of the region of refuge. Nevertheless, in all the Mestizo American countries there are developed zones and modern cities which are planned or grow up around industries and which are focuses of attraction. It is these metropolitan centers which are open to rural migration. Any country or region undergoing development simultaneously experiences a process of population redistribution. The central city and secondary centers of the regions of refuge become focuses of attraction only to the extent that they are influenced by the national economic development. Rural-urban migration is accompanied by an opposite migratory wave which brings people from the centers of development to the regional metropolises. This migration is composed of highly qualified professionals and technicians whose job is to contribute to regional development through the diffusion of modern technology (Koenig 1961:200).

Rural-urban migration is the type of spatial movement most clearly associated with economic development because the component activities of industrialization are secondary and tertiary in nature. They require little land, a lot of capital, and are located in cities for proximity to complementary functions. The very close correlation between economic development and rural-urban migration means that variations in the number and kind of migrants are determined by the stage of development of the city. In the first stage the flow of peasants to the city is sparse, because there are few urban centers in either the regions of refuge or in the depressed areas where these regions are found.

As urban centers grow and centers of development appear in the formerly depressed areas, opportunities for employment and better salaries attract migrants and lay the bases for rapid urban growth. The migratory flow remains constant until economic growth and urbanization reach the point where a substantial part of the population lives in cities. At that point the agricultural population declines drastically and does not regain its capability to supply great waves of people for the growth of urban nuclei. This third step in the process of rural-urban migration is not yet present in Mestizo America. In most cases the regions of refuge are still in the early stage of development.

THE MIGRATORY COMPLEX. In the preceding paragraphs we have analyzed the different types of population movements found in the regions of refuge. Some have all the characteristics of a migratory complex; others have several but not all of them. These characteristics and the concepts and theories explaining them have been described without reference to similarities or differences in the conditions of the various types of movements. Even at the risk of repetition, it seems appropriate to comment separately on the most important characteristics of migrations which are shared with or contrast to other migratory movements, since in doing so factors will come to light which were passed over or treated without proper emphasis.

The size of a migration is one of the most difficult types of data to establish in demographic studies. In internal migration, human movement does not go beyond the boundaries of a political unit and if, as commonly occurs, the unit does not exercise control over the movement of its citizens, the measurement of changes in residence poses serious technical problems. Data are available about the migrant workers recruited by plantations, but nothing is known respecting the numbers of Indians who take up residence in the great cities. We can prove the existence of such movements when we show that the inhabitants of the *villas miserias, favelas* or *colonias proletarias* of the great cities are recently settled peasants with a varying proportion of Indians. The number of Indians in Mestizo America is calculated at 30 million and it is assumed the the figure will remain stationary (León Portilla 1962). At one time the mechanisms of biotic balance were used to explain the constancy of the number, but since that balance stopped operating, it must be interpreted as the result of migration by the surplus inhabitants produced by population growth.

The volume of migration varies with circumstances, including the geographic distance between the region of refuge and the urban center, the extent to which the area where the community is located is depressed, the number of opportunities offered by the focus of attraction for certain types of migrants, the social and economic changes to which migratory movements are so sensitive, the stage of development or urbanization and economic growth, and various others.

Connected with these factors is the *direction* that migration takes: it is rural-rural in the opening of new lands, rural-urban in the important phase of economic development, and interurban when the city reaches maturity. Although in the final analysis migration is movement in only one direction, the actual operation of the process involves a coming and going from the community to the city and the city to the community, entailing considerable wasted energy. The number of peasants exposed to city life is infinitely greater than the number of permanent migrants. The loss of energy is obvious because the constant comings and goings have cumulative effects in the change of traditional patterns in the closed communities. Indians exposed to modern life tend to modernize life styles in the community.[8]

Migrations contain *differential* characteristics in terms of age, sex, and occupation. Young adults with work skills and experience predominate. Migrations add workers to the cities and increase the size of the active population. In general terms, men are more likely to migrate; this is manifested early before women follow. At certain points in urbanization women migrate as much as or more than men; this is the case when young Indian women go to the cities to work as domestic servants, replacing those who formerly filled these jobs and left to work in factories.

Most migrants come from areas where the educational level is at its lowest; there is an inverse relationship between schooling and migration. In preliterate Indian communities those with few skills and little practical knowledge most frequently migrate; however, they are the ones with the greatest creative energy and courage for adventure, mobility, and change. Traditionalist adults remain in the communities. The unemployed and dispossessed emigrate, those who have not managed to obtain their fair share in the allocation of resources.

When migration is considered in a broad perspective another differential characteristic is seen: the *succession* of migrants coming from different ethnic groups.[9] Some communities have a greater tendency to migrate than others. It is easy to measure this differential characteristic among workers recruited by the plantations, where some ethnic groups are more fully represented than others, which is explained by the differences in the man-land relationship observed in the different communities. Where this relationship is satisfactory because of agrarian reform, the peasants do not feel compelled to do migratory labor; this supposition, however, has not been fully proven.

The differences in the propensities of Indians and Ladinos to migrate are not obvious; both turn to migration as a last resort. The construction of access roads to the regional centers as well as general modernization has broken the economic structure upon which the central cities were based. Artisan production in particular has experienced a serious decline through competition with industrial products. The conservative nature of these cities has hindered the adaptation of the artisans to the working methods imposed by industrialization and has produced unemployment. Many artisans migrate to the developing urban centers to work as laborers. In addition, the controlling elite pays a high price for the advanced education of their children, who seldom return once their training is completed; there is no need for their specialized work. The cost of the preparation of the artisans and professionals who leave represents a serious bloodletting for the regional city; this is another factor contributing to its stagnation.

The migratory flow is not constant; it has *fluctuations*, highs and lows. Tied as it is to the economic conditions of the developing centers, the volume of flow and types of migrants vary according to the rhythm of economic growth. Rural-urban migration is basically a flow of workers following capital investment. Thus, when the flow of capital grows, so does migration. When the center of attraction declines—a mine is exhausted or a petroleum vein consumed—migration declines, stops, and even takes the opposite direction, that is, from the city to the countryside. This differential characteristic forces migrants to become dispersed throughout centers of attraction which are sometimes very far removed from their places of origin.

INTEGRATION AND IMPROVEMENT. The characteristics of human group movements, especially those in the migratory complex, produce important effects in the authority structures of the regions of refuge. There are many consequences both at the national and local levels, since both undergo modification in their internal structure and in the relationships which order the daily lives of their inhabitants. All those consequences may be grouped into two basic categories which we shall call integration and improvement.

The effect of integration depends upon the following characteristics of the migration: (1) the variety of typography and soil in a country; (2) the mixture of its racial groups; (3) the acculturation of opposing life styles; (4) the restructuring of the total society; (5) the unification of economic behavior; (6) the organization of political activity; and (7) the formation of a national ideology. The effect of integration operates as a unit; for methodological purposes, however, we may examine its parts.

Because of their immobility, the peoples of the regions of refuge must exploit the natural resources of a single habitat, where they are born, grow up, and die. This confinement to limited resources makes adaptation to the environment a rigidly deterministic process. In contrast, when modern peoples acquire the ability to move freely, they overcome the handicaps of adaptation to a single habitat through contact with more varied resources. Circulation of persons is always accompanied by the circulation of goods. Increased transportation and exchange enable a larger population to become prosperous independently of the local limitations of resources. The process of circulation opens the door to the exploitation of many environments, combines abundances and scarcities, and leads to the geographical integration of the country.

Migratory movements favor the cohabitation of different racial groups and contribute to the biological integration of the national population. The process of racial mixing began in Mestizo America with the arrival of the Spaniards in the sixteenth century, and produced the Indo-Ladino population which constitutes the majority group in those nations. In the regions of refuge the mixing process never acquired the intensity it had in open regions, where the various castes were able to interchange genetic codes without major obstacles. As a result, Indians and Ladinos remained differentiated while living together in a situation which did not favor mixing, as already noted. The movement of persons, responding today to economic imperatives that stimulate rural-urban migration, has fully rekindled the mixing process in those isolated areas.

Migration is a mechanism of cultural diffusion which exposes migrants to modern influences. It leads to contacts between different styles of life which, when combined, produce cultural integration. As with racial integration, the process of acculturation has a distinct dynamic in both time and space. In the regions of refuge, interchange and reconstruction of opposing cultural patterns are so infrequent that if we measure the process by its results we may well affirm that acculturation ended in the colonial era. In no other way can we explain the archaism from which those regions suffer. Forces now promoting human mobility give new impetus to cultural change, thereby leading to the achievement of a more complete cultural integration.

Migration, particularly from the countryside to the city, is a mechanism of social integration in the open class capitalist system.[10] When migrants move to the city they change occupation and rise on the social scale. If the process of economic growth is violent, their ascent is made easier by the fluidity with which mechanisms of capillary attraction or social mobility operate. Migration brings with it elements which change traditional stratification not only in the national society, where the process is most apparent, but also and principally in the regions of refuge. There the Indo-Ladino stratification is a caste system which cracks when groups on the move push past the obstacles isolating the regional center and go on to establish open relations with the centers of attraction of the developed regions.

Capital movements interact so closely with migratory movements that the aggregation and conglomeration of persons in the developed regions' centers of attraction are determined by the aggregation and conglomeration of productive activities aimed at achieving economic integration.[11] Circulation of goods and persons breaks the self-containment and self-sufficiency of the regions of refuge and makes them interdependent with the national economy. It modifies the basic orientation of Indian and Ladino economic behavior and makes them conform to national patterns. The results of migration as a mechanism of political and ideological integration are explicable on the basis of economic interdependence. Suffice it here to indicate these consequences, which will be discussed in greater detail in the following chapters.

Because of its importance for the national society, the effect of integration was studied primarily in terms of the results it produced in a given society. The effect of improvement will be briefly discussed against the background of the colonial situation. The effect of improvement operates by increasing (1) income, (2) the survival rate, and (3) the functional roles of Indians and Ladinos. Regional income rises because the means of exchange and purchasing power of the workers who are recruited for plantation labor increases, because prospective migrants inject savings during the comings and goings which precede their definitive establishment outside the community, and because those who have migrated to the city and prospered there make profitable investments in their home communities. The increased survival rate derives from the prospective migrants' exposure to modern medicine and sanitation, and the increase in their functional roles is due to exposure to the occupational changes imposed by migration to the city.

Migratory movements require energy consumption which increases in direct proportion to the distance between the region of refuge and the migrants on the one hand, and the developed regions on the other. The geographical distance which makes jungles, high mountains, and coastal plains such vastly different habitats entails a high cost in adaptation. The racial distance separating Indian and Ladino is greater than that between the Indian and the ordinary inhabitant of the growing urban center. Crossing the social distance between an ethnic minority and the national society is very costly. The economic distance between industrial capitalism and the subsistence-prestige economy of the Indian communities is incomparably greater than the simple difference between poverty and prosperity. The political distance defining the super- subordination relationship in the regions of refuge far exceeds any seen in a democratic system. The ideological distance between a magico-religious interpretation of the world and industrial civilization's scientific world view demands of Indian migrants a higher price than that paid by peasants who already share in the national culture. Thus, for the Indian the costs of crossing the distances separating him from national life are always high and they explain the weak representation which he has had until recently in the total process of human mobility.

NOTES

1. Hoebel (1961:320) states moreover that "the secondary functional effects of exogamy enlarge the area of sociability among peoples and at the same time favor cultural diffusion."

2. See Pozas (1959:126) for a better understanding of the system of debt peonage in Chiapas. See Hoyt (1955) for work in the Guatemalan plantations.

3. Loyo (1960:27) advises: "Regarding internal colonization, it is urgent that we carry out, in two or three years, several modest projects which vary along geographic, demographic, soil type, agricultural, financial, and organizational lines, all well planned and financed. Along the way we will acquire experience, rapidly correct, and quickly adjust systems and procedures to the realities and the concrete problems which appear. Then we can prepare and carry out, on a larger scale, new and fuller plans for the various types of colonization. It is necessary that the demogogical and inhuman era of miserable and disorderly attempts at reaccommodation of Mexico's agrarian population come to an end."

4. See Villa Rojas (1955), Chapter IV, "The Reaccommodation of the Old Towns."

5. Pelzer (1957:330) states: "The settlement of Europeans in tropical regions seems invariably to have brought great disadvantages to aboriginal peoples who were politically weaker and who had a simpler material culture, because the interests of the two groups are diametrically opposed. It deprived the indigenous population of either a part or all of its land, or at least of that part of the land which was not yet used regularly but was needed as a reserve for future growth; it led, in some instances, to confinement on reserves; and it exposed the native inhabitants to a great pressure to work for the incoming white settlers. Too often these settlers have the attitude that it is the native's prescribed place in world order to be an inferior working class. They rationalize, moreover, that since the peoples of the tropics are not accustomed to steady labour eight hours a day six days a week they will benefit greatly from developing this Western habit, and that they also will gain from learning the agricultural techniques of the Westerner. Actually the average Westerner has little or nothing new to offer which would improve indigenous agricultural methods, and, as I have mentioned, there has frequently occurred a deterioration in native agriculture and a reduction of food supply as a result of the prolonged absence of a large part of the able-bodied men while they are working in plantations or mines."

6. Bowman (1957:257) warns: "The pioneer settler cannot keep the books of the world. Wherever his community be located it is but a fragment of a larger economy, a thread in a web, not a completed garment. By overlooking these basic economic facts, the ardent advocate of a specific settlement venture can make any spot seem attractive to the unwary. Put in capital enough, screened houses, a purified water supply, fertilizer perhaps, tools, preferably 'native' labour, an assured price for export products in the world market, and add the hope that there will be tolerance for high temperature and humidity, and almost any tropical lowland area can be made to look like home. What is astonishing is not that such schemes are devised but that some men are willing to put money into them."

7. Barclay (1955:715) states: "Those forces in economic development which affect the distribution of people are by no means free from antagonism of purpose or effect. It is often observed that they tend to increase the movement, and the mobility, in a predominantly rural population, and some of the migrations that ensue have undoubtedly been uneconomic or disruptive. But there is an important element of consistency in the pattern as a whole. Where modern changes have proceeded apace, there has also been a substantial balance of migration in one direction–movement from the country to the city, from rural to urban areas.

There is nothing especially hidden or obscure about this relationship. It arises from the nature of modern industrial activity in its entry into a rural environment. Along with a general change in the manner of employing productive resources, there is some reallocation of manpower, which consists of opening up new non-agricultural occupations; and the shift in occupational structure happens to coincide with a redistribution of people."

8. See Landis (1943), Chapter XXI, "The Importance of Mobility for the Population."

9. See Lee (1964), Chapter III for different types of succession.

10. Comas (1957:169) states: "We know that the concept of race rests on the existence of groups which present certain similar somatic characteristics which are transmitted according to the laws of inheritance, although leaving margins for individual variation, also that there are no pure human races. At the most it would be possible to speak of racial purity in regard to one somatic characteristic but never for all or the majority of inherited characteristics. The mixing of the races has been going on since the beginning of man's life on earth, even in the beginning of prehistory. Better communications and the population increase have facilitated this mixing even more in the past few centuries."

11. Bogue (1964:487) reminds us that: "Migration is an instrument of cultural diffusion and social integration. The person who migrates from one community to another unites in himself two cultures. Temporarily, he tends to be a disruptive force in the community into which he enters. If members of one culture invade a community of another culture in large numbers, they tend to form a 'community within a community' and to create cultural diversity and ethnic tension."

Chapter 5

RESOURCES AND TECHNOLOGY

Potential Energy

THE INDIVIDUAL quotient of energy availability is one of the indicators created by development economists to measure the backwardness or progressiveness of populations. Use of the concept is possible because different forms of energy, from muscular to nuclear, may be converted into equivalent units. The basis of comparison commonly taken is the energy generated by one ton of coal or by one kilowatt hour, interchangeably. In the course of one year, a man leading a modern life is considered to expend the energy equivalent of 1.5 tons of coal. When this equivalent is below 0.750 tons per capita, the diagnosis of underdevelopment is unquestioned. Several countries which are presently or potentially developed are found between the two figures, among them only one Mestizo American country (Levy 1961:142).[1]

From the foregoing it is clear that developed nations consume a greater amount of energy than those left behind in economic evolution. The latter are characterized by the predominant use of human force in agricultural work as well as in the extraction of minerals, manufacturing, and transportation of goods. If animals are used for pulling and carrying, the labor is diversified but it is still classified as muscular energy and continues to be weak in terms of the effort put forth and its results. Under such conditions, development is seriously hindered by the limitations of archaic energy sources belonging to stages of human evolution which have been fully transcended by industrial civilization.

The prosperous nations of that civilization have energy sources at their disposal which are varied and different from the merely human or animal. The invention of equipment and machinery capable of transforming the energy stored in coal, petroleum, gas, the sun, water, and nuclear fission into heat and power, put into the hands of modern societies quantities of force which far surpass those produced by mere muscles. The use of external energy permits execution of a large part of the physical work involved in the production, processing, and distribution of goods and also permits protection from the rigors of climate in habitats which otherwise would be impossible for man to exploit. The sources of external energy extend developed peoples' control over nature and provide them with varied and abundant resources.

The different uses to which backward and advanced peoples put energy resources poses a question with a far-reaching implication; namely, what is the reason for such an obvious discrepancy? Explanations range from those which take into account limitations on invention resulting from an absence of outside energy sources in the habitat, to those attributing the differences to ignorance of techniques of exploitation when those resources are in fact present. The Mesoamerican Indians, we are told, discovered tar but in their ignorance of its possibilities used it only in rituals. However later, when those same Indians were subjugated by Western domination, they learned the industrial uses of this resource and did not put them into practice (Silva Herzog 1963:9). Thus the problem cannot be reduced to a simple lack of technical and scientific development or the archaic nature of the ethnic group. On the contrary, it embraces a complex of factors among which the process of domination stands out. The subjugation of underdeveloped peoples is as much responsible for their obsolete patterns of energy conversion as is the fact of their backwardness in terms of human evolution.

Examination of the problem leads us to review some elementary knowledge which, though obvious, is still important for our purposes. Man requires energy to maintain his organic life and to function in society. There is a relationship of mutual interaction between the obvious and hidden behavior that makes up a culture on the one hand and available energy resources on the other. The presence or absence of energy resources, their abundance or scarcity, their exploitation or lack of use, all determine the simplicity or complexity of any given people's cultural tools for contending with the habitat. In turn, the ideas and action patterns of that culture decide the use to which potential energy sources in the territory are put.

Sunlight, in the last analysis, is the principal energy source for humanity. The sun radiates a constant energy current of which only a minimal part arrives on earth. Of what does arrive, the greater part is reflected into space and the rest is absorbed by plants through photosynthesis, which in the presence of light converts carbon dioxide, combined with water and minerals, into organic material. As far as is known, only plants are capable of photosynthesis. Herbivorous animals profit from it, obtaining the sun's energy when they eat plants; carnivorous animals acquire it from their prey and man takes it directly from plants or indirectly from the animals that form his diet. As noted, the animals of the air, sea, and earth, including man, derive their energy from plants (Honigmann 1959:296).

The energy obtained by man and other animals can be measured through the oxidation of foodstuffs which give off calories; it is thought that something over one fourth of that caloric energy may be put to productive work. However, it should be noted that a man who works hard during the course of an entire year produces scarcely the equivalent of one tenth of a ton of coal. This is the amount of energy required by a member of one of the simplest hunting or fishing economies—the Seri, for example—to maintain life. The human organism is a highly efficient instrument for converting solar energy into work, but its productivity is very low. If internal energy sources were the only ones available, they would limit cultural development enormously (Daniels 1955).

Fortunately, in the face of the limitations of muscular energy, people have learned to make use of fossil energy produced millions of years ago by the decomposition of plants and other organic matter. These energy sources are external to man; among them, lignite, coal, petroleum, and gas are important. They represent the energy of sunlight which has been concentrated and stored through vast geological processes.

Those processes continue, of course, but the amount of stored energy which is extracted and exploited far exceeds that replaced, and therefore it is called capital energy. Its quantity is limited, but the rational use of stored solar energy brings great advantages to the peoples who know how to convert it to productive work.

The advance signified by the use of external energy sources may be evaluated if we know that a man living in a modern city requires the equivalent of one fourth of a ton of coal per year for light and cooking alone. This amount far exceeds that which the same man produces and is also greater than what can be obtained from beasts of burden. The normal energy requirement, taking into account all the purposes of the population as a whole, is calculated by Guyol (1955) at 15 times the amount of energy internally generated. The difference is greater for highly industrialized countries, reaching 80 times the energy produced by the human organism. Unquestionably, consumption of external energy is a good indicator for measuring backwardness or progress.

Conversion of potential energy into usable forms cannot be carried out without the expenditure of energy. The human organism adequately converts the solar energy obtained from foodstuffs into productive work, but in doing so, consumes a large quantity of that energy. The problem raised by the discovery and utilization of external energy sources has been to find the best procedure for obtaining the maximum return with the smallest possible expenditure of energy. Many methods of transforming energy have been conceived or manufactured by human society during its development and they have been increasingly efficient in diminishing the inevitable energy losses during the conversion process. The animal in harness, the mariner's sail, the windmill, the water wheel, the steam engine, the hydroelectric generator, and the atomic reactor all represent successive steps in the achievement of increasingly powerful and inexpensive energy transformers.

Peoples of advanced cultures possess the best techniques and have also transcended the use of solar energy in their compulsive and incessant search for additional energy sources. Water and wind have permitted generation of mechanical and electric power; atomic fission, the production of astonishingly strong atomic power. Energy sources, however, are not found evenly distributed throughout the earth, nor does their distribution have any relationship to the needs for them. With the exception of sunlight, which is unlimited and always replaceable but whose direct utilization has not yet been discovered, only hydraulic energy and that produced by burning wood, plant residues, or dung can be considered consumable. Use of this type of energy represents 20% of total energy consumption and is the only kind not controlled by peoples who have moved into dominant positions (Schumacher 1955).

In effect, the highly industrialized countries retain exclusive or preponderant use of strategic resources, including combustible fossils, for operation of their increasingly competitive technology. Rather than being diffused, efficient technical and scientific methods are preserved for their own use as instruments of domination, preventing technically backward peoples from utilizing the energy found in their habitat for their own welfare. This energy—especially in the case of petroleum and gas—is extracted through imported techniques for outside consumption. Even water resources, which are potentially important in the regions of refuge, are developed for use in culturally and economically advanced areas. Caught in the machinery of the process of domination, native communities are forced to consume noncommercial combustibles such as the aforementioned firewood, plant residues, and dung, which are cheap near their sources. With weak and limited sources and conversion into usable power through obsolete and feeble techniques, the possibilities of energy for modifying the conservative character of native communities is necessarily limited.

STRATEGIC RESOURCES. We have designated sources of external energy as natural resources several times, noting that use of the term is conditional on the use made of them. Edmundo Flores (1962) also points out the relativity of the concept, asserting that natural resources reflect the valuation made by the agent of a specific culture. Resources and their interpretation are determined by the value system of a community; their meaning is not universal. Petroleum, to cite a case, is a resource for an industrial society but not so when it abounds on the cultivated lands of an agrarian people which makes exclusive use of biotic energy.[2]

The example is apt because it is found in situations which confront culturally dissimilar populations, such as those who were successive masters of a territory bordering on the Gulf of Mexico where an important manufacturing zone flourishes today. In preColumbian times asphalt marshes inundated the fields and impeded the Totonac Indians from gathering their subsistence harvests. In the colonial era the Spanish *hacendados* took care to remove livestock from areas where the young easily became mired in the asphalt and died. As foreign control was coming to an end, scientists became mindful of bitumens or mineral tars, but it was not until the end of the last century that international cartels recognized their value and use as resources.

As noted, the concept is culturally determined. The existence of resources does not depend upon their physical presence alone; they are resources insofar as they have a function and are assigned a value by the human group which makes use of them. This feature is basic to the concept, but of course there are others. Spoehr has proposed a definition of natural resources which brings to light another important concept. According to this anthropologist, the term natural resources should be understood to mean those segments of the physical world which have current or potential use for the survival and physical well-being of man and which are developed, when possible, through the application of scientific knowledge (Spoehr 1956:97).

Spoehr's definition points out the rational focus in resource evaluation: resources have an objective existence. However primitive its level of organization, when a society confronts the problem of utilizing the resources of its habitat it acts in accordance with the physical principles involved, thereby demonstrating that its technology is based on the inference of cause and effect. Primitive as well as civilized man approaches the solution of his vital problems using judgment; the former's magico-religious view of the universe does not inhibit his powers of reasoning when questions of utility or survival arise.

A detailed account of this concept is relevant because one very widespread school of thought maintains that native peoples' improper exploitation of certain environmental features which are considered as resources by industrial culture results from an incapacity to perceive their potentials. The truth is that an ethnic group's technology, regardless of the degree of complexity attained, is based upon a thorough knowledge of the resources used through the very operation of that technology. The technology of the most primitive jungle band of the Amazon basin may be of a very simple order, but the men who use it necessarily have a profound knowledge of each sector of the natural environment which renders them satisfactions.[3]

Another aspect of the concept of natural resources is the crystallization of interests and knowledge around the segment of the environment upon which survival of the group depends. So-called primitive peoples do not exist in a state of ignorance regarding the natural world around them; even when their knowledge is essentially empirical, their technology leads them to center their interests on the specific resources upon which their life depends. Fishing peoples, for example, have an extensive empirical knowledge of aquatic animals, their biology, habits, migrations, and feeding places, and therefore they can fish effectively. The fact that they may accompany this act with magical rites or religious ceremonies aimed at psychological reinforcement of the rational practice means that to some extent they may hinder the probabilities of success.

Despite their simplicity, agricultural peoples have technical competence and adequate knowledge of the soils in which they sow their crops. They know the best times at which to engage in specific agricultural practices and they can empirically predict weather conditions. Incantations and prayers are credited for accurate predictions; by authenticating the results of experience they offer security for man's efforts. Nevertheless, compared to the total range of nature, this knowledge is directed at manipulation of a reduced area of experience; these peoples have specialized in obtaining specialized resources. The regional society knows its own habitat adequately but is ignorant of either neighboring or distant habitats. Its knowledge, empirical and specialized, prevents rapid adaptation to any surroundings other than its own. Its particular technology permits adaptation only to a single kind of environment; when that technology is put to work and given value, it applies only to a specific class of resources.

The crystallization of interest and knowledge around a particular segment of the environment does not necessarily imply a lack of complexity. Sauer (1956:50) notes correctly that nomadism is a specialized and complex mode of life, regardless of its appearance to the contrary; swidden agriculture is also complex and specialized. This specialization of the knowledge and use of resources adds the dimension of selectivity to the concept of natural resources. When peoples whose cultures are at very different evolutionary levels coexist in the same habitat, their technologies tend to center around different segments of the landscape. Consequently, they assign value and function as resources to different sectors of the habitat without obvious, that is, institutionalized, conflict. Moreover, that tendency and the corresponding adjustment make possible the use of a single sector of the environment with differing types of exploitation by virtue of dissimilar resource evaluation.

In the regions of refuge, with both Indians and Ladinos, the countryside is used for agriculture by some and for livestock by others. The Indians, accustomed to the itinerant cultivation of the cornfield, work the mountain slopes, whose tree covering they cut and burn. Ladinos occupy the plains, with their sparse trees and abundant pasturage. Both Indians and Ladinos assign the forest a function as a resource, but the value they give it varies. For the former it is noncommercial fuel and a primary material for the construction of their homes and furniture; for the latter it is an export product whose exploitation depends on the relationship at any given moment between the costs of extraction and the market place. Clearly the different functions and values assigned to resources are conditioned by the nature of the technology used to exploit them. Technology is one aspect of the total culture of a people and different interpretations of resources, as we have pointed out, can be understood only on the basis of differences in life styles.

The interest shown by industrial society in resource availability, renovation, and exploitation, arises from its singular propensity for technological invention Industrial civilization, viewed against all of human evolution, has developed in a very short time. This unusual growth is caused by incessant technological progress, a concomitant of the cumulative increase of science; we have reiterated that industrial civilization is characterized by its compulsive tendency towards change (Spoehr 1956:95). The so-called underdeveloped peoples, including native ethnic groups, do not share this compulsion. On the contrary, they are obstinately opposed to rapid change.

Through the invention of a specific technology, ethnic groups laboriously adapt to a particular habitat. Once firmly established, this adaptation encourages retention of the function and value assigned to resources and prevents capricious changes. Since these resources have demonstrated their usefulness as instruments of adaptation, the impulse to assign them a new function or value, which generally emanates from the interests or needs of the dominant group, is rejected. There are, of course, no predetermined rules for identifying the potentialities of the environment. Rather, a careful selection of the value and function of its resources takes place in accordance with adaptive experience.[4]

The fact that resources are (1) culturally conditioned, (2) rationally defined, (3) empirically manipulated, (4) centered in vital interests, (5) selectively determined, and (6) chosen for their function and value as instruments of adaptation to a particular habitat, all combine to produce two additional characteristics of the concept. These are (7) obsolescence and (8) limitation, both seen when resources are viewed from the framework of modern culture. In the regions of refuge, inhabited by Indians and Ladinos, the play of forces determining obsolescence acts with increasing intensity upon the resources. Their function and value deteriorate as they are superseded by others which are more modern and efficient; the use of firewood as fuel and of biotic energy as a work force are dramatic cases of obsolescence and technological lag.

The limitation of resources is also an indicator of this lag. Indians and Ladinos, isolated in the regional habitat, experience inevitable limitations in their respective technologies. Population groups survive and develop inside the limitations of this remote environment without physical or social communication. Their technologies become constricted and limited to exploitation of a reduced habitat.[5]

Chapple and Coon note that isolated societies with relatively simple organization are forced to use a single geographic typography, whereas industrial society thrives in any area, combining and redistributing products of the most varied of environments.[6] Thus, natural resources are of local concern in the regions of refuge and of worldwide concern when viewed from the broad perspective of modern society.

TECHNIQUES OF PRODUCTION. The use of natural resources, as noted, is regulated not only by a group's productive techniques but also by the nature of its social structure and political organization. The relationship of resources to men is not merely a matter of converting primary materials into goods to provide housing, clothing, and sustenance. The means of procuring strategic goods are derived from firmly established ideological models and are of prime importance in defining the limited use which some peoples make of their resources and the unlimited abuse committed upon them by others. In the regions of refuge strategic resources—agricultural land, livestock, forests, minerals, fuels—initially under the control of indigenous communities and assigned to their members for limited use, passed to Ladino hands for unlimited abuse. Landowners, livestock raisers, forest owners, and miners, all having appropriated strategic resources, created a persisting situation of control over the dispossessed Indian.

Together with production techniques, the situation thus created determines the unequal appropriation of resources. Doubtlessly, the interaction between many different aspects of a culture plays a part in the use and apportionment of resources. But within that multiple causation, technology (that is, the total complex of means of production) is the fundamental variable, the one upon which other variables are based and which produces the most fundamental changes in a society's life styles. Proofs of this assertion are supplied by comparative studies of primitive cultures and of cultures under domination in the regions of refuge. In the life styles of both a direct correlation may be observed between the culture's modes of production and the economic, social, political and cultural structures which it has created in order to survive.

The combinations of techniques, integrated to form technologies, are highly varied, of course, and some are more important than others. Chapple and Coon (1953) give particular weight to: (1) obtaining and producing materials, (2) their manufacture, and (3) their transportation.[7] Techniques for obtaining materials include (*a*) collection, (*b*) hunting, (*c*) fishing, and (*d*) extraction of quarry stones or minerals. Techniques for producing materials are utilized principally in the production of foodstuffs, fuels, and instruments for the growth and care of cultivated plants and domestic animals. The importance of techniques for obtaining and producing is such that Marxist philosophy, which makes economics the decisive factor in a culture, is based upon them.[8] Anthropologists also have based a typology of economic systems on these techniques. This typology consists of a progressive sequence beginning with the most primitive collecting economy and ending with the most complex industrial one. As Forde states, people do not live through economic stages, rather they have economies, which are neither simple nor exclusive but highly elaborate combinations. Nonetheless, such a typology is useful because it makes visible the cultural lag experienced by societies which use very rudimentary techniques.[9]

There are many technical processes invented by human groups for adaptation to the physical environment, all of them based on tools enabling man to modify his habitat. Of these the most essential are cutting tools for making arms to hunt and kill food: hatchets are made to fell trees and prepare the soil for seeding (with the help of fire, another basic technique), and hoes, plows, agricultural machinery, and various secondary tools are forged. The old cutting instruments, worked from chips of rock or polished stones, are a thing of the past. Even peoples with the simplest technology have had the opportunity through cultural borrowing to acquire metal tools, which are undoubtedly more durable and effective. The importance of these tools does not diminish the value of others, such as those used for the construction of the abode, its heating and lighting, those for processing skins and vegetable fibers from which clothing is made, or those used in basketry, ceramics, and the preparation and preservation of foodstuffs.

The third group of important techniques deals with the mobilization of people and goods. Ground transportation uses (1) human muscular energy for movement from one place to another and for carrying things or persons with the help of certain expedients such as the *huacal* or hand chair; (2) animal strength, for dragging, riding, and carting with the help of the harness, the saddle and carriage respectively; (3) natural energy, mechanically transmitted, such as the railroad, the automobile, electrical wires and ducts for water, oil or gas. Water transportation, the elements of which are a floating conveyance and the means of propulsion, uses three types of power source: (1) muscular energy, used with a lever, paddle, or oars, (2) wind, (3) motor power. Air transportation, belonging to industrial cultures, allows these to penetrate into the most isolated and hostile habitats.

If we examine the technology of any given people, we find that it consists of a combination of techniques, related in a specific manner, which the group uses in adapting to its particular environment. It is unlikely that such a combination will be repeated with exactly the same elements and the same mechanisms by another people in another place, for technologies vary with the environment and the special combination of principles used. The variety, of course, is great. In the regions of refuge, geographically distributed throughout Mestizo America, not all combinations nor even the principal stages of the economic typology are found. Only three such stages concern us, based on (1) a technology of gathering, hunting, and fishing; (2) a simple agricultural technology with small surpluses; and (3) complex agriculture with livestock and relatively large surpluses.

Peoples with a very simple gathering economy, such as the Tierra del Fuego Indians in the extreme southern part of Argentina and Chile, are characteristically organized into small bands. Within each band the work is divided into hunting and fishing, on the one hand, and gathering on the other. The entire community moves as a body in search of provisions and distributes strategic goods in a democratic manner. There is no specialization, only the simple division of work by sex. There is no surplus money, commerce, nor market. Interchange takes place through gifts and strategic resources—fishing and hunting grounds and gathering territories—are the band's property, assigned to its members for exploitation.

There is no inequality in the possession of wealth since productive resources are not individual property. Fishing Indians, such as the Seri of the Gulf of California and some others, would fit into this category were it not for their constant and sometimes intense exchange of ocean resources for the commercial products manufactured by more advanced economies. In any case, the primitive character of these ethnic groups does not tolerate any contact with outsiders. The size of their land or fishing territories is reduced daily as modern culture expands its communications and limits the possibilities of these bands' survival.

AGRARIAN CULTURE. When we divide agricultural economies into simple and complex evolutionary stages, we are actually characterizing the opposite poles of a continuum. If it were necessary to draw the line separating one economy from the other we would have serious difficulty because any technology is made up of an integrated complex of techniques which are different in every culture. The combinations of these techniques are potentially infinite and consequently some of the characteristics which appear to belong exclusively to primitive technologies may be combined with others considered part of advanced technology. Between the two techniques of swidden agriculture and plowing lie others which we could not include with certainty in either category. Nonetheless, the typological division is useful because it makes the differences obvious and facilitates comprehension of the ties between technology and other aspects of culture.

The simplest form of agricultural technology may be observed in the refuge of the Orinoco-Amazon River basin.[10] Ethnic groups there respond to problems of adaptation in particularly hostile situations. The tropical environment has never been easy to master; when a group has been able to establish itself firmly in the habitat, the success of their undertaking has not been lasting. Eventually it fails, and it is unusual for a new culture to be raised upon its ruins. This fact, little examined and poorly evaluated, gave rise to the stereotype of the impossibility of high cultures being born and prospering in the tropical habitat. We must remember that the tropical habitat is not uniform and at certain times in history and in specific places, conditions are such that astonishing civilizations emerge in the midst of the jungle. The complexity and advanced nature of the Olmec culture are attested to by the monumental constructions and beautiful statuary being exhumed in the alluvion of Mesoamerica. This was not only a high culture, but it preceded and nourished the Maya, the Toltec, and others that flowered before the discovery of Mesoamerica.

Of course, the above does not mean that the standard tropical setting favors human settlement. The opposite is more often true, as it is in the Orinoco-Amazon area. Adaptation to this habitat is precarious and has been achieved, as Meggers aptly notes, through man's conforming to the environment and not dominating it.[11] Ethnic groups living there demonstrate good judgment in creating and using a technology with which they certainly do not modify the basic landscape, but do make use of it and obtain the necessary resources for survival from it.

The hostile characteristics which stand out in tropical areas are the impenetrable rain forest and high temperatures throughout the year. The ethnic groups know how to accommodate themselves to these characteristics without attempting to basically modify them, through the use of the simple and efficient procedures that are part of swidden agriculture. First, a space is cleared, so small in terms of the immense vegetation that it scarcely disturbs the landscape. The fallen trees are allowed to dry and are later burned, before the beginning of the rainy season. In the field which has been thus cleared and burned there remain many stumps and large branches which resist fire. These are left to rot so that the decomposed material, mixed with the ashes, may enrich the soil. The cleared parcel is sown with a *coa* or digging stick, weeded to improve the growth of domestic plants, and then harvested. The planted tubers or seeds produce well during the first two years but very sparsely in the following years if the same plot is sown.

Only a few instruments are used, as noted: the hatchet for felling trees, fire for burning them, and the *coa* for sowing and harvesting. With such scant means of modification, the habitat undergoes the fewest possible changes. During the first year the soil is exposed to the sun's heat and to rain and wind after the trees are cleared and burned. The high temperatures upset the biological composition of the soil, hitherto determined by the shade of gigantic plants. Exposure to wind and rain alters its physio-chemical properties, especially in the high grade soils, and finally destroys the humus. Swidden agriculture takes into account the possible damage to the soil and saves it from becoming unproductive.

As soon as he gathers the harvest or, at the latest after the third year, the Indian abandons the cultivated parcel and opens a new clearing in the jungle, which he allows to invade the former plot. He rotates crops at the appropriate time, knowing that the longer the second forest growth is delayed, the longer the soil will take to regain its fertility. Taking additional protective measures during the agricultural cycle, he leaves tree stumps protruding from the ground, not only because of the difficulties in pulling them out, but because they are an obstacle to erosion. In order for grass to easily return and prevent rain and wind from carrying organic soil away, he does not destroy the undergrowth roots as a plow does. Rather, he leaves them so that they may form a protective plant cover. When grasses are torn out again with cultivation, they rot on the ground, covering it. Thus the soil's exposure to sun, wind, and rain is extremely short.

The tropical habitat undergoes almost no modification by man through swidden agricultural techniques, but rather is an effective instrument of production and survival. In his studies of the Mayas of the Yucatan peninsula, where rocky soil increases environmental hostility, Morley (1947) expressed the conviction that swidden agriculture, used historically by the Indian, has saved the fertile soil cover from destruction.[12] The advantages of the technique do not stop with soil protection. It also serves to preserve such crops as yucca, yams and other tubers, which are stored indefinitely in the ground, somewhat in the manner of bulbs, to be used when necessary and in the required amounts. The same is not true for grains such as corn, which deteriorate rapidly in the hot tropical humidity.

Swidden agriculture is part of a conservative technology whose basic orientation is not limited to the physical surroundings. On the contrary, it pervades the social field and makes for a simple, self-sufficient, and backward culture. Surpluses are scant in tuber crops and even low in grain harvests. The population density is low because there is much land held in reserve and itinerant agriculture compels continuous movement within the large territory claimed by the group. Division of labor by sex forces women to gather and men to hunt or fish as a complement to the fundamental agricultural activities. This complementary labor increases when surpluses reach a certain quantity, with the addition of such occupations as basketry, ceramics, and weaving, which are always part-time activities.

Allocation of strategic resources—hunting fields, fruit trees, parcels of land for cultivation—is a function of the community or family group. One or the other annually assigns its members the places where each nuclear family should obtain and produce its sustenance. Since private ownership of productive resources is unknown—except for some personal effects—there are no outstanding inequalities in wealth or status. The social structure is based on kinship relations, but the community leaders are elected to their offices in accordance with a hierarchical scale, in which cleverness and charisma count. Currency, taxes, or tribute are rarely found and intertribal wars are of a retaliatory nature; that is, they have the character of feuds between communities (Jacobs and Stern 1959:135).

THE EFFECT OF CONTACT. From the tropical lowlands with their swidden technology, the American peoples ascend mountainous slopes, reaching the altiplanos with their windy *punas*, inland lakes, and snow covered peaks. There diverse technologies have evolved, producing irrigation agriculture as exemplified in *chinampa* cultivation, and encouraging the emergence of confederations such as the Aztec of Mesoamerica and the Inca along the Andes, which represent very complex forms of organization. Horticultural Indians live in towns or cities of a given density. Cultivation takes place in the *calpulli* or *ayllu* with free men who are full members of the community, or with captives on territory which is held by a directing elite of members of the military, merchants, and bureaucrats. Agricultural surpluses, which are large, are taken to market to be sold together with specialized artisan products.

Social, economic, and religious organization are very elaborate. Politics allow tribal chiefs to perpetuate themselves through inheritance, and compel them to wage predatory wars for the purpose of acquiring tribute paying subjects. Human resources take on unusual importance. Servitude and tribute divide people into freemen and subjects, give rise to unequal appropriation of the land, which takes on some characteristics of private property without actually becoming such, and create social strata based on wealth and honor. The exuberant ceremonial life of these agrarian societies, extravagant waste of goods and men in religious festivities, exotic rites, tribute and servitude, make them appear in the eyes of conquerers and also in the judgment of archeologists as monarchical and imperial organizations of an oriental style. However, in comparative studies of the American Indian, ethnohistory has reservations in this respect. In any case, the real or supposed imperial organization collapsed upon its first contact with Western man.

Contact imposed a colonial situation upon the Indian peoples. As a general rule the gatherers and agriculturalists of simple cultures perished when subjected to domination. Gatherers were not even good as slaves, nor were tropical agriculturalists able to withstand plantation work.[13] The simple technology of each, so specialized in its adaptation to a specific habitat, prevented them from adapting to subjugation by a different culture which considered them as exploitable human resources. Why then had those same peoples accepted the domination of the so-called empires of the Aztecs or Incas? Doubtless the answer is that the social and cultural distance between masters and slaves could not have been great, nor the general orientations of the societies widely discrepant.

Native imperialism, if it did exist, was based on the tribute of goods and persons, respected the productive techniques of subject peoples and contented itself with the usufruct of very limited surpluses. Colonial imperialism was diametrically different, bursting aggressively into the cultures of the subject peoples and disturbing, albeit unintentionally, their precarious adjustment to the hostile environment which had been achieved through the trials and errors of thousands of years. The fate of these tropical peoples is an example of unreflecting intervention. The lands at rest, so extensive in swidden agriculture, were declared empty and granted to European settlers who established ranches with legal titles and raised cattle and sheep. This development not only favored direct damage to the Indians' cultivated land from wild livestock, but also disrupted the function of swidden technology by interrupting the rotating cycle of cultivation and rest which permitted the raising of profitable harvests. In the destruction of the Indies, a great deal of responsibility is borne by the unrestrained ignorance of the first European settlers and those who succeeded them.

The impact of conquest and colonization was survived by peoples in regions which in time have taken on the characteristics of regions of refuge. There the basis of Indian harvests is the cultivation of native plants, domesticated prior to contact. The technology used in raising such crops also dates from precontact times, with an important modification, namely the substitution of metal instruments for stone. But the principle, form, and function of the older items remain unvarying. And the practice of itinerant cultivation of maize and some tubers such as yucca in the tropics and the potato in the highlands persists, with the use of fire as the most effective instrument for soil preparation.

Some Indian groups—the culturally advanced ones—accepted the introduction of the Egyptian plow in raising harvests for the market. That innovation is now an anachronism, persisting by virtue of a tenacious conservatism. Similarly, artisan techniques which use native or sixteenth century Spanish patterns are obsolete and yield goods of imperfect quality as well as low productivity. The pre-Columbian backstrap loom or the pedal loom, introduced in the colonial period, both now obsolete, are still used to make clothing. Primitive tools are still used in the construction of housing, of furniture, and of utensils for household use and work. The structure surrounding this backward technology helps to limit the possibilities for change toward ways of acting and thinking which would be more in accord with the progress of the modern world.

The technological lag applies not only to Indians, but to Ladinos as well, and this fact is of great importance. As real or presumed heirs of the first dominant settler group that the colonial situation imposed in the regions of refuge, Ladinos orient their actions and technology toward keeping and defending the status quo which has placed them in a position of clear superiority. The Indians' subjugation presents them with plentiful human resources which make innovations undesirable and abort progress. Muscular energy, both human and animal, is used liberally because of its low cost. Goods are carried by animals or *tamemes* and persons ride on horseback or are carried in hand chairs by Indians. The oxcart and potter's wheel are perhaps the most important technical applications of the wheel. In the city, Ladinos support artisans whose production is organized on the guild model and whose techniques are obsolete. Artisan products are valuable as popular art, and they survive to the extent that the regions of refuge retain their obsolete characteristics since they cannot compete with articles produced by national industries. Because of its use as an instrument of domination, Ladino technology is far from embracing the forms, functions and meanings of modern technology.

NOTES

1. White is the anthropologist who has placed greatest emphasis on the importance of energy; for him, "Culture evolves as the amount of energy used annually per capita or the efficiency of the means used to put energy to work increase." White states: "From a zoological point of view, culture is no more than a means for maintaining life in one particular species. . . . The functioning of culture as a whole is consequently based and determined by the quantity of energy dominated and the way it is put to work" (1964:340).

2. Flores asserts: "The word 'resource' does not refer to a material or a substance but rather to a function that the material or substance can fulfill or to a process in which it can participate; that is, the function or process to achieve a particular end, such as the satisfaction of a desire. In other words, the concept 'resources' is an abstraction that reflects a human evaluation and relates it to a function or process. . . . Therefore, resources reflect all the changes in the goals of those who evaluate them. The concept 'resource' presupposes an economic evaluation of the environment by an individual or collective human agent. A resource, therefore, is a relative concept, which changes with the general scheme of means and ends; that is, according to the human agent who evaluates the resources and the means and ends for which he intends to use them" (1962:98).

3. Herskovits (1954a:70) states: "The ability of peoples with rudimentary technology to manipulate their resources effectively is thus the most fundamental aspect of their economic systems. . . . Food, in these regions, is obtained by hunting and the knowledge of these natives regarding the customs of the animals they hunt is traditionally famous."

4. Piddington (1957:462) states: "While the availability of raw materials in a given environment limits its technological exploitation it does not follow that all available resources are used. The new world provided the resources necessary to make bronze . . . but even the most elaborate pre-Colombian civilizations never knew a bronze age in the sense that this term is applied to the prehistoric development of the old world."

5. Forde and Douglas (1960:332) state: "Another common characteristic of a primitive economy, though also not a universal one, is a lack of diversity in the major resources. Some peoples are heavily dependent on a few products, which are processed so as to provide food, shelter, weapons, tools, and nearly all the main needs of the people. This tendency is particularly noticeable among hunters and herders. The Eskimo takes from the seals he kills meat to eat, fat for fuel and for lighting, fat for anointing himself, skins for covering, sinews for thongs, bones for harpoons and arrow heads. There is an economy of effort, but the risks are high. If, during a stormy winter, seals are absent from a usually sheltered bay, starvation and death for the whole community may result. The cattle-keeping Nuer of the southern Sudan turn the products of their cattle to meet most of their essential requirements: blood, milk, cheese, and meat for sustenance; horn and bone for weapons; dried dung for fuel; hides for covering and thongs and bags. But during the rinderpest epidemic at the end of the last century, when their cattle died wholesale, they were in desperate straits."

6. Chapple & Coon (1953:249) state: "The simplest type of technology so defined is that of the peoples who use only chipped flint or comparable cutting tools. These people are all food-gatherers and have no advanced techniques of transport. They can derive a living from the immediate environment in almost any environment. The most complex type is our own world technology, with complex and varied metal tools, all kinds of techniques of obtaining materials such as agriculture, animal husbandry, sea fishing, mining, etc., by means of power machinery where it is advantageous, great individual and regional specialization in techniques and products, and power-operated methods of transport by land and sea, and also by air.

We too can live in all environments, not by exploiting single landscapes separately, but by pooling and redistributing the products of all types of environment. Between these two extremes lie the other technologies of intermediate complexity, adapted to single landscapes or combinations of them."

7. See particularly Chapter X of *Principles of Anthropology* (Chapple & Coon 1953).

8. Stern transcribes the following passage of Engels: "The materialist conception of history starts with the principle that production, and with it the exchange of products, is the basis of all social order; that in all societies the distribution of its products has appeared in history, and with it the division of the society into classes and groups, which are based on what is produced, how it is produced, and how the product is exchanged. In accordance with this concept, the ultimate causes of all social changes and all political revolutions must be sought, not in the minds of men, in their increasing perception of truths and eternal justice, but in the operational transformations in the mode of production and exchange: it must be sought, not in philosophy, but in the economy and in the respective era." Stern comments: "The proofs he supplies give validity to this principle in regard to primitive societies. The studies of comparative cultures give proof to the fact that the forms of social relations, religious and political institutions and practices, arts and techniques clearly tend to correlate closely with the types of economic life of primitive peoples. It has been discovered that the decisive factor in determining the character and rhythm of these cultures is the presence or absence of surpluses, and these depend on the mode of production" (1951: 387).

9. Forde states: "The far-reaching significance of different modes of life was already recognized in classical times, and they were soon endowed with a developmental value as 'economic stages.' In the nineteenth century, when attention was first seriously devoted to the economies of primitive peoples, these hoary economic stages met with little criticism from the ideas of unilinear evolution, themselves transferred uncritically from biology to human culture. Man had begun everywhere, it was suggested, as a hunter, had later learned to domesticate some of his game animals

and so became a pastoralist, and finally rose to the stage of agriculture. Little distinction was drawn between the very different kinds of food gathering, or between the rudimentary digging of planted roots and advanced cereal agriculture with the plough. Nor were any valid reasons adduced for supposing that pastoralism everywhere preceded cultivation. Finally, the concept of cultural diffusion and the recognition of the part it played in affecting the economic pattern over vast areas was almost entirely neglected. The ideas of evolution and progress that dominated scientific and social thought produced a vague and abstract 'man' living nowhere in particular, who was always tending to struggle up to a higher stage. Criticism of this three-stage theory is no longer required: its inadequacy has long been realized. The German geographer, Edouard Hahn, performed the valuable service of attacking the dogma of pastoral priority, which archaeological discovery has since done so much to refute, and of indicating the great gulf that usually lies between digging stick and plough cultivation.

Peoples do not live at economic stages. They. possess economies; and again we do not find single and. exclusive economies but combinations of them. Development is not in one direction along a single line, and some economies have played almost no part in the historical growth of particular cultures. Pastoralism had, for instance, a relatively late and very limited development in the New World" (Forde 1953:461).

10. Ribeiro (1957:46) informs us about the actual conditions of the Brazilian jungle ethnic groups reduced to less than 100,000 individuals.

11. Meggers (1958:84) states: "The emphasis that should be placed upon the influence of man on his environment has not allowed us to see clearly other situations in which man, rather than dominate, conforms to it. Changes produced by hunter–gatherers and swidden farmers are comparable to the action of birds, other animals, and natural forces. All of them spread seeds, exterminate other beings, and produce minor alterations upon the environment. These modifications are the inevitable consequence of the struggle for life. Nevertheless, man is the only one that has developed the capacity to alter the environment with a goal in mind, on a grand scale and permanently. The development of this capacity is a decisive factor in cultural evolution. To say simply that all human beings modify the environment is to lose sight of the fundamental difference between transporting a seed and leveling a mountain or destroying a forest. All cultures have not developed the same capacities or, what is almost the same, all environments are not equally maleable. Some modifications, favorable to certain environments, provoke negative results in others. This latter case does not really depend on a less maleable environment but rather that its plasticity hinders rather than helps fulfill human needs. Given the diversity of climates and typographies it would be amazing if all areas were equally favorable and easy for man to dominate. In the Amazon basin man has hardly been able to leave a light trace of his presence. To negate environmental obstacles does not diminish the reality of this failure."

12. Morley (1947:162) states: "The experts of the U. S. Department of Agriculture who have studied the Mayan method of corn cultivation declare that it is the only method of farming that can work in the stony and shallow soil of the Yucatan. To try to use modern instruments and agricultural machinery in the northern Maya territory would be as inefficient as trying to add a fifth wheel to any vehicle."

13. See Oliveira (1964), Chapter III, "Occupied Territory."

Chapter 6

DUAL ECONOMY

IN THE REGIONS OF REFUGE the Indian and tribal groups are not completely independent although they are largely self-sufficient and self-contained. They live in close proximity to Mestizo or Ladino groups representing the majority or dominant group of the country, but with regional variations of the national culture. Generally the groups sharing in the national culture inhabit a governing center or metropolis while the subordinate Indian and tribal groups, scattered throughout a vast area, serve as the hinterland of the urban center.

Indians and Ladinos live in socioeconomic symbiosis, each group retaining its own identity. They form relationships that place them in separate economic, social, and political spheres which they cannot leave without causing serious conflicts leading to violence and repression. This economic, social, and political segregation engenders a dual structure, perhaps the most important characteristic of the regions of refuge, in which the dominant Ladinos subject the dependent Indian populations to unpardonable exploitation.

The dual structure juxtaposes two types of economic organization with separate orientations. That of the Indians is aimed at satisfying subsistence needs, and that of the Ladinos at strengthening the profit motive and increasing the accumulation of capital goods. But continued, first-hand contact between economies based on contradictory concepts forces interaction and merges antagonistic features. The original organizations change so much that the Indian economy is no longer one of primitive subsistence and that of the Ladinos is no longer a developing capitalist economy. In the latter case, which is also the more dramatic because of its national implications, contact and domination cause the persistence of a colonial economy which blocks progress and modernization of the region as well as of the country.

A STATUS ECONOMY. When two economic systems with different orientations come into contact, the conflicting forces produce a new system. The existence of a dual economy in a region of refuge represents the situation before the process begins, before the opposing elements have come together. The conflict between simple and industrial economies is seen objectively at different levels; sometimes the native economy appears little changed by contact, at others it may contain the basic ingredients of a modern economy. In both cases, considered in its entirety as the interaction of Indian and Ladino economies, the region's economy is obviously backward compared to the national, and even more so in comparison to the most advanced industrial countries. The dual economy is an economic model specific to underdeveloped countries.

To discover the characteristics of the process it is necessary to study its early phase. During the past century capitalist economies pushed colonial expansion; with new techniques and skills they burst into territories occupied by peoples with traditional life styles and relationships. Colonial occupation of agricultural lands and exploitation of resources and native manual labor satisfied the unlimited needs of the developing metropolitan countries with rational efficiency, helped their accelerated growth and provided an image of progress which Latin American countries tried to imitate. The fate of the people under colonial domination, suffering the consequences of European aggression, was not taken into account. Only the dazzling growth of Europe and the economic system oriented toward material gain which had allowed this rise were seen.

The influence of laissez-faire liberals brought pressure to transform the semifeudal society and economy of the colonial period into progressive systems. It was believed that civilization was a function of the amount of White blood in a given population, and because of this the immigration of European farm workers was desperately encouraged so that the land might be cultivated using entrepreneurial techniques and spirit. Communal lands, which had been undivided and held under pre-Conquest forms of ownership, were turned into private property so that they could be sold in the market. As in the territories under present day colonial rule, migratory work through *enganche*[1] was legalized on the assumption that the native would learn advanced cultivation methods through contact with modern plantation technology and improve his standard of living with the higher wages earned in the mines. The circulation of money in native communities would force traditional economic behavior to change and allow the imposition of more equitable and rational taxation.

Imitation of Europe by Latin American countries did not produce the desired development; on the contrary, it led to the establishment of the type of dual economy which Europe had introduced directly into its colonies.[2] Alongside the plantations run by Europeans and the mines, oil wells and refineries, alongside the profit-making factories and commercial firms, survived the native communities, stripped in part or completely of their former means of subsistence and rendered increasingly poor and unhappy with the deterioration of their spirit by the process of domination. Indian communities had their own concepts of land ownership and tenancy, compensation, and the value of work, distribution of goods, services, and resources, and appropriate sanctions to enforce conformity with tradition. Thus they had successfully resisted all pressures to change.

Rejection of the economizing norms of European culture made administrators and managers—those agents of change whose practical role was to force innovation—see that those norms, supposedly a part of human nature, did not function among the Indians as they did elsewhere. An explanation was needed for this unexpected fact; it was quickly found through rationalizations which attributed to the Indians limited needs, an absence of all instinct for material gain, a lack of legitimate ambition, as well as other characteristics which formed a stereotyped Indian personality dominated by fatalism and resignation.[3] In fact, they did not want to see that native behavior patterns were different from occidental ones, and oriented toward satisfying biological and social needs along models which were not motivated by the desire for material gain but only by the anxiety to increase status, honor and prestige, to expand the social ego.

In a context other than the Latin American one, differences in economic conduct between the native population and westerners were examined more easily when the administrators of large British colonial companies tried to apply the pressure and profit incentives which had been effective in metropolitan commercial enterprises; they discovered with surprise that these methods were not equally effective in mobilizing corporate native communities. The learned nineteenth century English jurist, Sir Henry Maine, analyzed the problem with great precision. He saw that there was a fundamental difference between Western society and native communities. He recognized that, to a large extent, the primitive communities were closed units with their own rights and obligations, organized into extended family groups whose economic and legal relationships had an inter-familiar rather than an interpersonal character. Western concepts of rights over property and its resulting alienability, sale, and relationship to the market, were not applicable to societies organized along different principles. To emphasize their distinct orientations, Maine termed the native community a *society of status* and the Western community a *society of contract.*[4]

ECONOMIC DUALISM. Maine never defined the differential features of status and contract economies. Holland was the first country to use a scientific approach, at a time when world opinion demanded that colonial powers implement an ethical policy which would give subject peoples some participation in the profits of colonial exploitation by raising their living standards. In 1930, the University of Leiden published a small work of Julius Herman Boeke, Professor of Eastern Economics, called *Dualistische economie.*[5] He proposed a theory of economic change which operates when a highly industrialized colonial power attempts to improve the subsistence of a subject population without changing the fundamental terms of the equation, without modifying the domination process that keeps mechanisms of superiority and subordination in operation. An analysis of Boeke's theory is important because it illuminates, in the colonial context, the situation of the regions of refuge. These regions are clearly colonial enclaves located in independent countries which are moving toward modernization.[6]

Boeke was employed in the civil service of Indonesia, the former Netherlands Indies. His theory of economic dualism emerged from observations of a colonial country where the capitalist economic and social systems imposed by Europeans conflicted with the precapitalist native economic and social system. Boeke thought that his interpretation of the Indonesian situation might apply to other countries which had undergone the colonial experience and where a similar conflict had taken place between the industrial and subsistence economies. He generalized especially in terms of Eastern Asia and expressed his opinions in the famous phrase of Rudyard Kipling, who vigorously extolled England's imperialist mission: "East is East and West is West and never the twain shall meet." However, dual economy is not confined to the Orient nor does its existence imply, as Boeke (1954) supposed, the impossibility of integrating disparate economies.

A dual economy has its own unique features. According to Boeke, one of them is the peculiar nature of needs, which are limited in the society of status, in sharp contrast to the unlimited needs of Western society. The Western reaction to a rise in the market price of goods is to produce more of them to obtain higher profits; in the dual economy the native responds differently. Production decreases when the price rises because with the sale of a smaller quantity the native can satisfy his limited needs. If salaries rise the same phenomenon takes place, since the worker receives enough money with less effort to fulfill his requirements. If he insures the subsistence of his family by cultivating two hectares, he will not sow twice that amount in order to improve his life. If he is working a pine forest or a grove of rubber trees and the price of resin or rubber goes up he will stop tapping a number of trees; if prices drop, he will increase exploitation in order to obtain money to satisfy his fixed needs. In other words, a primitive economy, in contrast to an industrial one, shows negative curves of supply, effort, and risk-taking.

Boeke's observations are valid, but not his explanation. Needs are neither limited nor unlimited in native communities; as we shall see they are simply of a different order. They are social or status needs rather than economic needs in the formal sense of the term as used in our modern culture. The truth of his observations, however, led to acceptance of the theory of the Indian's limited needs in the colonial context as well as in the regions of refuge. Forced recruitment of labor is justified by this theory, as is payment of low salaries to migrant plantation and mine workers and the policy of paying lower prices for native products than those prevailing on the national market.

The discrepancies resulting from more than one standard of value form another important feature of the dual economy. In an industrial society merchandise is valued according to its relative scarcity, and so-called rational factors intervene in the setting of prices. In the native economy, however, the rational factor is often passed over and primacy given to the non-economizing emotive factor, rooted in prestige. Cattle raising, extensively studied by Herskovits (1926), is an example of a different value system from the industrial one. Cattle are not valued for their weight or quality, but for certain anatomical peculiarities such as the size and shape of the horns. Similarly, in some native communities hogs are not valued for their weight and quality, but for the size and shape of their tusks (Du Bois 1961:198). In other communities the value placed on possession of large herds of goats or rams hinders the success of soil conservation programs or the establishment of an appropriate relationship between the number of animals and amount of pasturage. To reiterate, in the dual economy the purely economical nature of value is modified by prestige and status requirements.

One more feature of the dual economy is the little weight given to the profit motive. In an inventory of the data contained in anthropological literature on motivations to save, that is, on the determining causes of resource and labor movements in native communities, Herskovits (1954b) notes that preliterate peoples are generally considered to have a very weak response to the incentive for profit and for individual material gain so characteristic of a money economy. Such economic behavior is observable in terms of production as well as distribution. Commerce, transactions, and speculations take place of course, but the elements of regularity and continuity which characterize the idea of profit are lacking. Thus in native communities there are no strictly professional traders or entrepreneurs with the qualities of the Western businessman, tending to discipline, specialization, and commercial organization and dominated by "common sense reasoning" (Higgins 1959:276).

THE HOTHOUSE FLOWER. These features and others analyzed by Boeke led him to set forth three fundamental differences between the native and industrial economies. The latter is based upon: (1) limited needs; (2) lack of a money economy, and (3) an organization of corporate units. On the basis of these differences, this celebrated Dutch economist and colonialist arrived at two important conclusions which have provoked impassioned controversies (Boeke 1942). The first is a theoretical conclusion, that the concepts of Western economics are totally inapplicable to underdeveloped countries. The second conclusion is a practical corollary of the first, namely that the dual economy is irreversible and therefore any effort to develop Indian communities is useless and leads inevitably to their further disintegration.

Regarding the first conclusion, Boeke writes, "We shall do well not to try to transplant the tender, delicate hothouse plants of western theory into tropical soil, where an early death awaits them" (quoted in Higgins 1959:259). Western economic theory is aimed at explaining the behavior of a capitalist society and the native community is a precapitalist society. He particularly criticizes efforts to explain resource allocation and profit distribution in primitive communities in terms of the theory of marginal productivity.

Let us see what other development economists and economic anthropologists have thought in this respect: Herskovits (1954b) and Firth (1964) believed that economic theory is generally applicable to both industrial and primitive societies. However, since they postulated the relativity of cultural values they necessarily conceded the relative value of economic behavior, with different applications in each society.[7] The economist who has most closely studied Boeke's thought, Higgins, criticizes the arguments on which Boeke bases his conclusion, noting that the phenomenon of economic duality is observed even in the heart of the most advanced societies. For Higgins, Western economic theory necessarily has universal application or economics is not a science.[8] Bauer and Yamey, for their part, insist on the pertinence of economic generalizations and deny the possibility of theories or methods of analysis formulated specifically for indigenous communities or for the underdeveloped world. According to them, although it is necessary to take into account differences in institutional structures and culture patterns, economic behavior is fundamentally the same for all peoples and in all countries.[9]

The position adopted by economists and anthropologists who contradict Boeke seems fundamentally sound. Their conviction that differences in economic behavior among the peoples of the earth are of degree and not of kind includes the postulate that differences of degree are more easily overcome than those of kind. When the nations of Latin America obtained their liberty and independence 150 years ago, Indians and non-Indians alike were declared equal before the law, on the assumption that differences in political privilege were of degree and not of kind. The liberators' view of the situation was basically sound; their error lay in not putting or not being able to put into effect any action which would have made equality effective. A very similar phenomenon takes place with Western economic theory when its general application puts the Indian and industrial man on the same plane. Economists, entrusted with the practical direction of development programs and industrialization efforts, contradict their theoretical position, and *tend to disregard the preindustrial sectors*. Hirschman notes that there are reasons to believe that certain preindustrial economic activities have more probability of survival today than in the past.[10] In regions such as the refuge zones, where transportation by porters may be seen alongside airplanes, it is difficult to concede validity to the predictions of economic theory, created to resolve situations which are totally different. When economic planners encounter the problem they easily overcome it by disregarding it. In investment and development projects, the native regions of refuge are not taken into account or are assigned last place in the priority of programs, which in fact means that they are disregarded.

As noted, Boeke's second conclusion is a result of the first: the disintegration of primitive communities chained to a dual economy is irreversible. The contrast between old and new is so great, so deep and so wide that a meeting is not feasible; the distance is great and grows daily. We must accept dualism as an irremediable phenomenon, abandon Indian communities to their fate and put all efforts into the development and growth of the modern sector of the country's economy. Efforts to improve the traditional agricultural methods of Indian communities without changing their mental attitude probably cause more harm than good. Contrary to initial impressions, the agricultural system of these communities is not the manifestation of a lower stage of development, but the result of a careful process of adaptation upon which it would be difficult to improve.

Training of community leaders, technical assistance, and capital investment have no justification if economic development is limited by irrational economic behavior rooted in the very nature of the primitive mentality. Boeke did not consider its modification feasible, and in this he followed German thought at the beginning of the century, and especially the rational-prelogical dichotomy of Lévy-Bruhl, which has since been discredited.[11] Boeke believed that economic dualism must be accepted as a permanent feature of many countries rather than be considered a transitory phase in a process where the conclusion may be accelerated through a policy of integration (Boeke 1953).

A final comment on the theory of economic dualism and on its author's conclusions might well be that Boeke erred in his explanation of the phenomenon but not in the fact of its existence, about which there can be no doubt. The failure of the ethical policy implemented by Holland in its colonies was not due to lack of technical assistance or investment of foreign capital. In this as in similar programs failure was caused by nonparticipation by the colonial population, subjugated through mechanisms of domination that were often intangible. Economic as well as social and political development requires a climate of self-assertion which is certainly not found in the colonial situation.

THE SUBSTANTIVE AND THE FORMAL. Application of a dual interpretation of economic activities in the regions of refuge is useful because it forces economists to concentrate on a portion of their specialization which has been largely ignored in theory and in practice. In general, economists as well as sociologists have developed methods and techniques to explain and predict the phenomena of Western culture and have left the job of exploring native institutions to anthropologists. In the last 50 years they have accumulated considerable data, used by Herskovits in his well-known work on economic anthropology. In this largely descriptive work, Western economic principles were used to formulate theory, and as Herskovits himself notes, those principles were primarily constructed to explain the very aspects of modern economics which bear least similarity to the economy of primitive communities (Herskovits 1940:Chapter II).

The use of modern economic theory as an instrument for explaining primitive conduct always opens the door to serious error. It is natural for the researcher to try to project what has been useful in studying and analyzing his own society's economy, as well as to presume that those instruments can supply categories and insights for explaining different behavior satisfactorily. Elaboration of an economic theory for a dual society requires the interdisciplinary collaboration of the anthropologist and the economist. The latter must force himself to understand the economic activities and motivations of social groups which apparently do not respond to the incentives that permitted sustained development in industrialized Western countries.

The problem has arisen because of confusion and ambiguity concerning the importance of Western economic theory in explaining the economic organization of primitive communities. To a large extent that confusion and ambiguity are due to a lack of clarity and distinction between the concepts of economics and economic organization. It is obvious that the concept of economics as a science may be used to explain the economic activities of any human group, be it primitive or highly industrialized. On the other hand, the form of economic organization in which those activities are institutionalized and the motivations that guide people in accordance with established norms are not general, but particular to each human aggregation. They vary with the culture and the group's position in the scale of human evolution.

Polanyi and his associates note that the term economic has two distinct and independent meanings that are often confused. In its substantive meaning the term economic connotes simply the supply of material goods to satisfy biological and social needs.[12] In this sense, it is a universally valid postulate, the cultural response to a biological need; man's existence requires sustained support. In its substantive meaning, the term economic can be universally applied because all communities, independent of ecological, technical, and cultural differences, are made up of human beings whose biosocial existence depends upon the sustained supply of material goods.

Man not only has to fulfill the need for nutrients to maintain life; he must also satisfy social demands, personal tastes, religious rules and obligations imposed by personal relations, which are as important to group life as simple subsistence is to organic life. Man's economic organization is formed by the cultural apparatus of tools, goods, and services which must be produced, used, repaired, and replaced, and by the principles controlling production, exchange, distribution, and consumption of goods. Economic organization is general neither in structure nor function; it differs profoundly throughout various evolutionary levels and according to environmental differences. It depends on a number of legal rules and concepts of value which are defined by tradition, as noted by Malinowski (1944:126).

In effect, the exploitation of natural resources requires the use of techniques for the acquisition or production of material goods. In addition to use of techniques and natural resources, combined with the need to distribute the material goods among all inhabitants, defined institutional arrangements are required to assure the continuity of supply. Those who take part in the process are mutually dependent because the use of techniques, the division of labor, the very physical surroundings, and the fact that the economic process takes place in a social community, all make necessary the utilization of a specific pattern of recognized rights and obligations. What we call economic organization is composed of the rules which govern the use of natural resources and techniques, and which assure sustained cooperation in supplying material goods.

For Dalton (1961), the formal meaning of the term economic denotes the special combination of rules aimed at maximizing the achievement of some end or minimizing expenditures of some means. The formal meaning of the term is so important in Western culture that it often obscures the substantive meaning and takes on all the connotations of the verb to economize, that is, to make calculations to increase profits and decrease costs. The economic organization of industrial society is dominated by the formal meaning of the term. The market, which is the central institution of that society, is based on economic calculations, that is, on the use of mechanisms designed to economize. These include cost accounting, contractual obligations for assuring the sustained supply of resources, the imposition of manufacturing standards by an authoritarian hierarchy, and the setting of prices and salaries to economize in the use of scarce factors which fulfill unlimited needs.

The market centered economy is entirely motivated by the institutional need to seek material profits. It is based on the dogma that man's material needs are insatiable and therefore a scarcity of means exists by definition. The absolute quantity of resources available to a community is not important; if needs are unlimited, resources will always be insufficient to satisfy the unlimited demand for finished products. As a result, in order to satisfy his material needs man must economize, rationally calculating the use of his resources in order of preference.[13]

Dalton (1961) maintains that the syllogism—man's material needs are infinite, his material means are finite, maximum material acquisition therefore requires calculations for economizing—which is considered to be universally true, leads to error and serious misjudgments. It is incorrect to suppose that unlimited needs are part of man's very nature, just as it is incorrect to assume that economic motivations or the impulse to obtain material profits are based on utilitarianism. The social organization of the economy, that is, the economic organization characteristic of an industrial culture, is what impels man to want more material goods than he has at any given moment, and makes him value acquisition of those goods over the fulfillment of other social goals with which the acquisitive goal may conflict.

Acquisitive behavior in modern society is determined by the values and institutions of industrial culture. That is, it is determined socially rather than by nature or biology.[14] Industrial society puts great value on the acquisition of material goods as opposed to other goals, and its members behave in accordance with the institutional arrangements created by the society. Scarcity of material means depends on social rather than natural circumstances. If members of the Indian community do not economize in the use of scarce means and if they employ more than the minimum necessary to achieve a goal under specific circumstances, it is because their social organization dictates that certain means must be limited to only certain ends.

THE LADINO ECONOMY. Elucidation of the differences between economics as a concept and economic organization, that is, between the substantive and formal meanings of the term economic, enables us to understand why on many occasions the economic behavior of Indians appears antieconomic, that is, contrary to economic norms and principles. In reality it is only antieconomizing, or structured institutionally on the basis of rules and motivations different from those of Western economic organization; not all economies are based on economizing calculations. This semantic clarification also explains why financial incentives often do not lure native workers to industrial activities and why they do not always happily accept liberation from their traditional ties (Spicer 1963:19). The situation thus stated, we may begin our analysis of the dual economy of the regions of refuge with a characterization of the Ladino economy.

Ladinos commonly live in a central city which is the *chef-lieu* of the region of refuge and which controls the economic activities of the governing center and its hinterland. In most cases the Ladino city is a market city or a market supported by an urban concentration, as Marroquin (1957:33) aptly described it. The market dominates city life to such an extent that it imposes its particular rhythm and norms on it. Commercial exchange, functioning as a mechanism of economic integration, compels its participants to conform to the rules of the market. Peons sell their labor, landlords sell the use of their land and natural resources, farmers and artisans sell their products. The same mechanism works in the market to distribute the ingredients of production—work, land, natural resources, finances, transportation—as well as finished goods and highly varied services.

In the Ladino city the market has a specially constructed site called the marketplace, but in reality the market embraces the entire urban concentration. It includes the principles and norms which regulate buying and selling at a fixed price in money even though, as frequently happens, this does not take place in the marketplace itself where buyers and sellers congregate, and even though the object of the transaction is work or natural resources rather than material products. Labor is sometimes sold in the marketplace but more frequently this transaction takes place elsewhere. In any case the important point is that labor is bought or sold through the use of market prices. In the Ladino city land also becomes a commodity. Ownership or use is bought or sold for a price in money which is set by the same principles of exchange that determine the price of labor and of material articles. The price of maize or other basic crops affects land revenues and workers' salaries. The market's principle of integration puts all components of the economy into a mutually dependent relationship. Market prices direct resources among production alternatives and determine wages and salaries, profits, rents, and interest rates of resource owners.

An economy organized on the basis of commerce forces its participants to seek individual profit. It creates in them a mercantile libido; everyone must sell something with a market value in order to acquire the material means of subsistence.[15] The economic importance of a commercial organization is so broad and comprehensive that properly speaking, urban society is a mercantile society, in the sense that social organization is completely adapted to the needs, rules, and rhythms of the marketplace. It could not be otherwise; to include man and his surroundings in the market mechanism is to subordinate the very essence of the society to the laws of commerce.[16]

The currency of the Ladino market economy is "all-purpose-money," as Polanyi calls it. A single form of money serves as a means of exchange, savings, and payment and as a standard of value for all transactions in all sectors of the market. This single currency is conveniently interchangeable into checks, bank notes or coins. The use of all-purpose-money is a requisite for the functioning of an economy centered in the marketplace. Comparison of the values of different articles or services is made possible by transactions which involve work, products, and resources.[17]

Organized on the market principle and the use of all-purpose-money, the Ladino economy is pervasive, penetrating and interrelated, and tends to homogenize the sectors of production and distribution. The term money economy accentuates an important feature of the Ladino economic structure. Continuity of the supply of material goods in the market economy is assured through various practices, one of which is the use of all-purpose money. A money economy exists only when land and work, as well as manufactured articles, are treated as merchandise which can be bought and sold through the mechanism of the market.

NOTES

1. The *enganche* system of labor recruitment is one in which the worker is given a loan prior to his leaving for the plantation or other place of work, which loan is to be repaid through subsequent labor. At its worst this system has encouraged all the abuses of debt peonage.

2. Hirschman (1964:130) states: "A third factor, closely related to the others, is the coexistence and prolonged proximity of modern industry and pre-industrial, at times neolithic, techniques. It is often said that developing countries will probably go from the mule to the airplane in one generation. Nevertheless, if we look at the majority of these countries more closely, we will find a situation which apparently will continue for a long time, in which the airplane and the mule both fulfill essential economic functions. This dualistic characteristic of developing countries can be seen in the processes of production and distribution; it also exists in life styles and forms of carrying on business."

Lewis describes it further: "We find that a few industries highly capitalized . . . side by side with the most primitive techniques. . . . There is the same contrast between people: between the few highly westernized, trousered natives educated in Western universities, speaking Western languages, and glorying in Beethoven, Mill, Marx or Einstein and the great mass of their countrymen who live in quite other worlds" (1954:147).

3. Hoselitz tells us: "There was a time when one would have stipulated ideal types without vacillating, and even might have presented them as real descriptions and situations in which economic progress was related to growing affective neutrality. In other words, civilized man's economic behavior was considered to be coldly rational while the nude and primitive savage was thought of as an irrational child whose behavior was determined exclusively by his immediate necessities and his behavior toward social beings (human or otherwise) was seen as purely and predominantly affective. This theory, which until recently could have enjoyed a certain popularity among those who maintain vulgar notions of the superiority of certain races, has been demonstrated to be completely false" (1962:32).

Bauer and Yamey (1965:111) assert: "A very generalized belief exists that in the underdeveloped regions many people, especially the farmers, react to improvements in the level of income by producing and working proportionately less, because they need only enough income to pay for fixed or limited expenses. Sometimes it is said that this is true for most of the people of, for example, Africa, India, and Southeast Asia. But the most superficial examination of the changes that have taken place in the customs of consumption of many people in these territories, is enough to establish that the needs of many peasants and other peoples have not been fixed or static."

4. Maine (1963:164) states: "The word Status may be usefully employed to construct a formula expressing the law of progress thus indicated, which, whatever be its value, seems to me to be sufficiently ascertained. All the forms of Status taken notice of in the Law of Persons were derived from, and to some extent are still coloured by, the powers and privileges anciently residing in the family. If then we employ Status, agreeably with the usage of the best writers, to signify these personal conditions only, and avoid applying the term to such conditions as are the immediate or remote result of agreement, we may say that the movement of the progressive societies has hitherto been a movement *from Status to Contract*".

5. Belshaw (1965:95) informs us that Boeke formulated the original concept of dual economy in 1910 in "Tropish-Koloniale Staathuishoudkunde," which was accompanied by an article by J. S. Furnivall in the *Economic Journal* of that same year.

6. De la Fuente asserts: "Every local ethnic system, and the factors shaping it, resembles other local systems. These factors include the economic situation, generally superior for the Ladino group and inferior for the Indians; cultural duality, with generally acknowledged superiority, above all by the Ladinos for their culture and language, and undervaluation for the culture and language of the Indians, frequently accepted by them; racial duality, real or imagined, and at times used to rationalize the favored position of the Ladinos and undervaluation of the Indians; constant constrictions in relations between the groups; and the passing of Indian to Ladino by means of acculturation and assimilation, despite the barriers raised. Some of the differences among the local systems discussed before are more of quantity than of quality. The basic tendency of this change is the change in the caste structure, which operates with greater or lesser rigidity in the area, above all in the south, by means of the diminution and annulment of the differences between Ladinos and Indians which underlie their casts" (1965:216).

7. Fusfeld (1957:348) states: "This weakness of the early studies of primitive economies has led to the appearance of a new 'school' of anthropologists who have devoted themselves to studies of primitive economic life in great detail, using the terminology of economic theory in order to make comparisons between different societies. Less emphasis is placed upon the uniqueness of each society, and more is placed upon such things as incentives, exchange, trade and barter, money, use of capital, land tenure, and so on. The goal of this newer group of anthropologists is to derive some general principles of economic behavior among primitive peoples out of detailed studies of everyday economic affairs. Chief among them are Melville Herskovits, Sol Tax, Raymond Firth, and D. M. Goodfellow."

8. Higgins (1959:288) states with precision: "The question of usefulness of Western theory is an important one; clearly, the possibility of effective prescriptions for economic and social policy in underdeveloped areas by Western social scientists depends on the degree to which the tools of analysis, in the use of which the Western social scientist is an expert, can be applied in underdeveloped countries."

9. Bauer and Yamey (1965:9) declare: "In our opinion, many of the important differences among the underdeveloped nations are so profound and transcendent that the generalizations made about their economies are often of only limited applicability. When the generalizations are applicable, we give special consideration to factors which influence the growth of resources, as well as the factors that produce the different political responses to that growth. Although many of the differences found in various parts of the underdeveloped world are overwhelming, it is possible to apply widely some of the instruments and basic concepts of economy to the underdeveloped countries. For example, it is possible to apply them to the basic elements in the analysis of supply and demand. Analogously, the theory of inflation, the concepts of marginal substitution, and the complementary-competitive relation among the factors of production, are equally illustrative, whether used to explain events and circumstances in advanced countries or in countries barely beginning to develop. Special economic theories or methods of analysis specially formulated for the study of the underdeveloped world do not exist."

10. Hirschman (1964:131) states: "There exist reasons for thinking that certain preindustrial economic activities have much more probability of surviving now than in western Europe during the growth of industrialization. Now, much more than in the past, the power of industrialization tends to leave the preindustrial sectors in peace during a long period, rather than attack them directly."

11. See Aguirre Beltrán (1963:256) for a discussion of the sociological contributions of Lévy-Bruhl.

12. Polanyi was the one who made the distinction. For him: "The term economic is a compound of two meanings that have independent roots. We will call them the substantive and the formal meaning.

The substantive meaning of economic derives from man's dependence for his living upon nature and his fellows. It refers to the interchange with his natural and social environment, in so far as this results in supplying him with the means of material want satisfaction.

The formal meaning of economic derives from the logical character of the means-ends relationship, as apparent in such words as 'economical' or 'economizing.' It refers to a definite situation of choice, namely, that between the different uses of means induced by an insufficiency of those means. If we call the rules governing choice of means the logic of rational action, then we may denote this variant of logic, with an improvised term, as formal economics.

The two root meanings of 'economic,' the substantive and the formal, have nothing in common. The latter derives from logic, the former from fact. The formal meaning implies a set of rules referring to choice between the alternative uses of insufficient means. The substantive meaning implies neither choice nor insufficiency of means; man's livelihood may or may not involve the necessity of choice and, if choice there be, it need not be induced by the limiting effect of a 'scarcity' of the means; indeed, some of the most important physical and social conditions of livelihood such as the availability of air and water or a loving mother's devotion to her infant are not, as a rule, so limiting. The cogency that is in play in the one case and in the other differs as the power of syllogism differs from the force of gravitation. The laws of the one are those of the mind; the laws of the other are those of nature. The two meanings could not be further apart; semantically they lie in opposite directions of the compass."

13. Hopkins (1957:290) refutes the concept of scarcity: "... It cannot be 'scarcity as a fact of nature' which is relevant, then, but only 'scarcity' either as a critical shortage or as a generally acted upon cultural definition of situations. In neither case is 'scarcity' universal, since neither famines and floods nor money as a generalized means of exchange are recurrent characteristics of all societies.

The alleged response of society to the condition of 'scarcity' is 'allocation,' a term referring either to the process of distributing things or to the state of affairs consequent upon such a distributing. In either case, 'allocation' denotes what we already know, that members of society are continually being supplied with material means or that at any given time they have a supply. The process of supplying them consists, in the part denoted by the summary concept of 'allocation,' of a multiplicity of 'allocating' actions that are performed by individuals in their respective social roles and in accordance with the instituted values."

14. McClelland considers the acquisitive motivation an indicator of progress, when he states: "in Parsons' terminology, developed countries are characterized by the prevalence of achievement norms, universalism and specificity, whereas underdeveloped countries are characterized by ascriptive norms, particularism and diffuseness. That is, in developed countries people are evaluated in terms of what they can do (achieved status) rather than in terms of who they are (ascribed status); anyone is at least ideally able to compete for any job (universalism), rather than being permitted only to do particular jobs as in a caste system (particularism); and the relationship of one man to another is typically more specific, or limited to

the labor contract, rather than diffuse as in a traditional society where economic relationships are tied intimately to all sorts of other relationships involving kinship, political, religious and other social structures" (1961:154).

15. Malinowski and de la Fuente (1957:23) referring to the Zapotecs of Oaxaca, say: "If one wants to coin a neologism in the lingo of psychoanalysis and publicity one might speak of the *mercantile libido*."

16. Polanyi (1944:68) notes: "A market economy is an economic system controlled, regulated, and directed by markets alone; order in the production and distribution of goods is entrusted to this self-regulating mechanism. An economy of this kind derives from the expectation that human beings behave in such a way as to achieve maximum money gains. It assumes markets in which the supply of goods (including services) available at a definite price will equal the demand at that price. It assumes the presence of money, which functions as purchasing power in the hands of its owners. Production will then be controlled by prices, for the profits of those who direct production will depend upon them; the distribution of the goods also will depend upon prices, for prices form incomes, and it is with the help of these incomes that the goods produced are distributed amongst the members of society. Under these assumptions order in the production and distribution of goods is ensured by prices alone. . . . Such an institutional pattern could not function unless society was somehow subordinated to its requirements. A market economy can exist only in a market society. We reached this conclusion on general grounds in our analysis of the market pattern. We can now specify the reasons for this assertion. A market economy must comprise all elements of industry, including labor, land, and money. (In a market economy the last also is an essential element of industrial life and its inclusion in the market mechanism has, as we will see, far-reaching institutional consequences.) But labor and land are no other than the human beings themselves of which every society consists and the natural surroundings in which it exists. To include them in the market mechanism means to subordinate the substance of society itself to the laws of the market."

17. Polanyi (1975b:264) states: "The catallactic definition of money is that of means of indirect exchange. Modern money is used for payment and as a 'standard' precisely because it is a means of exchange. Thus our money is 'all-purpose' money. Other uses of money are merely unimportant variants of its exchange use, and all money uses are dependent upon the existence of markets."

Chapter 7

SPHERES OF ECONOMIC ACTIVITY

AN ECONOMY includes special kinds of social relationships, namely those of production and exchange. It comprises human services combined with each other and with material goods. Economic organization is a form of social action and therefore part of social organization in its broadest sense. The Ladino economy is made up of a machine technology, money exchange, and a developed credit system; it has the values, activities, and institutions of a banking system, private enterprise and an individualist structure in the Western style. It is internally coherent to the point that an economist can describe and analyze it without reference to social factors; that is, the economic phenomena can be abstracted from their social context without serious loss of meaning. In contrast, the economic and social institutions of the Indian community are so intimately connected that it is impossible to describe either the economy or the social structure without relating them to one another.

The Ladino economy comprises all the dominant characteristics of a market economy, with the important difference that it is an underdeveloped, restricted, and obsolete economy. The Indian economy, on the other hand, is neither a market nor a money economy, but rather a subsistence economy. This means that the economic units of which it is formed are highly self-sufficient and self-contained, since, basically, they produce only what they require for their own subsistence; between the units no extensive exchange relationships exist. The Indian economy is not underdeveloped; it is different. It may be (1) a subsistence economy able to sustain a sphere rich in prestige, or (2) an economy which is barely sufficient to maintain life at the lowest subsistence level.[1]

INDIAN ECONOMY. The following are the characteristics, methods and processes of the subsistence economy:

(1) Material equipment is simple and use of machines is unknown. Technology is backward; sometimes it is simply the carry-over without basic changes of methods in use before contact with Western culture, as in swidden technology. But in most cases it is made up of surviving "ways of doing things" introduced by Europeans during the colonial era. In either case muscular energy is used; human beings manipulate the *coa* and animals draw the wooden plow. Under such circumstances resources allocated for technical development are sparse and change is slow and limited. The community is conservative, tending to maintain traditional forms unaltered because the economic mechanism is insufficiently sensitive to change (Marroquín 1958).

(2) A consequence of technical backwardness and the use of muscular energy is a total absence of adequate means of communication. Not only is the region of refuge as a whole isolated from the outside world, but neighboring communities within it are also separated by physical and social barriers which make relations between them difficult and sometimes hostile. Under such conditions, commercial exchange is limited to the transportation of highly valued goods and services. Winding trails, designed to be used by beasts of burden, tie the communities to the Ladino city (Marroquín 1956).

(3) Technical backwardness means that the division of labor is simple; sometimes it is determined simply by sex and age. Knowledge of agriculture is general among men and to a lesser extent among women. In the most developed communities one may observe various specializations in manufacturing or

services but in such cases artisans, shamans, musicians, and other professionals do not practice full time. Their specialized activities are complementary sources of income. They never cease to be farmers; no one attempts to earn his living by a single skill. Speaking in technical vocabulary, we should say that there is no periodical unemployment or fluctuating market for manual labor whose subsistence depends on capitalist initiative, because occupational specialization is incomplete.

(4) The productive unit is small and the level of productivity very low. Although in some cases there may be a wide network of producers, as units of differentiated functions they are limited in scale. The economic producer is not the individual but the collectivity, which may be the extended family, the hamlet, or the community. The family group or extended family possesses greatest advantages for economic activity in the subsistence economy and is one of its most distinctive features; it is an autarkic economic unit, satisfying by itself all the demands of self-sufficiency. Kinship ties and obligations provide a basis for cooperative work and capital circulation within the group as a means of collective security. Low productivity is caused by backward technology, the poor quality of available resources and the lack of cheap capital.[2]

(5) As a consequence of the family's importance in the subsistence economy, women and children find themselves in an unfavorable position of dependence in respect to other members. Women not only perform the work imposed by the division of sexes, but frequently agricultural chores as well, considered by other economies the exclusive province of men. The latter situation appears especially in Indian communities where salaried work has penetrated but it is seen also in reciprocal labor. Child labor is used during important phases of the agricultural cycle and although it undoubtedly has economic bases, its use is determined largely by the apprenticeship and teaching patterns of peasant societies (Levy 1961:144).

(6) The level of capital investment in the productive unit is minimal. Indian communities use certain types of goods in production and sometimes these are accumulated in advance for that specific purpose. The construction of a house, for example, entails the laying aside of capital goods, but because of its nature, such capital has many uses and the goods thus accumulated may be put to many other goals if circumstances so warrant. Capital is very mobile and may be used without waste in other enterprises. However, there is no constantly expanding market for capital although new channels of investment may be sought. Capital goods exist as well as effective ideas for their use and upkeep, but an investment is never made with the definite purpose of obtaining profits in the form of interest.[3] In general, capital goods are scarce, family inheritances small, if there are machines they are few and crude, land is not sold, livestock is often a source of social distinction or may be worshipped as something linked to the supernatural, and to place capital value on anything entails a difficult problem of conceptualization.

(7) As a result of the above there is no enterprise system seeking to create new demands. Businessmen generally come from the Ladino city and participate in the organization of goods and services to satisfy traditionally conditioned needs. When community members begin commercial enterprises little capital is used. Such businesses act as enclaves of the money economy within the subsistence economy. Even in these cases, they do not restrict their operations to businesses or commerce (Aquirre Beltrán 1953a:106).

(8) The system of control over capital goods utilizes different coercive mechanisms from those commonly used by the Western economic system. Social limitations on accumulation are different in that they provide specific and regular institutionalized spending channels. Holding an office in either the secular or religious sphere of the community government obliges persons who have accumulated more than the allowed capital goods to redistribute them in the lavish spending of a *mayordomía* or the conspicuous consumption accompanying a wedding. The use or threat of magic against those who accumulate goods, charge interest or hoard money is one of several traditional means created to level inequalities (Cancian 1965: 135). In the Indian communities there are differences in the possession of capital; there are rich and poor, but the distance between wealth and poverty is not great (needless to say, such a situation is not prescribed here as a norm).

(9) Salaried employment as such does not exist. Labor is not sold and bought in the market, nor does it generally have a money price. Even when money is used in commerce, production tends to be based on a system of compensation that is not tied to money.

Workers can obtain compensation by sharing in profits or they may be moved to donate their services by a wide range of incentives, among which kinship ties and loyalty are important. Alliances between producers tend to go beyond their common interests in production and compensation. As Firth (1954) points out, the production relationship is only one facet of the social relationship.[4]

(10) As a result, the distribution system of income from production tends to be complicated and not easily sorted into a classic economic scheme of rent, interest, salaries, and profits. The Indian system may be very simple, as for example, when all production agents are compensated with a banquet, or it may be very complicated with each agent compensated according to his social rather than his economic contribution. In the construction of a house, compensation often varies with social position and food is offered even to those who contribute on a small scale.

(11) The Western economizing principle which gives compensation in proportion to total productivity is not always followed. It functions in the Indian economy, but its operation is conditioned by social factors. Under such circumstances, economic relations can be understood only as part of a total combination of social relationships. For Firth, economic ties within the Indian economy depend on the social status and relationships of the persons concerned. In other words, labor is a social service and not simply an economic service; compensation is calculated in terms of the total social situation and not merely in terms of the immediate economic situation. Economic means tend to be translated into social ends. This contrasts with economic relations in an industrial system, where the individual in an economic situation normally has a high degree of anonymity and impersonality. Even if he is not simply a name on a payroll, what is important is his function as an energy factor, as a provider of capital or in his organizing capacity. His specific industrial characteristics rather than his total social characteristics are what matter. It is feasible to replace him because he is defined by the magnitude and quality of his contribution to the economic process, apart from his personal status or position in society. Firth continues: in primitive communities the individual as an economic factor is personalized, not anonymous. He tends to maintain his economic position by virtue of his social position. Therefore his economic displacement also indicates a social disturbance.

(12) Economic units in the subsistence economy not only produce what they need but also provide their own productive resources, including capital. The principal form of savings is what Myint calls the subsistence fund, contributions to which make it possible to sustain a greater number of workers or the same number for a longer time. As Indian communities pass from a subsistence to a market economy, the quantity of articles in the subsistence fund diminishes, and opportunities to acquire outside capital become important. Initially self-financing, Indian production becomes dependent upon the Ladino sector, especially when cash crops are cultivated. The principal reason for this dependence is a lack of real savings, but other contributing factors include weaknesses in the credit system (Myint 1965: 67).

(13) As a consequence of the Indian communities' unique features, the members' per capita incomes, measured by their earnings or consumption, are extremely low. In applying the analytical categories of Western economics to Indian communities, some researchers have arrived at measurements of per capita income that are surprising to the point of absurdity. One of them has calculated a per capita income of barely three dollars a year. Malinowski and de la Fuente noted that such figures are more sensational than accurate as they do not take into account problematical features of the Indian economy in terms of what should be considered and measured as income.[5] In any case, even considering that housing, certain foodstuffs and reciprocal services are free, it is obvious that the Indian's real income is very low—so low in fact that occasionally it only permits life at a subsistence level.

The features noted above, which give form and substance to the Indian economy, originate partly from the behavior patterns found in Indian societies before contact with Western culture. But for the most part they represent archaic patterns of economic behavior found among European peasants before the emergence of capitalism. The fact that these are termed Indian features does not mean in any way that they are strictly Indian in origin.

Finally, the discussion of features such as the personalized character of relationships, reciprocity of work and redistribution of goods is not intended to introduce moral significance or judgments. Nor is the tendency of these features to mitigate inequalities meant to imply equity, justice, or a lost golden age when all people participated in production, distribution, and consumption of goods.[6]

FUNCTIONAL EQUIVALENTS. When features, methods, and processes of an Indian economy are given names used in the industrial economy, such use of modern terminology makes those who do not know the ethos of the native culture suppose that they are functional equivalents of their Western counterparts. Both societies have substantial economic organization whose purpose is to provide daily sustenance and each has instruments, money, a division of labor, commerce, and markets. But they are not identical because their organizations are not equivalent nor do they have the same goals.

One of the basic conditions of a money economy is the use of all-purpose-money, without which an economy of commercial exchange could not function.[7] The Indian economic system is characterized by the absence of all-purpose-money, of a price mechanism, and of a true market. Without these the principle of integration which is characteristic of commercial interchange is impossible. Money is used in the Indian economy but it is special-purpose-money. Distribution of natural resources, of material products, and of work often function separately. Labor may be the object of transactions that do not entail money; land is not part of market operations, nor is it exchanged through the mechanism of buying and selling. Work and land are exchanged in different economic spheres, according to different social rules in which kinship obligations prevail and compel the interchange of reciprocities.

Different uses of money indicate differences in the principles of economic integration. The Indian community uses livestock, liquor, foodstuffs, and other products sanctioned by tradition as currency in marriage transactions; the bride price is paid in such currency. It is special-purpose-money which is redistributed among the bride's relatives; its use legalizes the transaction. If legal tender, or all-purpose-money, were employed in such an operation, economizing goals would be introduced for the first time and a transaction with deep social meaning aside from its economic implications would be abstracted from its social context. Because only one kind of currency, specially earmarked for the transaction, can be used to acquire a bride, the Ladino stereotype which says that Indian women are sold in the same way as Ladino prostitutes is easily refuted. In the latter case a commercial operation takes place while in the former it is a social operation.

The payments made by Indians to their authorities when they seek justice or some other service are made in special-purpose-money; liquor is used in Mesoamerican communities. Use of such currency is socially approved and neither authority nor client incurs criminal responsibility through its offer or acceptance. In Ladino society the use of all-purpose-money in such cases would constitute a bribe, and indeed this would also be the case in the Indian context. As noted, the use of currency in both economies does not imply a functional equivalent. Money has different meanings and values according to its use in the Indian or Ladino context.

There are other economic characteristics, methods, and processes common to both economies which also lead to confusion when the analytical categories which have proven useful in the industrial context are applied to the Indian economy. In Indian communities the purpose of foreign trade is to export what is produced domestically and to import what is not, while in the Western economy foreign trade is based on the economizing principle of least cost. Products are always imported when they are cheaper than domestic goods. This functional difference explains the persistence in many places of relatively expensive Indian textiles despite the availability of cheaper, better quality manufactured cloth. Foreign trade is not always based on the principle of least cost.[8]

In Indian communities markets are invariably restricted to commerce in manufactured articles. As already stated, land and labor are never the object of transactions based on the mechanism of commercial price formation. Market prices do not determine the allocation of work and other resources which go into production. Neither the use of land nor the location or function of labor are responsive to market price fluctuations because the means of livelihood in Indian communities do not depend upon the market. In a primitive economy the market is local, specific, and closed; its prices have no effect on noncommercial economic spheres.

An Indian community often has a physical marketplace but not a commercial or market system, that is, an economically broad complex of commercially integrated resources and products by means of which people acquire their subsistence. In the Indian community the term market signifies the physical site where exchange transactions take place, the marketplace. In the industrial economy the term market is applied not only to the specific site of the market or to places where ownership of goods if not the goods themselves change hands. It is also applied to the forces which constantly encourage commercial exchange, to the pervasive mechanisms of supply-demand-price which systematically regulate resources, work, and products, independently of the specific site where transactions are consummated (Dalton 1961).

Polanyi states that the economically broad mechanism of commerce with its individual economizing material profits and domestic and foreign trade based on money does not exist as an integrative pattern in Indian economies. Production and distribution of material goods are organized on principles of trade which are essentially different from those of commercial interchange. Production is rarely motivated by profit incentives, labor is sold only in special circumstances, and the matrix of the distribution process is not economizing, taking instead the form of presents, gifts, and ceremonial interchange.[9]

The integrative patterns particular to the native economy are (1) reciprocity, or giving and counter-giving which result from socially derived obligations, and (2) redistribution, or the channeling of goods or services to functionaries of the communal government, in allocation centers, who totally redistribute them and provide municipal services or specific goods to individuals according to their religious or political status. These integrative patterns were the dominant economic principles in ancient Mexico and Inca Peru and are still important to the surviving Indian communities. According to Malinowski, this give and take impregnates all of Indian life. Every ceremony, every legal or customary act is accompanied by a material gift and a counter-gift. Giving and receiving riches is one of the principal instruments of social organization; it is central to the power of those who hold political or religious offices, to the ties of kinship and to legal relationships.[10]

One of the distinctive characteristics of Indian life is the predominance and frequency of forms of economic integration based on reciprocity and redistribution. Economic and social institutions are fused to the degree that it could well be said that there is no consciousness of an economy as a combination of practices separate from social institutions. Transactions involving material goods are a manifestation of social obligations and have no meaning of their own apart from the ties and situations that they express.

RECIPROCITY AND REDISTRIBUTION. The examination thus far of the Ladino and Indian economies shows the clear importance of integrative principles in both. While in the Ladino economy the integrative principle of mercantilism predominates, in the Indian economy the integrative principles of reciprocity and redistribution prevail. The dominance of one or the other principle gives rise to different spheres of economic activity regulated by their respective norms and values, by different organizational rules, by occasionally contradictory sanctions aimed at forcing conformity in group members, and by institutionalized economic mechanisms which vary from one sphere of activity to another.

As noted, no economic system is formed of a single piece not even the industrial system, whose integrative principle—the market system—is so pervasive that the greater part of the components of production, distribution, and consumption converge in the market. The industrial economy has introduced and continues to introduce features and organizational processes regulated by market norms into the Indian economy with its double integration principle. Thus in the Indian economy there are three spheres of economic activity: (1) the subsistence sphere which fulfills the basic needs of the unit of production and consumption, (2) the prestige sphere, directed at achieving a social position with good opinion and reputation, which will build self-respect and expansion of the ego, (3) the market sphere, through which the Indian economy interacts with the regional economy (Bascom 1948).

The subsistence sphere is ruled basically by the principle of reciprocity or cooperation. A low technical level and little specialization are tied to particular work forms. These utilize cooperation to give impetus to the productive process, which is organized on the basis of reciprocities. One of the most characteristic features of work among Indian peoples is its cooperative quality. The family unit is a cooperative institution; the community itself is a large cooperative unit.

Cooperative work, however, functions differently according to whether the family, the hamlet, or the community is involved. Whoever receives a service must return it when asked by the person who gave it. This is not the appropriate place to discuss the forms of cooperative work in which the family participates; Julio de la Fuente (1964b) has described them for Mesoamerica, as has Charles J. Erasmus (1965) for South America.[11] Suffice it to say that cooperative work is used in the critical periods of the agricultural cycle when abundant manual labor is needed or for enterprises which are too much for one man, such as construction of a house or fixing a roof. The goal of cooperative work in such cases is not exclusively economic, but social as well. That is, it is directed at maintaining cohesion among members of the extended family, including consanguinal, ritual, and affinal relatives. Cooperation through reciprocity is one way to strengthen the ties which convert the extended family into an economic unit, one of the functions of which is to give security to its members.

The second type of cooperative work is aimed at obtaining necessary resources for the social needs of a hamlet or barrio and is performed by the extended families which form the smaller units of the community. The contribution of the barrio members is not returned directly but through common benefits. The barrio relies upon its power to impose legal or supernatural sanctions on those who do not conform to traditional dictates. As in the case of family cooperation, this type of work is an integrating factor which unites group members in a common undertaking (Aguirre Beltrán and Pozas Arciniega 1954).

The third kind of cooperative work embraces the entire community and like the others is aimed at fulfilling municipal needs which will benefit all members. In this as in the other forms of cooperation, women and children participate. Labor is not specialized, so that participants should all do the same work, the only differentiation being imposed by the individual's status or position in the community hierarchy. The Indian community overcomes the problem of scarce capital through cooperative work; thus available capital may be invested in works of broader scope which benefit the whole group. Abundant manual labor is substituted for scarce capital in a non-monetary economy.

The principle of redistribution regulates the prestige sphere and determines the norms according to which the community consumes production surpluses (Aguirre Beltrán 1952). In effect, productive activities of Indian communities are directed at two basic goals: the first is fulfillment of the biological needs of subsistence; the second, acquisition of prestige. Once the first goal is attained, production or income surpluses are put toward achieving the second. The Indian's drive for prestige is induced from childhood, when he is given responsibilities and taught skills to raise him above his companions. During his youth and early adulthood he continues to render services to the community for which he receives no pay apart from an increase in his status in the society. He finally reaches maturity as a man of "distinction" who is consulted in any important business involving the community. He has attained a distinguished position, but to do so he has had to expend so much labor, wealth, and products on the group's behalf that at the end of his life he is left with the same amount of capital that he had as a young man beginning his productive activities. If he does not save money, he and those closest to him enjoy an imponderable amount of prestige. In the standards of Indian culture, prestige is worth more than money.

One of the most common ways to buy prestige is to hold a cargo in the community government. The cargo holder's dignity derives from the accumulation of services rendered and is paid for by the free spending of his own goods. A *mayordomo* is committed to conspicuous consumption and institutionalized waste of such magnitude that he must accumulate savings before his election, borrow while in office, and pay off debts for years afterward. The effort required for a cargo, the accumulation of capital goods, and their careless expenditure during the abandon of the fiesta are always great and serve to level inequalities in accordance with the integrating principle of redistribution. All community members participate in one form or another in the ceremonies offered by cargo holders; each member receives a portion of the conspicuous outlay of food and alcohol and takes an active part in the rite according to his status in the local hierarchy.

The struggle for prestige is never an individual business. The contagion spreads to the wife and to a lesser degree to the children, but in any case the infection is confined to those closest to the office holder. Furthermore, its diffusion is restricted by the limited number of positions in the power hierarchy. However, other means of acquiring prestige are available to the community and the extended family takes part in them. Ceremonies pertaining to the crises of life—birth, marriage, and death—are exploited in order to purchase prestige. In all such cases the pattern of waste appears with surprising magnitude.

Less obvious forms of conspicuous consumption are seen in the communities' daily life but primarily in what Veblen calls devout consumption, that is, in the cost of religion. This is comprised of visible squandering of goods and services in constructing churches, making ceremonial vestments, and acquiring the paraphernalia required by the ritual.[12] To a great extent devout consumption is imposed from outside and does not carry the same prestige as the community's traditional patterns of waste. The principle of redistribution is operative in devout consumption, but indirectly, so that it does not constitute a powerful means of acquiring prestige.

On the other hand, redistribution is apparent in the waste following the harvesting of maize, the Indian's basic crop. Its pre-Columbian provenance seems confirmed by the survival of very archaic features and the absence of similar waste in commercial harvests introduced by Western culture. In some places the harvesting of maize has all the characteristics of a fiesta in which the entire community participates. The conspicuous distribution of the harvest takes place in accordance with harvesting rights, but in addition the owner of the crop must pay a ransom for the success of the harvest in the form of lavish food and drink.

As noted, the pattern of waste by which prestige is acquired has various functions. Among them two, already mentioned, merit special emphasis. The first is to give cohesion to the group. The extended family must work cooperatively as well as competitively to fulfill the demands of ceremonial interchange when life crises take place. This kind of work as well as that performed by members of a hamlet or barrio and by the entire community, are all very effective in maintaining the cohesion of the family or wider social groups and, in the final analysis, of the community as a whole. This cohesion is so strong that outside elements scarcely touch it. It is a powerful barrier to forms of integration which may penetrate the weakened borders of the community.

The other important function of the redistribution principle is to mitigate serious inequalities of wealth through conspicuous consumption of surplus production accumulated by persons seeking prestige. In Indian communities, status and power are not achieved through accumulation of wealth and the exploitation of labor which accompanies it, but through the conspicuous consumption of accumulated capital goods. Through waste, the Indian community keeps its members in a state of economic equality which discourages the development of capital (Herskovits 1940:355).

THE DOMINANT ECONOMY. It has been noted that the spheres of subsistence and prestige often overlap; cooperative work includes reciprocities as well as redistributions. The conclusion of an agricultural cycle with both relatives and neighbors participating is cause for celebration with conspicuous consumption of food and drink. Both spheres originate from the play of internally generated forces; actually, these two spheres are what define the Indian economy. The market sphere, on the other hand, is a product of external forces and acts to connect the Indian and regional Ladino economies.

We have noted previously that although the Indian community is largely self-sufficient and self-contained, it is not independent in any sense. The degree of its autarky is determined by the extent of its market sphere. As this sphere grows larger and more pervasive, the community's dependence on the modern economy and its degree of integration into the national society grow. In such cases the market's integrative principle is able to operate in a broader field. However, the relationship is mathematical only when we compare the subsistence and market spheres, leaving aside the sphere of prestige. Because the latter has a counterpart in the modern economy there is always the possibility of its being reinterpreted in such a way that it may survive in a money economy. In fact, some Indian communities which are already highly acculturated, which have a greatly reduced subsistence sphere, and which earn their livelihood selling their labor as salaried workers still hold to the patterns of conspicuous consumption which bestow prestige. In particular they keep alive the religious festivities based on the syncretism of the ancient spirit cults and Catholic saints.

The continuous increase in the market sphere at the expense of the subsistence sphere is commonly attributed to the economizing incentives put into play by the market economy. It is believed and asserted that hunger and material needs force the Indians to work as poorly paid employees. This explanation is not new; it was used by the English during the Industrial Revolution to oppose labor legislation. To their minds the fear of hunger was the most effective natural force for persuading people to become salaried employees (Dalton 1961). However, it appears that in the Indian communities this is not the motive for members to seek work outside the community, as the often compulsive character of migratory work would seem to demonstrate.

There is increasing evidence that the imponderable needs of the prestige economy rather than subsistence material needs compel Indians to work for wages. Many of the stereotypes on which the theory of the Indian's limited needs is based derive from economic behavior motivated by the search for prestige. For the Indian, salaried work does not represent a way of earning a living but rather of accumulating capital goods for redistribution through conspicuous consumption. This is the reason why the Indian frequently breaks the discipline and continuity required by salaried work, a fact often noted by the capitalist employer. The latter can never rely for the success of his business on manual labor which is poorly qualified, low in productivity, and irregular in its attendance and punctuality

The Indian obtains money through wages, through the sale of cash crops, and through borrowing with interest; such money may be used to buy prestige or to fulfill subsistence needs, but in either case it ties him to the market economy and forces him to respect its laws. Soon he becomes bound by networks of relationships which make him dependent on decisions taken outside his community. The distinctive nature of the Indian culture, of its economic organization, and the subordinate social position of the Indian community all explain the relationship of domination between Ladinos and Indians when the two converge in the market economy; by definition this is a Ladino economy and a sphere of Ladino activity.

The mechanisms of control used by this economy are varied and subtle and only three of them will be the objects of our consideration. The first is so-called migratory labor, discussed above, which is generally aimed at filling the need for manual labor in the mines and plantations of colonial countries or enclaves. Recruitment of workers from the subsistence sphere to a wage economy entails various control mechanisms ranging from the use of force at the outset to more subtle but nonetheless effective procedures. These include the imposition of taxes or head money with payment demanded in currency, the alienation of community lands by hacienda and plantation landlords, the forcing of peons into debt through their prestige needs—the marriage of a child, the demise of a relative, assumption of a *mayordomía*—and similar expedients.[13]

Initially the migrant worker does not consider his salaried activity as permanent, full-time employment. It is a temporary job which he feels compelled to take due to internal or external pressures, which allows him to earn a certain sum of money to complement that which he obtains by working in the subsistence economy. During the migration period the Indian does not abandon cultivation of the family cornfield. Other members of the extended family take it upon themselves to maintain the productive activities of the economic unit in the absence of one of their members. When a large number of family group members succumb to the incentives of migratory labor, the cohesion of the group is broken and it becomes part of the wage economy rather than a unit of production in the subsistence economy. When this happens the formerly independent Indian peasant becomes a number on a businessman's payroll and henceforth depends upon the initiative of the latter for his security.

Because wage labor represents only a complement to the peasant's basic income, the theory of the Indian's limited needs justifying low salaries is of no real consequence for the family's sustenance. But once the Indian enters the wage economy he joins a society of unlimited needs in which payment commensurate with those needs is required. Payment of low salaries and the Indian's acceptance of them in the new situation can only be explained by the operation of control mechanisms which are reinforced by the worker's increased dependence on capitalist initiative.

High interest-bearing loans are the second mechanism used by the Ladino economy to insure the Indian's dependence. Loans freely offered to the peasant by the hacienda owner, the shopkeeper in the Ladino city, the recruiting agent or other persons occupying strategic positions in the regional hierarchy, carry very high interest rates. Pressured by an unforeseen event, by status obligations, or by the need for agricultural investments, the peasant accepts loans which force him to depend upon outside financing. He becomes imprisoned in a network of manipulations which force upon him concealed charges in the form of high prices for merchandise bought on credit in the Ladino store or in the form of obligations forcing him to sell his harvest at low prices before it is gathered.

A third control mechanism is the introduction of cash crops for foreign markets, which builds ties of dependence through a system of market prices which have no relation to the Indian's needs. In times when Indian communities had excess lands and manual labor, once subsistence needs were filled cash crops allowed a money income which helped to increase conspicuous consumption without any diminution in subsistence production. Both cash and subsistence crops could be produced, fulfilling different functions. In this first phase production for export was a complementary activity and price fluctuations had serious repercussions in the prestige sphere but not in that of subsistence. In the second phase, land and manual labor formerly used in subsistence production are turned over to export production, and the peasants must depend on the outside world for their livelihood. This dependency exposes them to a chain of other reinforcing control mechanisms.

As a result of this process the Ladino economy becomes clearly dominant, and fundamentally changes the integrative function of the market. This function is now limited strictly to economic theory; as we have noted, economic phenomena may be extrapolated from social contexts for analysis and economic predictions will not suffer as a result. The Ladino economy practices a similar method of abstraction in its interaction with the Indian community. It extrapolates economic activity from social context through control mechanisms and blocks the integrative principle of the market from expanding beyond purely economic relationships. This is important because this segregation of the Indian from his community pervades the very foundation of the dual economy.

THE REGIONAL ECONOMY. One of the characteristics most consistently observed in economies with low per capita income is the very high proportion of the economically active population engaged in agriculture, the very low proportion in manufacturing, and the generally low proportion of persons living from commerce, transportation, and services. There is a notable statistical relationship between distribution of the population by occupation and economic development. This relationship, discovered in the nineteenth century, has been brought to light by Colin Clark (1951).

According to Clark, industries can be classified as primary, secondary, and tertiary. As a country develops, the proportion of workers in primary activities declines and consequently the secondary industrial sector increases, eventually giving way to the rapid growth of the tertiary. The first sector includes agriculture, animal husbandry, hunting, fishing, and forest exploitation. The second comprises manufacturing, the construction industry, public works, mining, and the production of electrical energy. The third sector includes commerce, transportation, and public administration as well as domestic, personal, and professional services.

Primary production activities in the dual economic structure are performed by Indians. The greater part of the active population—not to say its entirety—is engaged in agriculture, low-level animal husbandry, fishing, and wood cutting. The ethnic groups which are most integrated into the national society and economy and which, before or after contact with the West, established a tradition of intercommunal specialization, have a number of persons in manufacturing activities. However, in only a very few cases are these activities full-time occupations; the artisan continues to be primarily and fundamentally a farmer. Thus the domestic production of Indian communities is basically agricultural and is composed of the following, in order of importance: (1) native crops, such as maize, beans, yucca, potatoes, and quinoa, for the needs of the community itself; (2) cash crops—wheat, coffee, rice, sugar—to fill the nutritional needs of the Ladino city; and (3) raw agricultural materials—cotton, henequen, sesame—for international trade (Barre 1962:19).

The secondary activities of processing and the tertiary activities which include public and private services, commerce, transportation, and communications, are reserved by the Ladinos for themselves. The processing industry, with few exceptions, is confined to the artisan production demanded by the Ladino city and the Indian hinterland's prestige economy. Although the Indian is potentially the biggest consumer, his low purchasing power limits the growth of manufacturing, which also suffers from competition with the cheaper, higher quality products of national industry. As compensation for these limitations, the tertiary sector proliferates into a plentiful bureaucracy, a large group rendering personal services and a commercial lumpen-bourgeoisie of intermediaries and traders who range from the humble *atajadora*[14] to the money-lending shopkeeper.[15]

As a direct result of productive activities being distributed along ethnic lines, agriculture remains stationary and immovable in terms of the type and quality of harvest, the clan basis of land exploitation and technological inefficiency. The agricultural population is excessive for the needs of either modern technology or the obsolete techniques actually used. The repercussions of this are seen in the unproductive use of the work force as well as in the disguised unemployment which encourages the cultivation of latifundios and minifundios, both of which are increasingly barren (Navarrete 1963). The labor force created by underemployment must work on plantations and haciendas in the more favored regions. But these workers' low technical skills and ignorance of the national culture, as well as the operation of control mechanisms that keep them subjugated, all keep the costs of manual labor low. Whether self-employed or hired by a Ladino landlord for agricultural work, the Indian uses his work energy unproductively.[16]

The division of productive activities between Indians and Ladinos engenders an interdependence that affects the fate of both ethnic groups equally. Unproductive use of the work force in primary activities affects the rational development of secondary and tertiary activities, subjecting them to the uncertainties of good and bad harvests, to fluctuations of quantity and quality in produce raised using a primitive technology, to price fluctuations, to the false euphoria of overproduction, and to cyclical recessions. In addition, the Ladino economy is dependent upon both the national and international economies. It is based on a commercial and speculative capitalism that deflects the human and financial resources of the region away from industrial activity. With the economy thus oriented outward, the internal market is reduced, income leaves the region, and wages are limited in both amount and number paid.

Through such means the regions of refuge are kept in a permanent state of exploitation, poverty, and underdevelopment. The low level of real income of both Indians and Ladinos makes savings insufficient and limits capital formation. There is no stimulus to invest because demand is low. The market is broad in geographic and demographic terms, but narrow economically because of the small volume of production and low productivity. There is no manual labor qualified to apply modern techniques, nor an adequate infrastructure to insure the success of large businesses. Income distribution is unequal and those with high incomes—the local oligarchy—hoard savings, deposit them abroad, earn interest by lending them as agricultural credit, speculate with them in land or real estate, or use them to import non-essential or luxury consumer goods.[17]

In more favored regions, development of modern industrial and commercial centers attracts a disorderly assortment of men, merchandise, services, capital, intellectuals, and artists, which bleed and impoverish the regions of refuge. The people of these regions, puzzled, see the younger and more valuable elements of the population emigrate while their scant savings are drawn into the banking system and directed toward rapidly developing regions. Traditional industries and old crafts disappear in the face of competition from modern industry. The development of centers of attraction also serves to diffuse modern economic forms, balancing the effects of impoverishment. However, the effects of diffusion penetrate very slowly into the regions of refuge, so slowly that without a planning effort on the national level, the regions remain underdeveloped (Myrdal 1964:43).

NOTES

1. Myint (1965:40) clarifies: "In this phase it is necessary to distinguish the two possible meanings of the term subsistence sector or economy. It may signify that the economic units, such as the family village or tribe, are self-sufficient, producing only what they need for their own consumption and with tenuous or absolutely no relations of exchange among them. This is the sense in which we have used the term until now, and in our context subsistence always implies non-monetary. The term also includes the suggestion that people in the subsistence sector live at a minimal level

of subsistence; that is, that the resources and technology that they possess are only sufficient to allow a fixed number to live at a minimal subsistence level. Clearly, the subsistence sector, in the former sense, does not necessarily signify that the people within it are struggling along at a minimal subsistence level in the latter sense."

2. Foster (1942:98) referring to the Popolucas of Veracruz, states: "Of great importance is the almost complete lack of any privileged groups or persons in a position to siphon off the economic surplus of the group to be used to satisfy their own wants. Since each family is the producing and distributing unit, it enjoys the right to consume the fruits of its labor. There is no leisure class that exists because of its rights to part of the productive efforts of others."

3. Firth (1958:68) adds: "The investment of capital with the definite idea of getting a return from it in the form of interest is, however, not at all common in primitive economics. Where goods are contributed by others to assist a man in productive enterprise, these are usually given either in accordance with kinship obligations or as part of a general scheme of reciprocal arrangements, and are transferred back again with no additional increment" (Firth 1963a:87).

4. Mendieta y Núñez (1938:69) was the Mexican sociologist whom, it seems, was the first to point out that "Indian economy is not really tied to salaried labor," but he did arrive at a discovery of the principle of reciprocity.

5. Steininger and van de Velde (1935:9) referring to a Zapotecan community in the Sierras, state: "Accurate arithmetic apparently is nonessential to existence, for in the economics of this Zapotecan village two plus two equals three. Total annual income falls short of supplying actual necessities by at least twenty-five percent. Manifestly it takes less to sustain life than logically would be supposed. Economically San Pablo is a study in negatives. It is not so much a question of what these Indians have as it is of what they have not. Judged by American standards their condition is practically standardless.

Figured at the rate of exchange current while this is being written each inhabitant lives on the equivalent of a little less than one cent American money per day. From the sale of charcoal San Pablo derives its greatest income, which amounts to, roughly, $43.00 a month and it would be difficult to imagine any American village of 700 inhabitants whose leading industry returned a gross profit as small as this. For a woman's wardrobe one dollar and a half a year is an extravagant allowance. The average expenditure is less than one half of that amount!"

6. Neale (1965). This clarification is indispensible because anthropologists are often accused of being romantics in their descriptions and interpretations of native societies, conferring upon the concepts they use unwarranted axiological implications. See González Casanova (1965:84).

7. Polanyi (1957b:266) who originated the concept, considers that: "Early money is, as we saw, special-purpose money. Different kinds of objects are employed in the different uses of money; moreover, the uses are instituted independently of one another."

8. De la Fuente (1965:156) notes that, "Among the Chamula, Zinacantan, Mazatecan and even Mixtecan men and women, the Indian suit or dress is considerably more expensive than the non-Indian outfit."

9. Polanyi (1944:68) adds, "never before our time were markets anything other than accessories of economic life."

10. Malinowsky (1961:167) in a study of the Trobriand Islanders, noted the importance of reciprocity, saying: "The whole tribal life is permeated by a constant give and take; . . . wealth taken and given is one of the principal instruments of social organization, of the power of the chiefs, of the bonds of kinship and of relationship in law."

Fusfield (1957:345) upon analyzing the contribution of anthropologists in explaining the problem, states: "Perhaps the most important single work was Malinowski's multivolume study of the Trobriand Islanders. He showed how thoroughly the production of goods and services was embedded in political, religious, social, and kinship institutions. The economic activities of individuals were motivated by social and political obligations, by kinship, by friendship, and by magical rituals and beliefs. Exchange was carried on by gift-giving and ceremonial distribution of goods: barter existed only with persons outside the tribe; buying and selling were nonexistent. The Trobrianders were a typical nonmarket people, with an economic system and motivations that can hardly be understood by modern market-conditioned man.

Supplementing Malinowski's pathbreaking work were the studies made by the followers of Boas, particularly those of Benedict and Mead. Proceeding from a different methodological base than Malinowski's, some of the conclusions are nevertheless startlingly similar. Especially important is confirmation of Malinowski's view that primitive economic institutions are so thoroughly entwined with other social institutions that one can hardly speak of economic motives in the modern sense of that term. Mead's description of the gift-giving Arapesh is a classic example of kinship and friendship obligations as motivations for economic activity. Indeed, the numerous descriptions of the potlach of the Northwest Coast Indians illustrate a general principle: acquisitive motives are usually channeled into activities other than the provision of goods and services to meet material needs. Also of importance along these lines has been the work of DuBois, emphasizing the importance of prestige elements–a noneconomic factor–in channeling economic activity in primitive society.

Thurnwald also placed great stress on gift-giving, or reciprocity, as a pervasive element in primitive economic life, a pattern far removed from the acquisitive motives of the market economy and requiring a symmetrical pattern of social relationships for its operation. Indeed, Mauss has suggested that gift exchange is the fundamental principle underlying all primitive trade" (Fusfield 1957:345).

11. See de la Fuente (1964b), Chapter XII, "Indian Cooperation and Modern Cooperation."

12. Veblen (1963:312) states: "The most patent economic importance of these observations we see in the devout consumption of goods and services. The consumption of ceremonial accessories demanded by all cults in the form of medallions, shrines, temples, churches, vestments, sacrifices, sacraments, holiday clothing, etc., serves no material goals. Therefore, all these material objects can be characterized, in no way pejoratively, as articles of conspicuous waste. The same can be said in general terms of the personal services consigned by these same practices, such as the education and services of priests, pilgrimages, fasts, festivals, domestic devotions, etc."

13. Moore (1951:60) states: "Since the decline of slavery as a mode of labor mobilization, the most frequent system of recruitment and retention of reluctant native laborers has been the long-term indenture, supported by a penal sanction for nonfulfillment. This relationship is nominally contractual, but not breakable at will . . . the use of various forms of more or less moderate coercion to secure hacienda, mining, and even factory labor is endemic in Latin America. The forms vary from the common peonage, or debt servitude, to the long-term indenture contract similar to that used in many colonial areas."

14. *Atajadoras* are middle-men (actually women) operating in the regional produce market. At their worst they force the Indians to sell their produce to them at a reduced price, destroying that which the Indian refuses to surrender. They then resell the produce to Ladino vendors.

15. Baran (1964:199) invented the neologism.

16. Nurkse states: "These countries suffer large-scale disguised employment in the sense that even with the traditional agricultural technology a large part of the population working in agriculture could abandon it without reducing agricultural production. . . . In industrialized countries unemployment is an obvious waste of resources, visible to all, and perhaps because of this has been given more attention. In an overpopulated peasant economy, we cannot point to a particular person and say that contrary to appearances, he is unemployed. There can be total employment and nobody may consider himself to be unemployed. Nevertheless, the fact is that less agricultural labor could be used without affecting at all the size of the harvest" (1963:41).

17. Kuznets says, "Perhaps in the underdeveloped countries a greater proportion of these savings serve to finance the consumption needs of the lowest paid groups, adopting the form of payment to the transfer of land and other property, putting them into the hands of money lenders. A greater proportion of these savings, instead of being invested productively may be destined for the acquisition of precious metals and the purchase of luxury items" (1964:88).

Chapter 8

CASTE AND CLASS STRUCTURE

UNTIL THE BEGINNING of the last world war, sociologists classified the social structure of Latin America as neofeudal because of its duality. The tip of the social pyramid was composed of a small elite of large property owners, professionals, merchants, financiers, and public figures who monopolized wealth and power and who transmitted it to their heirs. The unity of these governing families was strengthened by a dense network of relations of friendship and kinship which assured loyalty to the elite. At the base of the pyramid was an enormous mass of people, miserable and illiterate, who worked in agriculture, crafts, and as intermediaries. Between the top and the bottom there was no third group such as the bourgeoisie or middle class of Europe. The pyramid was composed of only the elite and the unlettered masses. Within the dual structure there was little social mobility; the oligarchy discouraged it.

Today, these structural characteristics are beginning to change or have already been modified in the great urban centers and in more favored regions. But in the regions of refuge they have not varied and history has made an important addition, for the dual structure is not only an arrangement between classes but a caste system as well. The top of the pyramid is occupied by the Mestizo, Ladino, or national group and the base by tribal or Indian peoples. In those regions the class struggle between the elite and the illiterate masses takes on the tones of an interethnic battle engendering serious tensions between the two groups and provoking continual conflicts when either one attempts to interfere in the other's territory, activities, or rights. The Indian's subordination does not prevent the cyclical appearance of nativist or messianic movements which endanger the Ladino's security; nor are the Ladinos' superordination and privilege sufficient incentives for the integration of Indian and tribal populations into modern life. Social mobility scarcely exists. Passage from Indian to Ladino status is obstructed by pressures originating at both the top and the bottom, pressures stabilizing a social structure which resembles the caste system characteristic of the colonial period. Such a social structure reinforces the patterns of economic exploitation based on segregation of productive activities and on the unequal distribution of freedom and wealth.

COMMUNITY vs. SOCIETY. To call the system of relations which orders daily Indo-Ladino life a dual structure is of course a convenient expedient which allows a complex process to be made intelligible. However, complete and accurate comprehension of the situation is possible only if we analyze the significant factors in the situation: Indians, Ladinos and those marginal to both groups, who seek positions in the social structure.

In studying American Indian and tribal communities it is quickly seen that all of them place their members in distinct positions on a graduated scale, that is, in a structure of regularized inequalities where men are situated in accordance with the value placed on their various roles and activities. Even the most primitive tribal groups show a stratification in their social organization so that certain individuals become chiefs, leaders, or principals in order to lead productive, offensive, or ritual activities. As communities become technologically more complex and consequently more specialized, the fulfillment of particularly important social needs requires a greater degree of internal differentiation as well as the creation of more and more varied roles to satisfactorily resolve the problems that arise. Thus institutionalization of the differences, as well as their stratification, is unavoidable in a system which structures social relations, integrates the community components and keeps them united.[1]

Although man has perfected the ideal of equality throughout the history of his development, both the Indian communities and the national society still use stratification as the bases of their internal and external structures. Both societies place their members in specific positions in the social structure and persuade them to fulfill the roles assigned to them. Since the assigned roles are not of equal importance to the group's survival nor require the same capabilities, this social allocation is necessarily differential. The society must grant compensations as incentives to action and use varying forms of distribution for such compensations. Differential compensations and their distribution in terms of social positions become part of the social order.

The compensations available to societies for filling necessary positions and assuring essential services may be granted in the form of goods and services, of prestige and power, and as the rights and privileges tied to those positions. The functional importance of the position, combined with the scarcity of persons qualified to fill it, lead to unequal distribution of compensations. The varying rights and privileges of different positions enable societies to be sure that the most important positions will be occupied by qualified persons (Davis 1965: 358). The way of determining a person's qualification is important in social differentiation; ability is ascribed or acquired. Ascribed ability is the basis of the caste system, while acquired ability defines the class structure. In the former, children ideally inherit their parents' roles and never change positions in the social scale; in the latter, also ideally, children fill roles independently of the parents' position.

Sociologists and anthropologists who have investigated Indian communities agree that such communities have neither social classes nor the necessary structural conditions for the emergence of a class system. Allocation of material resources and the instruments of production are in the hands of extended families or of the territorial, *ayllu* or *calpulli* clan. Production relations are based on reciprocity and the redistribution of surpluses through conspicuous consumption. On the other hand, in the Ladino or national society there is an obvious conflict between workers and the dominant elite. Here patterns of appropriation operate to divide the society into classes, or interest groups, which act to change the obsolete structure. Let us say finally that classes are interest groups, based on acquisition, which emerge from vertically differentiated social structures.[2]

According to Marx's social theory, contrasts between the classless Indian community and the Ladino society with classes, rest on their conflicting ways of organizing production.[3] Other scholars of human society have used different criteria to establish other dichotomies, such as Tönnies' (1963) contrast of community and society;[4] Maine's (1963) opposition of the society of status with that of contract;[5] Becker's (1950) formulation of the secular and sacred society;[6] and Redfield's (1942) brilliantly constructed conceptual scheme contrasting urban and folk societies;[7] to cite only a few. Using all these criteria, we would classify the Indian community as a society without social classes, organized as a status group, sacred and folk in nature, all of which define what we generally call a community. The Ladino society, in contrast, would be a contract society, essentially urban, secularly oriented and divided into classes, which form what is commonly called a society.

In characterizing the Indian community as a classless society, we are not suggesting or outlining the ideal image of a society without differentiations among positions of value. We desire simply to emphasize the fact that this society has not generated, as part of its structure, conflicting interest groups. A society without classes is not necessarily an egalitarian society. The clarification is important because a group of precursors of the Mexican social revolution, led by Enrique Flores Magón, proposed the Indian community as a structural model to replace the obsolete one then prevailing. The anarcho-agrarianists idealistically conceived the Indian community to be a society in which income, esteem and authority were equally distributed among all citizens (Blanquel 1963).

The anarcho-agrarianists had an important influence on the direction of the agrarian reform, reinterpreting pre-Columbian forms of land tenancy into modern models, but their idea of a self-sufficient and egalitarian Indian community was completely false. Dahrendorf (1959) maintains that a society with no outstanding variations of income and inheritance is conceivable—that is, a society without social strata—but never a community without differentiation of roles in terms of power.[8] We shall see eventually that the Indian communities have positions in their political structure with varying rights to authority, but they do not empower any one group to occupy those positions regularly and exclusively. Neither individuals nor the groups to which they belong achieve monopolies on positions of authority. They fulfill them and turn them over to other individuals or groups who in turn transfer the power, so that the emergence of interest groups is virtually impossible. However, the social organization in these classless communities demands a certain differentiation among valued positions.

Nonetheless, all investigators agree in describing American communities as fundamentally homogeneous. There are no obvious inequalities in the possession of resources, goods, or services. The knowledge and skills necessary to earn a living are equally distributed or accessible to all, with the exception of supernatural capabilities such as those of shamans. All members of the community participate in the social order in positions that vary within very narrow limits. They form a status group which has a single culture, subculture, or life style and which limits the approved area of social interaction to the territorial boundaries of the community. The economic units—*calpulli* or *ayllu*—formed by extended families are largely self-sufficient and the population—*altepetl* or *llacta*—is endogamous.[9] Marriage with outsiders—persons belonging to other Indian communities, even with the same language, are considered as foreign as Ladinos in these enclaves—is strictly forbidden. Social restrictions, cultural simplicity, and low technical specialization make homogeneity possible.

The community's internal system of stratification emerges from the general pattern of homogeneity. The system is composed basically of a political-religious hierarchy whose functioning depends on the holding of cargos. Nash states that the cargo system is the axis around which the social structure of the group revolves and that the function of the system is similar to that of the kinship structure in Black communities or the class structure in the Ladino society (Nash 1956:145). Different positions on the hierarchal scale are held by community members, who, through the consumption of goods and services, exchange cargos in the parochial government. Fulfillment of these cargos necessitates considerable effort and expenses which not all are able to pay. Most frequently the Indian hierarchy is formed on the basis of acquired status, but there are cases in which ascribed status becomes particularly relevant. The latter situation is found in some Andean communities where the *ayllu* which controls the strategic cargo of governor tends to establish itself as a superior status group apart from the common status group. However, there is no freedom from the obligation of conspicuous consumption of goods and services in order to maintain the inherited position (Friede 1944).

ETHNIC STRUCTURE. Indian communities, containing a single status group or one group superior to the rest, establish relations among themselves following an ethnic structure characterized by mutual antagonism and reciprocal hostility, thus separating one community from another. When Sol Tax studied Mesoamerican communities he proved that the Indians' ethnic, social, religious, and political unit is the municipal group (de la Fuente 1965:179). The same is true in Andean communities where *reservas* or *parcialidades* are the largest units of Indian organization. There is no larger unit which might include a sizeable linguistic or cultural group and even less, a wider conglomerate capable of forming a nation.

The myth of aboriginal empires and kingdoms, described as nations by the chroniclers of the conquest, is continued today in the myth of small nationalities. There neither were nor are there any Indian nations; there were and are Indian ethnic groups organized into segregated parochial communities. Before contact with Western man, these communities formed tribal confederations which allowed each member community to maintain its independence. Alternatively, one community subdued the others and formed tribal empires which sometimes achieved prolonged stability. In both cases the communities forming the "nation" were in constant conflict and controversy, thus establishing and preserving the group's identity and boundary limits.[10]

The present situation has not changed essentially. In the regions of refuge the Ladino group, acting as an *etnia* (unified ethnic group), functions as an imperial tribe, imposing its domination so that the structure can survive in a situation of conflict. Each Indian community considers itself hostile and different from the others and from the Ladino society or its enclaves. It accepts Ladino superiority as inevitable, but with ambivalence, since it is convinced of the superiority of its own culture or life style, to which it remains tied.

Ladinos constitute the dominant *etnia* in the regions of refuge. They commonly inhabit a city which becomes the *chef-lieu* of the regional ecology or they establish enclaves in the ceremonial centers of the Indian communities. Sometimes, through a process of expansion, they displace the Indians from the civic center and the latter then settle on its outskirts. Ladinos are part of the population which share the modern national culture; they do not consider themselves a separate *etnia* from the rest of the nation, but rather a segment of it which in the regions of refuge represents the interests of the national majority group.

Consequently, time and effort would be saved by describing the Ladino structure simply as a class system similar to that of any industrial society. In doing so we would reinforce the impression received by a superficial examination of the Ladino group; actually Ladinos support the obsolete structure which existed in all the Americas before the onset of economic modernization. It is composed of two social classes: the first dominates the resources and the instruments of production and calls itself the aristocracy; the second is formed of manual laborers and masters or workers in various professions, commonly called artisans. Of course, there is no industrial working class that could be designated a proletariat. Included in the aristocracy are some rich merchants, university professors and descendents of old families which were once powerful, but essentially this class consists of large property owners. These are men who own town houses situated around the main plaza of the city and great haciendas in the countryside, the latter land acquired by taking advantage of the general defenselessness of the Indian communities, *reservas* or *parcialidades* (Whiteford 1963:65).

The dual class structure, composed of aristocracy and artisans, has been replaced in the great urban centers and industrialized cities of Mestizo America by a modern capitalist structure in which, besides the two traditional classes, there is an intermediate stratum commonly called the middle class. The emergence of a middle stratum still has not occurred in the metropolises of the regions of refuge, but there one does see a structural phenomenon which cannot be ignored, namely the existence of a marginal population known in South American countries as *cholos* and in Mesoamerica as *revestidos*. This population is sometimes the product of biological, sometimes of cultural mixing, but in either case it has no established position in the social structure of the regions.

The existence of a marginal population such as the one described is due to the persistence in those regions of the caste relationships that characterized the colonial situation. In effect, the Ladino population, which is divided into classes, operates as the dominant caste in its relations with the Indian population. It does not matter that the Ladino occupies the lowest position on his group's social scale. The mere fact of belonging to the dominant caste puts him by ascription in a superior position to the Indian, even when the latter may be a leader or principal of his own community. Since the nature of Indo-Ladino relations will be examined and the theory upon which they are based will be analyzed below, let it suffice here to accept the phenomenon of duality in order to explain the origin of the marginal population.

The existence of a caste that usurps privilege and power and which subjugates other castes engenders contradictions which tend to modify the social order. The Indians, who occupy the subordinate position of the caste system, accept the situation as inevitable but do not conform passively to it. At various times the community as a group produces nativist movements which expel the Ladinos from Indian territory until bloody governmental repression joins the Ladinos to subjugate them once again.

Indians who rebel as individuals against their own group when experiencing the demonstrable effects of Ladino culture seek to pass from Indian to Ladino status at any price. Adams calls this process ladinization or the rejection of the culture of the community of origin and assimilation into the Ladino culture and society.[11] Ladinization is not synonymous with acculturation nor with integration into the national society. In the caste system, social mobility is hindered by the very nature of the structure; consequently, Indians who adopt Ladino status try to pass for Ladinos. To do so requires that the mother tongue be denied and that the native culture and its status symbols such as dress, occupation, and obligations of reciprocity and redistribution be abandoned.

When *cholos* or *revestidos* break affiliation with their community of origin they lose their identity as Indians and do not acquire a new identity as Ladinos or *criollos*; ladinization does not mean their acceptance in the privileged status group. Settled in the cities, they hold menial jobs that are classified and valued as suitable for Indians. *Revestidos* or *cholos* thus join a money economy in which they earn monies that they invest in commerce or land. Differences in possession of goods and services arise; these differences do not connect them to the Ladino classes in the caste situation. Both systems remain segregated by the barrier of caste. Colby and Van der Berghe (1966) describe a situation such as this in the Indo-Ladino city of Quetzaltenango, where the ethnic line segregates the Ladino from the Indian *revestido* society although both are structured into socioeconomic classes.[12] In reality, the Indian *revestidos* and *cholos* constitute an intermediate caste with no place in the caste structure. Let us examine the castes as well as the caste systems in order to understand the gravity of the problem and the need for drastic and revolutionary change in the existing structure.

INHERITED INEQUALITY. Kingsley Davis (1965:355) has said that the Hindu caste system is the most thorough attempt known in human history to introduce inherited inequality as an orienting principle for social relationships. The social order based on caste did not remain cloistered in Southeast Asia; it spread through different parts of the ancient world and powerfully influenced other systems of social differentiation and evaluation. During the era of the discovery of America, the Arabs, who conquered North Africa, established a caste structure in the Berber lands in which warriors, priests, peasants, and tribute peoples formed differentiated strata similar to the four original varnas of the Hindu system.

When the African slave trade was extended to the New World the first contingents of Blacks were made up of Berbers classified in the Moorish caste. The term caste, introduced early by the Portuguese slave traders, was adopted and with time determined the quality of the entire colonial order, based on the institutionalization of genetic differences. After viewing the colonial situation the astute observer Humboldt wrote, "In Spain it is a sort of title of nobility to have descended from neither Jews nor Moors; in America, a skin which is more or less white decides the rank which a man occupies in society" (Beltran 1946:101, 271). In the colonial social structure, status, and occupational role were determined by phenotype; it had structured a society divided into castes.

Europeans occupy the rank of highest honor and esteem in the caste system. They retain wealth and power and are said to come from a *clean caste, without flaw or blemish*. Defeated in the wars of conquest, the Indians form the subject caste, but they are assured of obligations and privileges giving them a definite function in the colonial structure as the tribute payers. The Indian rebellions which took place throughout the centuries of foreign domination are an index of the defeated peoples' refusal to conform to the status assigned them. However, because that position is clearly defined by duties and rights, the Indians had no difficulty in reconstructing the ancient values which gave them identity.

Disruptive elements which ultimately ruined the system were introduced into this Euro-Indian dichotomy. As African and Asian slaves of varied ethnic backgrounds entered the colonial society they were also classified as castes, but their freed offspring of mixed blood and enfranchised slaves did not achieve a definite status in the order as it existed. Negroes and other immigrant castes were classified as infamous and contact with them was forbidden as religiously impure. The fact that the European population as well as the migrant Negroes were predominantly male represented a serious contradiction for the caste system: replacement could only take place through migration, and it is well known that human mobility is regulated by economic factors which have little to do with an organization of status. As an inevitable consequence of this contradiction, there was a proliferation of mestizos, mulattos and other mixtures before there was a legitimate position for them in the colonial order. But it was the marginal position of these intermediate castes which determined the end of the economic system of slavery and therefore of the caste system (Beltran 1965).

The structural and ideological remnants of the colonial regime permitted the system to continue in the regions of refuge of politically independent countries, although Indians and Ladinos acquired citizenship. Violent interference by Ladinos in the rights and privileges which the colonial government had accorded the natives led to armed conflicts of the kind that had taken place in the colonial era, significantly called caste wars. As had happened centuries before, revitalization movements were bloodily repressed and many Indian communities were destroyed. In addition, the Indians lost their territorial bases through the mechanisms which secularized land in order to distribute it as private property. They joined the money economy as either salaried peasants, proletarian status, or hacienda peons, serf status. However, communities in the regions of refuge managed to survive the impact of liberal laissez-faire and retained the old colonial relationship vis-a-vis the Ladino population, that is, the caste relationship.

The preceding historical digression is necessary because today certain members of the structural school of sociology deny validity to the term caste when it is used to designate relationships other than those characterizing Southeast Asia. Louis Dumont (1960) and Oliverio C. Cox (1948) have objected vigorously to use of the concept in describing interethnic relationships in certain capitalist countries such as the United States. For Dumont the Hindu caste system is a social order based on inequality, while the color bar is a social evil which contradicts the egalitarian ideals of a democratic society. Such features as endogamy, mutual segregation in some circumstances, and low mobility are similar in both cases, but that similarity does not allow the scientist to endow them with all the features that form a social system and which give it functional coherence.

The mutual rights and obligations of the different castes turn them into functional entities composed of a particular combination of cultural characteristics. Castes are a specifically Hindu cultural phenomenon, with roots in the Hindu value system and philosophy, apart from which they are incomprehensible. When caste becomes the principle of social organization, all other social divisions yield. The caste system, it is insisted, is found only in societies which are small in scale and relatively uncomplicated, such as Hindu villages; the system loses its structural characteristics when contemplated on the scale of a state or nation. Modern political and economic complexity puts an end to the system (Stavenhagen 1962).

In the United States the common use of the term caste was apparently initiated by Dollard (1937) during the 1930s, when he described social stratification in a southern Black town. Upon analyzing barriers to social contact and certain forms of relationships, he called the social groups castes. Since then, the use of the term has been strongly argued. Acceptance that a caste system exists in the United States means negation of an image of the American social organization that has been so patiently constructed by philosophers and that politicians attempt to impose in underdeveloped countries. If existence of the caste system is accepted, North American life and democracy as the just model of human relations totters; picturing the United States as the society of the common man or as an open class structure offering opportunities to everyone becomes indefensible.

Furthermore, those fighting for Black liberation believe that to acknowledge a caste system means to create an unbridgeable obstacle which would prevent remediating the situation. In the open class system of a democracy where the equality of all persons, without limitation as to sex, color, or creed is constitutionally affirmed, the struggle for the liberation of the Black is politically and juridically easier than in a situation where inequality and the fixed and immutable nature of interracial relationships is accepted. In the former case, resolution of the problem is a much more accessible goal. It is possible that those who oppose Dollard from a theoretical frame of reference are as much in the right as those who do so from practical considerations. We think that social problems are more open to resolution if their premises are adequately clarified. But whether this or the preceding approach is correct, the fact is that the term caste found favor and that in the United States as well as Europe various scholars have used it to designate rigid social systems in which social mobility is nonexistant or minimal.

Max Weber (1960), Talcott Parsons (1954), Kroeber (1948), Nadel (1957), Warner (1960), Ganth and Mills (1948) and other sociologists and anthropologists, considered the caste system a useful concept for dealing with particular forms of relationships. These are characterized by specific structural features, among which rigidity of the system, membership ascription, slowness of change, endogamy and a hierarchical value scale are all important. According to these criteria the caste system represents an extreme, fixed, and motionless case of stratification.

PLURAL CULTURES. Use of the term caste to designate relations between Whites and Blacks was extended to Latin America when North American anthropologists encountered the problem of characterizing interethnic, Indo-Ladino relationships. Gillin (1951) and Tumin (1952), knowing as they did that use of the expression had an ancient history, explicitly described the situation as a caste relationship when they studied a Mesoamerican town in which interaction occurred between Indians and Ladinos inhabiting the same locality. Both groups had their own cultural patterns but the reciprocal pattern which characterized the community as a whole was a caste relationship.

Tumin entitled the book containing the results of his investigation, *Caste in a Peasant Society: A Caste Study in the Dynamics of Castes* (1952). On the basis of sociological inquiries the author analyzed Ladino-Indian relations in different places and circumstances and reached conclusions confirming the aptness of the term as well as the existence of a marked antagonism between the castes. Both conclusions were seriously argued by those who denied validity to use of the term and those affirming the conviction that interethnic relationships can take place without hostility. Tumin was forced to defend the correctness of his observations and the justness of his interpretation in a seminar where the opposing criterion prevailed.[13]

In Peru, Holmberg also felt obliged to categorize the structure of relations between the subordinate Indian groups and the dominant mestizos as a caste system. Contemplating the Andean situation as a whole, he undoubtingly designated the conflicts arising from confrontation of the Indian community and the national government (which he characterized as hostile and aggressive) as caste relationships.[14] The social structure is based on a value system which is essentially static and inflexible. In the two worlds of the mestizo and the Indian, deep cultural and attitudinal differences persist; although in terms of language, social organization, politics, and values they represent two completely different ways of life, both of which depend on the other, based on a caste system.

Julio de la Fuente (1952:77) believed it possible to resolve the controversy—which arises partly from observation of the many variations found in interethnic relationships—by constructing a continuum which would include: (1) class relationships; (2) quasi-class relationships; (3) quasi-caste relationships; and (4) caste relationships. Field investigators with ideographic mentalities thus would have no difficulty classifying the conclusions based on their data on social behavior in any of the stratifications of the continuum. De la Fuente believed that Indo-Ladino relationships generally fall into the category of quasi-caste, that is, they are similar to caste relationships. The Reichel-Dolmatoff's also designate relationships between Indians and non-Indians in Colombia as similar to the caste system.[15] Other ethnographers also adhere to the indirect designation in order to avoid further complications.

Sol Tax (1956), Beals (1954), Nash (1957) and others, however, have thought to overcome objections to the term caste by describing the social situation characteristic of the regions of refuge as a multiple society with plural cultures. In doing so they follow Furnivall (1939) closely; he proposed applying the term plural societies to the Southeast Asia situation, specifically Burma, where immigrant Chinese, Hindu, Moslem, European, and other populations established themselves as enclaves among the native population. Each national enclave tends to establish its relations and means of securing sustenance as an autonomous entity, which leads to a plural economic system. Obviously this hypothesis cannot be extended to the mestizo countries of America, in the same way that it is impossible to extend the concept of small nationalities, held by the kind of sociologist whose mentality tends to dogmatism. The two constructs are not functionally equivalent, despite a large number of similar features.

Nash (1957) defends his position by calling attention to the fact that although the entire population of the national territory is included in the political and economic ties forming the nation, only a part of that population is conscious of the existence of a national entity. Only this segment participates meaningfully in social and cultural life; it controls resources and communications; it is distributed throughout the territory; it monopolizes political power; its control of relations with other nations as well as its economic decisions have national repercussions. On the other hand, there is another sector composed of small societies with varying cultural traditions, local organization, scant economic resources, and without political power. The cultural distance separating these societies from the national segment includes differences in language, customs, occupation, dress, and even physical features. All this is true, but it is equally true that analytically those plural societies are reduced to a single social category, that of the Indian, in encounters with Ladino domination, regardless of differences among their cultures. The sector of the national population which has contact with those societies endows them with a single social meaning, one particular quality, and a general position of subordination; within the structure of social relationships, this is what counts.

The descriptive criterion for social classes, which is such a useful instrument for accurately placing components of North American society in the six class categories created by Warner, was followed by Beals (1954) in analyzing Latin American social structure. His work sheds considerable light on the differences between the strata in countries which still have not completely overcome their feudal past. He recognizes the extensive use of the term caste in colonial times and accepts the fact that Indian groups have special attributes. Of these, perhaps the most important are the existence of independent value structures and an internal prestige system; but he adds that these groups should be called plural cultures rather than castes.

Wagley and Harris (1965) carried the descriptive orientation to its logical conclusions when they proposed a typology of Latin American subcultures. This typology was aimed at resolving the perplexing problems arising from the diversity of institutions and cultural patterns within Latin America. They began with the supposition that there is a series of generally shared values and ways of behaving that form a common cultural denominator, made up of nine subcultural types: (1) tribal Indians; (2) modern Indians; (3) (mestizo?) campesinos; (4) traditional sugar plantations; (5) modern sugar plantations; (6) provincial city; (7) upper class metropolitan; (8) middle class metropolitan; (9) urban proletariat. It is easily seen that when Wagley and Harris constructed their taxonomy of subcultures they used cultural, social, economic, and ethnic dimensions indiscriminately in forming different categories. From a logical point of view, a multiplicity of measures is not a good basis for a classification system. Wagley and Harris point out that there is a quasi-caste relationship between the subculture of modern Indians and that of the (mestizo) campesinos who live with them; it is presumed that a class relationship exists among the others.

Imprecise use of the terms caste and class, their combination with cultural and racial categories, and above all, their use as descriptive categories have provoked a justified rebuke from younger anthropologists. (Hermitte 1962; Stavenhagen 1964). Unfortunately they have gone beyond a balanced criticism and deny the usefulness, justification, or meaning of the term caste in the Mestizo American situation. For them the structure of Ladino-Indian relations is a rigid, closed class structure which reveals the conflict and exploitation to which the Indians, who in the class society constitute part of the rural proletariat, are subjected. Formulation of this thesis is not new. In Mexico, during the decisive moments of the revolution and particularly in the discussion stage of the agrarian reform, ethnic groups were designated as the *Indian class*. The unlimited confidence of the governing elite in its own capacity to resolve the country's age old problems led them to suppose that the Indian's problem was merely a question of liberating him from the Ladinos or mestizos of the bourgeois class which exploited him.

Direct contact with Indian peoples through participation and observation soon made it clear that things were not as simple as they originally seemed. It was not always possible to distinguish with certainty between Indians as members of the exploited class, and the mestizos who lived among them and who by definition formed the exploiting class. Of course racial characteristics were valueless in distinguishing natives from those of mixed blood, nor could cultural characteristics offer any practical guarantees for differentiating the exploited class. A definition of the Indian community based on a North American psychological orientation which put a decisive emphasis on the feeling of belonging was not a useful criterion either because of its high subjectivity.

Elsewhere (Beltrán 1957) we have discussed the development of all those attempts at definition and how they died a natural death when the theory of regional integration, which we developed, clarified the unavoidable need to consider the total situation in all its complexity; that is, the structure of relationships formed by the two basic components of the regional situation, Indians and Ladinos. These are not class but caste relations; there is not one class of Indians and another of mestizos; there is an Indian caste and a Ladino one, subordinate and dominant castes which together form a caste system. A solution for the Indian problem is not easy; it implies moving from a caste relationship to one of class and this change, as Julio de la Fuente pointed out, is not a peaceful process but rather a revolutionary one.[16]

A DEFINITION OF CASTE. The preceding discussion has led us to propose a definition for the concept of caste which may serve as an analytical tool for the Latin American situation. Castes are status groups maintained by ascription, which originate in vertically differentiated ethnic structures. The terms of the definition require a detailed explanation:

(1) *Castes are status groups*: The compensations granted by the society to its members for fulfilling a role which is functionally important for the group's survival include economic incentives which contribute to sustenance and well being, symbols of esteem and honor which contribute to self-respect and the expansion of the ego, and power. The economic system is the means whereby goods and services are distributed and used. The status system is the means whereby honor and prestige are distributed in a community. Connections between the two systems are close but they are not identical. Max Weber (1960) points out that status groups are stratified according to the principle of consumption of goods as represented by a special life style, while classes are defined according to their relations to the means of production and acquisition of goods. The status group is made up of individuals who occupy a similar position in the prestige hierarchy and who consequently tend to treat each other as social equals. To do so they form closed or exclusive circles which are restricted, self-sufficient and self-contained.

The cultural circle is closed. The status group shares in a special life style, that is, in a fully differentiated culture or subculture which often has a particular idiom or dialectical variation, a differentiated language and a shared value system constituting what Durkheim (1961) calls a moral community. In caste situations life styles tend to perpetuate themselves. The acculturation process is slow and although it is manifested at different levels, the manifestations are generally minimal; therefore the culture of the status group is readily designated as traditional.

The social circle is restricted. The social intercourse of members of the status group is severely limited to within the narrow confines of the circle. The individual is authorized to seek his equals, form friendships, or choose a spouse only from inside. When the caste shares its physical location with another caste, the social circle assigns the individual a place where he must reside and earn his living (Honigmann 1959:441). The social circle is also restricted by prohibitions against eating, drinking, participating in ceremonies with persons outside the group, and assuming occupational roles other than those traditionally ascribed.

The economic circle is self-sufficient. The group, in its entirety, acts as a unit of production, distribution, and consumption. Its original economic spheres of subsistence and prestige predominate over the market sphere introduced by the money economy. In fact, when the latter sphere predominates, the group is no longer defined by the status system and becomes an interest group in the economic system. Self-sufficiency necessitates a very low level of specialization and small size, such as in the folk community studied in Yucatan by Redfield and Villa Rojas (1962).

The breeding circle is enclosed. The closed life style, restrictions on social intercourse and self-sufficiency of economic relations confines members of the status group to marriage within a limited pool of potential mates characterized by endogamy. Marriage outside the group is strictly prohibited and those who break the prohibition lose their group identity and membership. The territory occupied by the group constitutes the limit of social interaction as well as the area in which endogamy is practiced.

(2) *Castes are maintained by ascription*. In status groups membership is hereditary, ascribed patrilineally and ideally fixed for life. The principle of inherited status entails inheritance of social inequality; the member of a given caste is born and dies within it. He does not aspire to another caste if it is of an inferior status, and he is not accepted into the superior status of the dominant caste for obvious reasons. He should remain in his place, in the position given him by birth. Nonetheless, even in the most extreme systems, movement from one caste to another always takes place. Complete immobility does not exist because it is impossible; the system never achieves total perfection (Davis 1965:355).

(3) *Castes originate in an ethnic structure*. Castes are consolidated when status groups have carried the confinement of their life styles to the furthest extremes and when distinctions of esteem, prestige, and honor are firmly entrenched; that is, sanctioned by conventions, law, and ritual. However, the status structure reaches those extremes only when ethnic differences underlie it. Frequently the two are identical to such an extent that it is impossible to say where the caste ends and the ethnic group begins. Max Weber (1960) says that

castes are, in fact, the normal form in which ethnic communities live side by side, usually as societies. Like castes, ethnic communities organize their relationships and activities on the basis of kinship responsibilities and rights; they exclude exogamous marriage and restrict social intercourse to the area occupied by the community.

Julio Luelmo points out that in prehistory ethnic groups dealt with one another on the basis of the caste system. Prior to European contact those American states now called kingdoms and empires were constituted in this way.[17] The external contradictions of the situation acquired an importance of the first order; the tribe which usurped superior status ruled the subject tribes for a period of time which was determined by the interplay of external contradictions. These eventually led to the elevation of another tribe, formerly subjugated, to the rank of imperial tribe, and thus status was passed successively. Through this process ethnic groups formed caste systems, each with its exclusive population, maintaining the conviction that it was superior to its neighbors. In every case the ethnic group considered itself the chosen people, true men, the center of the world.

(4) *Vertically differentiated ethnic structure.* Nevertheless, an ethnic group is not a caste if it does not form part of a system; the caste does not exist as an isolated entity but as part of a vertically differentiated system. The caste structure transforms horizontal ethnic coexistence into a vertical social system of superiority and subordination. As long as this phenomenon does not exist, the ethnic structure does not give birth to a caste system. Ethnic coexistence encourages ethnocentrism, which leads to mutual exclusion and disdain for the worth of others and permits each community to consider its own worth the highest. The caste structure carries with it social subordination and a recognition of higher worth in the privileged caste. According to Max Weber (1960) this is due to the fact that within the caste structure ethnic distinctions as such have become functional distinctions in political socialization. But even in the caste structure the status group occupying the lowest position is able to continue cultivating a belief in its particular worth which, as stated, is of equal importance in the ethnic structure.

Mutually exclusive communities are ethnic minorities which are subordinate to a national majority but which in no case are small nationalities, for the existence of the latter implies the absence of a caste system. In the caste structure, Indian communities are in actual or potential conflict. Even in cases where cultural differences are not significant and when ethnic groups can communicate adequately through a common language, competition for privilege and rank hinders the unity of thought and action which characterizes a nationality. Cases in which the regional ethnic structure receives a single name such as Maya, which includes both the dominant mestizo group and the subject Indian groups, are most confusing to those who dogmatically postulate the existence of small nationalities.[18]

Relations of superiority and subordination as well as other similar social and political complexes are established for the purpose of developing and maintaining privileges held by one of the castes and for establishing competition between ethnic groups for advantages and rights. Barriers that prevent or impede the free attainment of social goals generate hostility which is manifested when subordinate groups perceive the privations and frustrations to which they are subjected. Caste antagonism is the force that always underscores the causes of Indian rebellion and which is expressed as nativist or revitalist movements.

The absence of open signs of hostility in societies divided into castes does not mean that subordinate ethnic groups accept the social arrangement willingly. It simply indicates that the means of domination, such as humane methods of oppression, benevolent despotism, and paternalism,[19] operate efficiently. It is asserted that in Southeast Asia such mechanisms were able to keep a caste system functioning for 40 centuries; in mestizo America they have operated for four centuries in the Indo-Ladino model. As a repercussion of the application of control mechanisms, the internal unity and synergy of the subject group are reinforced, making it isolated, restricted, self-sufficient and enclosed. Thus barriers are raised to acculturation and to the evolution and progressive development of the *etnias*, who undergo segregation and segregate themselves, limiting free circulation or the access of peoples to one another.

Any attempt to construct a system of absolute social inequality is intrinsically contradictory. The very scale of values by which one caste judges itself better than another makes its members try to improve and acquire prestige and thereby affects the position of the group as a whole. A change of position or of economic fortune, an alteration in the observance of rules and taboos, all affect the system. The idea of absolute inequality is not only internally incoherent, but incompatible with the fundamental needs of society; it would require a completely static system. Any society, by the simple interaction of its structure, engenders frictions which change that structure, as Kingsley Davis (1965:355) has pointed out. Furthermore, the external conditions in which a society lives change constantly. The caste system is an archaic social structure which is obsolete and which has neither reason to survive nor any possibility of doing so beside a modern industrial society.

Indo-Ladino relations in Mestizo America fulfill the conditions of the proposed definition of caste. They are caste relationships and historically and sociologically it is correct to designate them as such.

NOTES

1. Barber (1964:17) says: "Contrary to first impressions, which may accentuate differences among people, the essential function of the system of stratification in a society is that of integration. That is, to the extent that the system of stratification is the expression or result of differential judgments by the hierarchy, following a common set of values, it serves to unify the society."

2. Dahrendorf (1959:31) states: "By stratum I shall understand a category of persons who occupy a similar position on a hierarchical scale of certain situational characteristics such as income, prestige, style of life. 'Stratum' is a descriptive category. By contrast, the concept of class is an analytical category which has meaning only in the context of a theory of class. 'Classes' are interest groupings emerging from certain structural conditions which operate as such and effect structure changes."

3. It is well known that Marx forcefully stated the problem of social classes more than 100 years ago. Before the advent of capitalism and industrialization the terms, states, ranks, orders, and corporations were used and prior to that, one spoke of castes. Gurvitch (1960:30) says that for Marx the prototype of the class struggle seems to be the relationships between the city and countryside. He writes: "Opposition between the city and the countryside begins with the passage from barbarism to civilization, from the tribal regime to the State, from the locality to the nation, and it is found in the entire history of civilization up to our time. . . . Here for the first time the division of the population into two great classes appears, based directly upon the division of labor and instruments of production."

4. Polanyi (1957a:69) states: "In Germany, Maine found a disciple in Ferdinand Toennies. His conception was epitomized in the title of his work *Community and Society* (Gemeinschaft und Gesellschaft 1888). 'Community' corresponded to 'status,' 'society' to 'contractus. . . .

The emotional connotation, however, given to status and contractus as well as to the corresponding 'community' and 'society,' was widely different with Maine and Toennies. To Maine the pre-contractus condition of mankind stood merely for the dark ages of tribalism. The introduction of contract, so he felt, had emancipated the individual from the bondage of status. Toennies' sympathies were for the intimacy of the community as against the impersonalness of organized society. 'Community' was idealized by him as a condition where the lives of men were embedded in a tissue of common experience, while 'society' was never to him far removed from the cash nexus, as Thomas Carlyle called the relationship of persons connected by market ties alone. Toennies' policy ideal was the restoration of community, not, however, by returning to the presociety stage of authority and paternalism, but by advancing to a higher form of community of a postsociety stage, which would follow upon our present civilization. He envisaged this community as a co-operative phase of human existence, which would retain the advantages of technological progress and individual freedom while restoring the wholeness of life."

5. Polanyi (1957a:69) comments: "Sir Henry Sumner Maine undertook to prove that modern society was built on contractus, while ancient society rested on status. Status is set by birth–a man's position in the family–and determines the rights and duties of a person. It derives from kinship and adoption; it persists under feudalism and, with some qualifications, right up to the age of equal citizenship as established in the nineteenth century. But already under Roman law status was gradually replaced by contractus, i.e., by rights and duties derived from bilateral arrangements. Later, Maine revealed the universality of status organization in the case of the village communities of India."

6. McKinney and Loomis (1963:13) explain: "The *sacred society* is isolated vicinally, socially, and mentally. This isolation leads to fixation of habit and neophobia, relations of avoidance, and traditional in-group-out-group attitudes. The concrete is emphasized at the expense of abstraction; social contacts are primary; and tradition and ritual play a large part in the life of the individual. There is the dominance of sacredness even in the economic sphere which works toward the maintenance of self-sufficiency, and against any development of the pecuniary attitude. The division of labor is simple. Kinship ties are strong and are manifest in 'great family' relationships. All forms of activity are under sacred sanctions, and hence violent social control is at

a minimum. The forces of gossip and tradition are powerful tools of control. Nonrational behavior is predominant, with an important element of supernaturalism present. Rationalism, particularly in the form of science, is largely absent. The value system is impermeable.

A sacred society is one in which resistance to change is at a maximum or, to say the very least, where change is in the highest degree unwelcome. These societies might also be called traditional, customary, ceremonial, conservative, immobile, or prescriptive, but for our purposes sacred and like terms carry the meaning well enough (well enough, that is, as long as holy, supernatural, spiritual, divine, or religious in our ordinary sense are not regarded as synonyms). Baldly put, societies which impress upon their members habits making for a high degree of resistance to change are sacred societies."

7. McKinney and Loomis (1963:17) state: "To Redfield, the folk society is a small collectivity containing no more people within it than can know each other well. It is an isolated, nonliterate, homogeneous grouping with a strong sense of solidarity. Technology is simple, and, aside from the division of function between the sexes, there is little other division of labor; hence the group is economically independent of other groups. The ways in which problems are met by the society are conventionalized by long intercommunication within the group, and these ways have become interrelated with one another to constitute a coherent and self-consistent system: a culture. Behavior is spontaneous, traditional, personal, and there is no motivation toward reflection, criticism, or experimentation. Kinship, its relations and institutions, is central to all experience, and the family is the unit of action. The value of traditional acts and objects is not to be questioned; hence they are sacred. The sacredness of objects is apparent in the ways in which objects are hedged in with restraints and taboos that keep them from being commonplace. All activities, even those of economic production, are ends in themselves. The more remote ends of living are taken as given; hence the folk society exists not so much on the basis of exchange of useful functions as in common understandings as to what is to be done . . . the folk society . . . is the polar opposite of urban society."

8. Dahrendorf (1959:219) maintains: "In view of examples of this kind, it seems plausible to argue that where there is no group which is capable of monopolizing the positions of authority, it is virtually impossible for coherent conflict groups to emerge, and the society or association in question is therefore classless."

9. Rodríguez Sandoval (1949:25) states: "Generally speaking, the woman, once married, goes to live in her husband's house, thus moving from one *aillu* to another if the husband does not belong to the same *aillu*. When the husband dies the widow frequently remains in the husband's *aillu* and continues to offer her services, as though she were a daughter to her parents-in-law. If she remarries she can take a husband from either of the *aillus*, but not beyond her own people or *llacta*. Thus we can explain how the various Indian groups have maintained their unmistakable characteristics over time."

10. Coser (1961:26) commenting upon Simmel's propositions about conflict, states: "Simmel deals with interrelated although distinct phenomena. First he states that conflict fixes the boundaries among the groups composing a social system, thus establishing the identity of those groups. Secondly he says that reciprocal rejection maintains the total system because it creates an equilibrium among the diverse groups. For example, conflicts between the castes of India may separate and establish the distinctions among the various castes, but it can also guarantee the stability of the integrated Hindu social structure by provoking an equilibrium among the various demands of the rival castes."

11. Adams (1956:213) proposes: "The word ladinization can refer to various and distinct processes which occur in Guatemala. The first may refer to the biological mixing of various races; in this sense it is the same process that we call miscegenation. . . . Within the general conception of ladinization of culture or behavior, we can distinguish two distinct processes: social mobility and transculturation. The former relates to the change an individual undergoes when he divests himself of the customs of his own class or ethnic group, in order to become a member of another class or ethnic group. As a consequence, an individual can become a ladino without essentially changing the cultural character of either of the ethnic groups in question. In contrast, transculturation refers to the change that an entire community or society undergoes upon becoming culturally more similar to the other."

Beals (1956:245) commenting on Adams' position, notes that, "The process of transculturation consists primarily in the loss of the original culture and the adoption of aspects of the new culture . . . the processes are not always that simple. In some cases syncretism may occur, in which elements of both cultures are merged, creating something new and different from what existed before." This latter process is called acculturation.

Varallanos (1962:181) coincides with Adams, calling *cholificación* "the process of Indian-Spanish transculturation in Peru." Varallanos, nevertheless, idealizes the Mestizo, in his *chola* variety, to a point very close to racism.

12. South American anthropologists have been hard pressed to describe the social structure in Andean regions of refuge. Reality presents them with three population groups distinguished traditionally on the basis of ethnic origin: Indians, *cholos*, and *mistis*.

Because of the historical development that shaped the colonial heritage, these population groups are stratified hierarchically in such a way that the *mistis*, descended from conquistadors and European settlers, are in a superior social position in the scale of values, despite the nation's political independence and its democratic ideology.

On the basis of rights and privileges of birth, the dominant group subjects and exploits Indians and *cholos*. It claims to be racially White and although most of its members are effectively so, mixture with the Indian has changed the original genetic composition and continues to do so with increasing force. In some regions of refuge the *mistis* are really Mestizos and that is what they call themselves. White or Mestizo, *mistis* have a deep sense of nationality and represent the modern face of the national society in their respective regions. There are inevitable regional variations and they are clearly backward in their conception of industrial civilization, but their forms of living articulate easily with the national structure.

The *indiada* emerged directly from the American population that the Europeans encountered in expanding their colonial enterprise. *Mestizaje* plays a certain role in the peripheral fringes of the regions of refuge, but in the Indian centers the physical features that are objective manifestations of race persist with surprising vigor and in fact some colonial peoples, initially categorized as Europeans, have undergone a process of Indianization. Physical features are important as signs of social categorization because the color range places individuals in different places on the social scale, reserving the lowest and least desirable levels for the Indians (Lipschutz 1956:60).

Economically, the *indiada* work in agriculture and with livestock, whether as free, salaried laborers, as *hacienda-runa* serfs, or as independent peasants. The Indian has no other alternatives, aside from agricultural and livestock work except for some subsistence crafts, that allow him to make clothing, build a house, furnish it, and construct rudimentary tools for work and recreation. His economic life is based on the reciprocity of the *ayni* and *minca* and the redistribution of surpluses through ceremonial consumption in religious festivals.

The market is tribal and limited to satisfying urgent local needs. Land tenancy is communal or individual and land holdings are small. In either case, land is very rarely considered merchandise (Nash 1964). In the case of an *hacienda-runa* Indian, property is owned by the *misti latifundista*. The Indians are generally monolingual in a native language, illiterate, and wear clothing identifying them as belonging to a local community. Sometimes they have Indian surnames and adhere to customs, ideas, and practices in marriage, religion, communication, and ways of living together that segregate and set them apart as a group, culturally and socially immobilized.

In addition, a population group grows and evolves in the Andes called the *cholada* that is marginal to the two mentioned above. Because of the universal nature of the conditions underlying the social structure of each Mestizo American country, this group shows great similarities in different regions of refuge. For example, the differences between a *cholo* woman from Cuenca (Ecuador) and one from Cochabamba (Bolivia) are less than those separating these two from Indians and *mistis*. This apparently surprising phenomenon results from the fact that the *cholada* emerges in domination situations found wherever a dual economy segregates the inhabitants into opposing ethnic sectors. The *cholo* is born where an interethnic barrier blocks the integration of groups. He is a marginal man with notable similarities wherever he appears. The name *revestido* given in Mesoamerica to the *cholo* does not mean that he is different from his Andean counterpart; both are the result of the same structural situation.

The *cholo* is an Indian who has broken his affiliation with the community of origin. In his struggle to enter the *misti* or Ladino society he remains in the middle of the road–*nepantla*, the Mexicans would say (Durán 1951:268)–unable to overcome the domination mechanisms put into play by the superior group to block his integration. Consequently, the phenomenon of the *cholo* as part of an organized group, the *cholada*, can be found only in the structure of the regions of refuge. The group remains a minority in respect to the regional population. If the *cholo* emigrates to a culturally and economically more developed region, the social class structure there is not theoretically an unbridgable obstacle to his articulation into the national society.

Once the *cholada* is formed it increases not only through the addition of individuals from the Indian group but also by virtue of its own dynamism. As it grows it aggravates the internal contradictions of the ethnically structured society more and more until it is impossible for the latter to function. When its numbers surpass those of the Indian population it is no longer a marginal group but becomes the majority. It then changes the structure of relations between Indians and *mistis*, making them untenable. At that moment the *cholada* and the entire region are integrated into the nation as a single bloc. The most notable case of massive integration in the past 50 years is that of the *cholada* of the Mantaro Valley in Peru, where a caste structure changed into one of classes (Adams 1953). The Mantaro Valley changed from a region of refuge to a region of development (Arguedas 1957).

The Indian becomes a *cholo* when pressure for land forces him to renounce rights he may have to the family parcel. Agriculture is based on minifundia, caused by inheritance customs operating on a population that is growing at an increasing rate; those who cannot conform are pushed into salaried work outside the community (Pozas 1945). The place of easiest access for the Indian is the district city, where he goes weekly on market day. This is the small metropolis of the municipal ethnic group. To take up residence there does not mean a total rupture of the loyalties tying one to the community of origin.

The most important step is taken when the Indian establishes residence in the *misti* capital of the province, *chef-lieu* of the region of refuge. The obligations connected with service or *mittani* lead both male and female Indians into domestic service in the cities. After several years, if the Indian can manage to overcome the factors forcing him into this service, he commonly remains in the city as a *cholo* (Vázquez 1961). But it is the young men undergoing military conscription who experience the effects of contact with the outside world perhaps most violently and who most frequently enter the *cholada* upon returning to the region of their origin. Becoming conditioned to military norms, learning the official language and acquiring literacy all make readjustment to the Indian agrarian culture difficult.

Passage from the Indian to the *cholo* level entails a minimum participation in the national culture and consciousness even when ties to the local community are not lost (Mangin 1955). The *cholo* knows he is different from the Indian, with whom he does not want to be confused, and he seeks unsuccessfully to be accepted as a *misti*. To this end he rejects the symbols of integration in the Indian group, among them the community government and system of festivals, and imitates *misti* attitudes in respect to conspicuous and religious consumption. When the *cholada* is numerous and rich, as in Sucre, the group's power is established through various means such as adorning the Virgin of Guadalupe's mantle with jewelry and precious stones.

The economy of the *cholada* is the basis on which he maintains his superiority to the Indian and his continued inferiority to the *misti* in the hierarchy. The passage from Indian to *cholo* entails important changes in the norms regulating productive activity and the nature of its components. When the Indian is a member of his community, he shares in the rights and obligations of tenancy and use of the group's resources, including land. Land that has been cultivated traditionally has features that are very similar to those of private property. Thus there are limitations on the kinds of crops raised on it, preventing its inclusion in the integrating ambit of the market. The *cholo* conceives land ownership in the same way as the *misti*, that is, as total ownership, and sees land as merchandise subject to the market's mechanisms of price formation. He treats resources such as pasture land, fields of rushes, and others in the same manner, rejecting their communal character in order to free himself from the obligations attached to them. The *cholo* may own a cultivated parcel and may even cultivate it himself with his relatives; however, his relationship with the land has changed. It is no longer the sacred relationship relying on the sanction of traditional society, which makes a man of the glebe one with the reciprocal ties between the land and those who cultivate it. The *cholo* focuses the problem of production from the conceptual scheme of the profit economy. He sows the field to obtain goods for market and he figures in economizing terms that render him a profit in money. Thus he rejects the rights and obligations of the *ayni* and other forms of mutual help. Give and take is no longer the normative principle of his economic behavior. He prefers the rules of salaried work and when he needs agricultural labor he pays Indian peons in money.

The change also extends to such forms of cooperation as the *minca* or *faena*. These are used by Indian peoples outside the money economy to meet the needs of the municipal police force, and particularly for construction of such works as schools, roads, bridges, or for repair and conservation of public buildings and services. The *indiada* responds to calls from local authorities and even tolerates abuse of their willingness to cooperate by national development programs. A large part of the transportation system of the *queshua* and *puna* have been built with *mincas*. The *cholo* is reluctant to cooperate in nonremunerative labor even in public works that directly affect him. When he feels forced by social pressure to contribute to those works he does so in money and not in labor or kind; he contributes in terms of the market economy, resorting to the expedient of paying a daily wage to the Indian who does the work in his name.

But the basic change, the fundamental one for the Indian who becomes a *cholo*, is in occupation. He leaves the primary activities forced upon him by the dominant structure and enters the sphere of manufacturing and services, changing from an agrarian life to an urban or semiurban one. The *cholo* who retains a plot and cultivates it with salaried labor is no longer a fully peasant member of the agrarian society. Instead, he is generally an artisan, merchant, or local functionary for whom agriculture is a subsidiary activity and rarely the principal basis of his subsistence, which is maintained by working in the urban population center. Beals (1951) sees this process of urbanization as equivalent to that of acculturation.

In the capital cities of Andean regions of refuge there are certain kinds of employment that have traditionally been considered appropriate for Indians and which therefore are never practiced by *misti* artisans. To do so would be to descend on the social scale and in one's own estimation, to be employed in a very low status specialization. The kinds of work appropriate for Indians vary from country to country and from region to region. Rodríguez Sandoval (1959: 62) mentions the following as valid for Ecuador: stonecutter, bricklayer, mine digger, muleteer, porter, and street cleaner. Núñez del Prado (1962:10) gives a longer list for Cuzco: artisans, textile workers, domestic servants, drivers, small merchants, drivers' helpers, wool dealers, bricklayers, and small businessmen. He also notes that the lower posts in the governmental hierarchy such as *gobernador, teniente gobernador* and *agente municipal* are occupied by "Indians in the process of transculturation."

Those who have had the opportunity to travel through the inter-Andean alley can add other occupations such as the barber who sets up his stand in rural fairs; the tailor who makes much of the clothing for both men and women; the baker who produces so-called Indian bread; the dealers in leather and skins who seem to be exclusively *cholos* in some places; the ironworker who forges tools for native cultivation; the shoemaker who makes *oshotas*, and various others. But perhaps no occupation is more common than that of the plaza merchant, almost always a *cholo* woman, or that of producing and selling *chicha*, which also seems to be a speciality monopolized by them.

During the morning hours of market days the district cities become surprisingly active and take on a new appearance. Flower-decorated poles extend from house doors and the different colors of the flowers indicate the kind of merchandise for sale: good *chicha*, rum, coca, bread, corn. On such days the urban population seems to adorn itself to receive the Indian clientele arriving in large numbers with agricultural products to interchange for manufactured goods or services. *Cholo* women acquire the produce on the outskirts of the town, on access roads as *atajadoras* or in the market place where they set up their stands. Economic interchange causes concomitant changes in various aspects of the culture. Perhaps one of the most important is that which inverts the traditional status of the woman, who goes from a very low value as an Indian to levels as a *chola* that are higher than that of the man. This rise in status results from the economic activities of the *chola*–in her role as plaza vendor or merchants–which afford her a cash income that liberates her from dependence on her husband. Frequently her income is greater than that the *cholo* man receives in manufacturing or services. In these circumstances the balance of power in the domestic unit inevitably is tipped toward the woman, who is then presented with alternatives that she never had as an Indian nor will have as a *mišti* if she enters the dominant group through her offspring. One of these alternatives is to enter into free union relationships in which the man is not a basic factor in the family unit and therefore may be and frequently is replaced.

In censuses taken by the male dominated national society, domestic units in which a woman is head of the family are categorized as "abandoned by the husband," while in fact the contrary is true. Moisés Sáenz (1933:275) relates his impression of the *cholo* woman: "It is true that the Indian woman plays a very important role in the domestic economy. It is also undeniable that in plazas and markets it is she and, at least apparently, not her husband, who is the element of greatest importance and nevertheless, this does not fully explain the marked superiority of the *cholo* woman over the *cholo* man, the truly surprising jump by the Indian woman as soon as she reaches the next highest step in the ethnic-social scale. The superiority of the *cholo* woman over the Indian woman seems unquestionable. Her spirit is more agile, more active. She walks proudly along the roads, her manner is open when greeting acquaintances, she speaks in a strong voice, somewhat brusquely, although her inflection is never disagreeable. She takes the initiative in informal conversations. Her physical appearance is also distinguished: tall and robust, never obese, neither is she mannish, but forward and sure of herself. The *chola* travels all the roads of the sierra, carrying her products and merchandise to the Sunday market, humming half in Spanish and half in Quechua, radiant in her tightly fitted waistcoat and her flaring underskirts of bright colors. She takes part in the social life of the fiesta; at the sound of guitars and bandurrias she sings, dances, and gets drunk. If she reaches a higher social category her deportment is of such dignity, such balance and sobriety as to inspire envy in any woman of distinguished family. The caste of *mamá señoras* is well known. They are the notable woman of the community; they own property and have a monopoly on *madrinazgos*. They dress in black, wear *llicllas* of plush and embroidered shawls; they are great ladies. In the countryside as well as the city, in El Salvador and Ecuador, Peru and Bolivia, the *chola* has become a powerful class. They are merchants and politicians. They dominate the human landscape of Peru. In the improbable markets of Huancayo and Ayacucho the *cholas* swarm, haughty, sure of themselves, challenging."

Uriel García (1930:210) adds, "The *gatera* who sells meat, fruit, tools in the market, is base in her language, aggressive and ironic, shameless in a fight. From this type came the famous *cholas* in the history of the Republic. Pacha-Anka, Huallpacaldo, la güera Melchora, Orko-Asno, women bosses of trade unions, carriers of the bier of the Virgin of Bethlehem, women who guide religious mobs, mayordomas of parish *santidades*, fervent partisans of political caudillos, instigators of rock fights, capitans of thieves and highwaymen, quiet at the first peal of the María Angola–the great tumultuous and *cholesca* bell of republican Cuzco. At cries of 'Long live the Virgin of Bethlehem!' or 'Down with so-and-so!' she would stone a newspaper or set fire to a neighboring house or beat to death the tormentors, hanging their bodies from the balconies."

The *cholo* is necessarily bilingual, speaking Quechua or Aymara and Spanish. His human condition contains a linguistic and cultural duality that is highly useful as a link between the Indian and the *misti*. "He is the leader, directing social and economic changes; he knows how to read and write and if he does not, he sends his children to school" Martínez (1961:234). In some regions, for example Tarabuco in Bolivia, the women of the *cholada* are monolingual but they differ from the Indian women in that they prepare their children for a different way of life. Their preoccupation with education and life in the urban center reveals the general aspiration to ascend the social scale. *Cholos* "are in reality highly acculturated Indians who are conscious of forming a stratum that is different from that of Indians" Galdo (1962a). They unite social mobility with geographic mobility. The *cholo*, in contrast to the Indian, moves frequently and over long distances. He travels and comes into contact with the outside world.

The exchange of the status symbols that place the Indian in a community culture for those identifying the citizen as a member of the national society is not complete in the case of the *cholo*. His clothing, one of the most visible symbols in the process of change, has remained midway between Indian dress and the Western pattern. Sometimes the differences are found in the quality of materials; Indian clothes are rougher, made of *casinete* or coarse cashmere. Or the distinction may be found in the omission of an article of Indian clothing such as the man's *chucllo* and poncho, the woman's *anaco* and *lliclla*. These are replaced by the hat and overcoat, by the skirt and shawl respectively. The shoe replaces the *oshota* and the difference is also seen in the hat–regional in form and style–used in place of the showy local Indian garb. For people living in the inter-Andean alley the dress of the *cholo* woman is so distinctive that there is not the least difficulty in identifying her. "At first glance anyone can tell who is mestizo, who Indian, and who is in the *cholada*" Ortiz (1962:57).

In addition, the manner in which the skirt, the hat, and the shawl are worn identifies the region from which the *chola* comes. The Indian woman is parochial, the *chola* is regional, the *misti* is national, at least in terms of clothing. Changes in housing and food are less obvious. The *cholo* lives on the outskirts of the great cities, in rented rooms that serve as living room, bedroom, dining room, kitchen, pantry, and pen for guinea pigs and chickens. There is a notable absence of sanitary facilities. In the secondary cities living conditions are no better; the houses are placed back to back and there is no open space for recreation. The inhabitants sleep on low boards or on the floor and frequently there is no heating such as that found in peasant houses. The diet is midway between that of the countryside and the city, and this represents a disadvantage from the point of view of nutritional balance. The *cholo*, like the Indian, consumes *chicha* and other intoxicating beverages, sometimes in considerable quantities, but he no longer chews coca when he moves to the city, a practice which remains an inseparable part of the agricultural work of the Indian.

Finally, we shall look at changes in the family structure, above and beyond those already noted in reference to the status of women and the nature of marriage. Marriages may follow the customary norms of free unions or the civil and canon laws observed nationally, but *cholos* choose their spouses from within their own group. Marriage with an Indian is rejected because it entails a regression in the search for a higher social status and marriage with a *misti*, although desired, rarely happens since the *misti* group maintains its superior position through endogamy. The *cholo's* upward aspirations on the scale of values explain his tendency to repudiate the symbols tying him to his Indian roots, among which is his surname. Sometimes the change is easy phonetically; it is said in Puno that many of the *cholos* named Arispe have Indian ancestors named Quispe. The change in surname represents a definitive break with one's origins. The family name is one symbol that the *misti* as well as the Indian holds on to tenaciously, to the point that it is considered "the prime determinant indicating whether a person belongs to one caste or the other" Adams (1959:83).

The description of *cholada* characteristics has been minutely detailed so far, necessarily so in order to clearly establish the marginal condition of the group. It is precisely this transitive condition that provokes greatest confusion among anthropologists whenever they attempt to find a system in the social structure of these three population groups. For some–naturally the ones most tied to Marxist orthodoxy–Indians, *cholos* and *mistis* form a class system. For others, less limited by a rigid position, they form part of a caste system. Mangin (1955:22) asserts that, "it is a matter of choice whether the groups are to be considered as classes or castes," although he concludes that "the term caste could be used at least to divide Indians from non-Indians."

Initially, in Mexico as well as Peru, relations between Indians and Mestizos were classified as class relationships; one spoke of the Indian class, the Mestizo or *misti* class and even of the *cholo* class. In order that this division into ethnic classes would conform to the economic class stratification generally used among North American sociologists, the Indian class was assigned the status of lower or "lowest" class, the *cholo* that of lower or middle class and the Mestizo that of provincial upper or middle class, Schaedel et al (1959). After Karl Marx's definitive analysis in which greatest diagnostic significance was assigned to production relationships in the determination of the social structure, scholars studying American societies could not ignore their importance. They compared the Indian with the working class and the Mestizo with the bourgeoisie, basing their comparisons on the fact that the so-called Indian class is subjected to exploitation by the so-called Mestizo class. In fact, classes based on ethnic differences cannot be compared in any way with classes based on the means of production since the systems within which they function are totally different.

The increased confusion regarding the terms made the younger generation of anthropologists avoid the impasse by taking the neutral position of categorizing the different groups as social or cultural strata. Ortiz (1965) is inclined to treat the different ethnic groups as subcultures while Vázquez (1961) refers to the *cholo* as a cultural group. Nonetheless, in monographs published recently by the Plan Nacional de Integracion de la Poblacion Aborigen (PNIPA) in Lima, authors describing the social structure of the community or region which is the object of their research refer to the *indiada*, the *cholada* and the *mistis* as social strata. They take great care not to declare themselves for or against a definition based either on class or caste; they simply limit themselves to description, thus avoiding controversy. Galdo (1962a) takes a step forward without leaving the descriptive level when he analyzes the social classes that form the *misti* and Indian strata, although he calls them substrata. Thus he divides the *misti* into: "(1) the rich, traditionally the big land owners and now also the big merchants; (2) the middle class, to which belong middle-level property owners, merchants and certain employees, and (3) the lower class. The *indiada* is divided into *colonos–hacienda-runa* or hacienda serfs–and *comuneros*. These, in turn, he classifies as the rich, or *camiris*; (2) the middle or *taipis*, and (3) the poor." The *cholo* stratum, significantly, appears to be undivided in Galdo's scheme.

The presence of social classes among the *mistis* is unquestionable. Perhaps one might object to speaking in terms of a middle class in the regions of refuge, since an emerging middle class is barely coming into being in the culturally and economically more developed regions, Crevenna (1951). The substrata into which the Indian *comuneros* are divided are not called classes by Galdo but the terms rich, middle, and poor, which he implies carry an implicit connotation of classes. Differences in possession of material goods are undeniable and in specific places–Otavalo, for example–there is an effective division of the Indians into classes.

In this latter case, as in Quetzaltenango, Guatemala, there are Indians who as a direct consequence of their position in the social economic system, have taken advantage of the work of other Indians with whom they maintain a wage relationship. These exceptional cases are significant, as we shall duly see, but they are not indicative of the general rule of communal relations.

Differences in the possession of capital goods are general. They are not sufficient as a basis for a class system, however, unless they are accompanied by institutionalized relationships allowing the formation of interest groups in which some take advantage of the labor of others who are unprotected and dependent. *Camiris* are called rich because they possess more land, more livestock, and better access to other resources than do the *taipis* and the poor. But all three are subject to the norms of reciprocal labor and to the principles of redistribution and conspicuous consumption. Costales (1957:205) reports that among the campesino group of Chimborazo, a person is called poor or *huasharango* "who is not distinguished from things of the country, who goes unnoticed like the wind," or who "because of some circumstances, perhaps economic, could not achieve his desires for social prestige, and is an unknown Indian in his community, living isolated in humiliation and shame." As noted, a man is poor who holds no cargos and has no fame in his community. The Indian scale of values does not measure men in accordance with their economic but with their social status, acquired through redistribution of surpluses and the holding of cargos in the community government.

It is clear from this discussion that the Indian population known as the *indiada* is not divided into social classes. Nor as whole does it constitute part of a class system with the status of lower class. It is simply a preclass population that organizes relationships among its members on the basis of kinship ties, ties to territoriality, and service to the governing hierarchy, all of which form the structure of the native ethnic groups. The *misti* population group, as an incorporated part of the national capitalist society, is divided into social classes. But in its relations with the *indiada* it acts as a unit, as an ethnic group situated in a superordinate position. Consequently the relationship between *mistis* and Indians is a relationship of castes.

The *cholada*, sometimes called the lower class, is a group that is marginal to the two basic castes. It constitutes an intercaste whose mere existence represents a serious contradiction that endangers the traditional order and ultimately destroys it. The case of the Mantaro Valley mentioned above, is a clear example of the growth of the intercaste which breaks the old structure and gives way to the emergence of a class system. The absence of an intercaste in the region of refuge is a sign of the prevalence and force of the caste system. Under these circumstances the subordinate caste cannot find ready channels for ascent to *cholo* status because the superior caste blocks it. The Indian resolves his frustration over the impossibility of crossing the caste barrier by enclosing himself within his own group, producing the conditions for the emergence of a class system of his own. The case already mentioned of Otavalo is an example of this evolution, which unfortunately discourages national integration. It hinders the formation of the intermediate marginal group and facilitates the formation of conflicting castes, containing social classes within themselves. These castes are in persistent disarticulation, separated by the unbridgeable wall of the caste barrier. Such is the social structure of the Andean regions of refuge, objectively interpreted.

13. Tumin (1956:178) says: "I am not trying to falsely lead you to believe that John Gillin totally supports my point of view. Nor do I want to place too much emphasis on the differences which exist between Redfield and Tax, on the one hand, and myself, on the other. As Roberts insinuates, it is possible that my sympathies for the Indians of the community I studied have induced me to see certain sentimental dimensions in the relationships which do not really exist. Nevertheless, I have studied my field notes carefully again, I have gone over the original interviews written at the time, and I do not believe myself willing to substantially change the estimation of the situation I presented in my report of 1952."

14. Holmberg (1965:104) says "Of a total of approximately three million Indians living in Peru, one million are landless and work as peons on haciendas; one million, independent small landholders, live in Indian communities; and the remaining million, separated from their land, work in mines, in mestizo towns, as migrant laborers and as servants. If it is true that the majority of Indians live separately from mestizos, as much because of caste barriers as of geographic isolation, it is the Indians who work on the

haciendas who occupy the lowest rung of all the Indians, socially as well as economically. At the pinnacle of the social hierarchy, concentrated along the coast, is a small elite, considered to be White. Relations between the individual and the community, and between the community and the nation, are quite different than those commonly found in the United States and some Latin American countries, due, at least in part, to the caste ordering of the social hierarchy which, until recently, maintained a type of static equilibrium. Dependency and submission, more than independence and liberty, characterize social relations within the community, and these, in turn, tend to rule the relations between the community and the nation."

Adams (1959:82) speaking of the Peruvian community of Muquiyauyo, adds: "To an outsider, the townspeople appear to be dressed generally alike, to live in similar houses, to speak the same language, and to resemble any group of people among whom are both rich and poor. Little by little, however, differences became clear. At certain fiestas, for example, some people ate the fiesta dinner in one part of the building, others in another, and certain people always took the lead in certain kinds of activities. When it became clear to me that the terms 'Indian' and 'mestizo' had a social meaning beyond their racial connotation, I began to question informants concerning them and found that at least up to the beginning of the present century there existed a series of social distinctions which constituted a caste system."

15. Reichel-Dolmatoff (1956;1961) says: "Nowadays, if you ask any member of the population, Spaniard or Indian, rich or poor, about the clan system and the details of the criteria for classification, he will answer that each one forms a separate class and finally he will enumerate 3, 4, 5 or 7 economic classes, but upon trying to assign people, one by one, to those classes, it can immediately be observed that criteria of surname, lineage and race prevail and that the factor of caste is still taken strongly into account in the social structure of the town" (1956:445).

16. de la Fuente (1965:217) says: "that the change from caste to class is not, in the area, a peaceful process, is made apparent by the results—some temporary, others long lasting—of the two social movements referred to."

17. Luelmo (1965:22) says: "Among the castes and social classes we find a new differentiating characteristic. To the extent that the contradiction expressed by the antagonism encountered by the social classes fighting among themselves, represents an internal contradiction in the very organic-social process—the nation—the prehistoric castes represent a contradiction of different organic processes expressed within the imperial tribes before the tribes were subjected by military victory."

18. Berzunza Pinto (1941) as president of the Indian subcommittee of the Mexican Communist Party, begins the statement of the Indianist platform of the party with the following criticisms: "The Communist Party has before it, as a part of its revolutionary Mexican organism, the vèry important problem of the Indian groups living scattered about our country who number several million active people. The Communist Party, in accord with its proclaimed objectives and also in accord with the attitude that a revolutionary party should assume in all colonial or semi-colonial countries, should lend itself with decision, firmness and dedication to making a careful study of Mexico's Indian groups, which would give an exact picture of the situation and lead to appropriate steps. . . . Such studies, clearly focused upon by the Communist Party, would also put an end to the dominant imperialism within the party itself, which under its old leadership was limited merely to saying: 'we are for the self-determination of oppressed nationalities, which is a guarantee of liberation, etc., etc.', and to reciting the general objectives regarding Indians . . . which produced over a long period of time within the ranks of the party, not only the confusions regarding the problem which now occupy us, but also created a limited and inefficient way of focusing and dealing with these problems."

19. Vázquez (1961:34) describes the paternalism of Peruvian bosses, as follows: "The bosses assume a certain paternal behavior toward the peons, but for their own benefit. They consider that by accepting or, as they say, by *tolerating* peons on their land, they are performing a humanitarian act; thus they believe themselves to be living according to Christian principles, doing right by their fellow creatures. Whenever they are censured for the miserable lives of their peons they feel and believe themselves to have been offended. The criticism is considered as disloyal and an offense to their honor. They think that their personal sacrifices and gifts as good-hearted men are not appreciated by envious and stingy people and they think themselves victims of slander. As exploiters they appear as the exploited. They believe themselves to be the protectors and benefactors of the peasant because at certain times of the year, generally when the harvest is over, they give them food and liquor and grant economic help or aid the functionaries of the local fiestas."

Chapter 9

THE POWER HIERARCHY

MESTIZO AMERICAN countries are national states in the process of formation, with established rights in a defined territory where they exercise governmental functions. The entire population of the territory is subject to public legislation, order, taxation, and benefits from services provided by the administration. The majority of those born in the territory, with the exceptions resulting from age, sex, income, and education, have citizen status and therefore the right to vote and the possibility of election to a role in the power structure. That structure has three important levels: (1) the highest or central government, located in the capital of the republic; (2) the intermediate, that is the state or departmental government, located in the most important city of an administrative zone, which is often very extensive; and (3) the lowest, which is the local government. This is located in a secondary city or ceremonial center, the nucleus of a lesser territory called a *municipio*, parish, or district. The national states with federal forms of government elect functionaries at all three levels while countries with a centralist organization fill many of the second and third level posts with appointments made at the highest level (Scott 1959; Silvert 1962).

In general the regions of refuge contain a greater or smaller number of *municipios*. Occasionally some regions of refuge coincide with the jurisdiction of a state or department, but this is not the norm. More frequently the region comprises the area of a canton, province, or some other medium-sized territorial division. Furthermore, regions of refuge are not administrative units and if their metropolitan cities become centers where decisions affecting the *municipios* of the region are made and executed, this is due to the position of those cities as religious, social, economic, and cultural centers and not as important administrative centers. In the formal sense, the metropolitan *municipio* has no jurisdiction over the rural *municipios* that form its hinterland. However, traditional behavior patterns validate urban interference in supposedly autonomous political entities which are located within their sphere of influence and which form a power structure with special characteristics. This is due to the fact that Mestizo American countries are not really fully constituted national states. Rather, they are nations in the process of formation; in the regions of refuge they govern heterogeneous populations which interact in dialectical relationships.

Although the population in these regions is under a single political system, only a part of the people are fully conscious of what the nation means as a comprehensive social entity. These people are the ones who take an interest in national political activity and who feel that they form part of a motherland whose frontiers extend beyond the narrow limits of the parochial community. In the regions of refuge this segment of the total population is represented by the group calling itself Ladino. Although a clear minority at the local level, when it is tied emotionally and structurally to the country's majority or dominant population, it acquires the rank of the superior group within the regional equation.[1]

Native ethnic groups in parochial societies find themselves in the subordinate position of dependent peoples. Their members have no clear concept of what nation signifies, nor do they participate actively or consciously in the national political machinery. The social world of these ethnic groups is confined to the parish. They have their own forms of government, which are only weakly articulated with national patterns. Because their languages are different from the official tongue and their cultures different from the national one, communication between the parochial world of the Indian and the national world of the Ladino is difficult and based on relationships of superiority and subordination that place the Indians in an anomalous position.

The parochial Indian societies differ from one another, sometimes to such an extent that they form separate cultures with their own languages or dialects, thus hindering or preventing communication among themselves. Each group constitutes a local community and the communities of a region form a horizontal structure which sometimes appears to be a plurality of cultures or a motley mosaic of different idioms. This situation has led several scholars to consider the Mestizo American countries as multinational states composed of a large number of plural societies.[2] Each of the parochial communities with a different culture would constitute a separate society, a nation with a relationship of inequality vis-à-vis the dominant or majority national society. The total compendium of plural Indian societies plus the dominant Ladino one would constitute the general society of a non-national or multinational state.

This manner of interpreting reality only distorts the picture since it ignores the differences between the Ladinos of one and another region of refuge and between these Ladinos and the general population sharing the national culture. In addition, it treats the situation as a finished phenomenon rather than a constantly changing one which continuously integrates parochial societies, one by one, into the national society. Of course, despite their cultural plurality, the Indian communities as a whole constitute a single social world, that of the Indian, in encounters with the Ladino societies. These latter, despite their regional cultural variations, constitute another single social universe, that of the Ladino. Both worlds, the Indian and the Ladino, struggle to form a new social universe, that of the nation, which has already been achieved through historical development in the culturally more advanced regions. The Mestizo American countries appear to be multinational states only if they are analyzed as static entities. When viewed as processes, they are national states in formation. Therefore, those who propose the formal establishment of multiple nations or of a non-national state are proposing, possibly unknowingly, to brake the development process of the existing social duality.[3]

THE INDIAN REPUBLIC. The arguments and controversies arising from the problem of nationalities derive to a large extent from an inadequate or false interpretation of the nature of the Indian community. Somewhat unjustly, Adams called the community a myth.[4] To understand it we must refer to the origins of this institution, created by Spanish colonialism as an instrument of indirect rule which allowed the foreign minority to peacefully exploit the human and material resources of the newly discovered land. The institution was organized following the model of the Spanish *comuna* to the letter. Its rules and regulations were copied, its goals and functions were reproduced, and it was given a staff whose titles and responsibilities corresponded exactly to their European equivalents. This cultural pattern was imposed on the defeated population, but it was not accepted by them without reservations.

It is predictable that when cultural historians study the Indian *comuna* they use data from the wealth of documents regulating the institution, that is, the cedulas and ordinances dealing with particular cases. Focused upon from this perspective, the institution is shown unquestionably to be a community of the Spanish type; Antonio Garcia did this in a famous essay.[5] According to him, the community designed and bequeathed by the colonial power was imposed upon ethnic groups lacking a monetary mentality or an extensive scale of values. These groups did not have political concepts, a rationally oriented economy, nor knowledge of ways in which to widen the scope of their cultural achievements. The metropolis imposed the *comuna* upon the defeated population in the belief that the Indians had lost their political, economic, and cultural concepts upon the decapitation of their culture through the destruction of the governing elite. Those of the elite who did not perish in the conquest and agreed to collaborate with the dominant group were given noble status according to the Spanish model. Governing functions were conceded to them in order to expedite exploitation of the peasant masses through their mediation.[6] This nobility was given privileges and duties which—as long as the colonial interests considered them useful—made them appear to be a mechanical transference of European forms to the essentially different arena of the Indian political structure.

Both the colonial authorities and present day cultural historians whose judgments depend upon the documents of the dominant group have erred in not observing that while the form of the Indian *comuna* is fundamentally Spanish the content is eminently Indian. In fact, the *comuna* received the traditional name of Indian commune, republic, *reserva* or *parcialidad*; its functionaries were called *gobernadores, alcaldes, regidores, capitanes* or *alféreces*, all accepted designations in peninsular political terminology. It is true that the Indian *comunas* did not have the high status of the Spanish *ayuntamiento*, nor did their functionaries have the dignity and lineage of the European counterparts. To emphasize their lesser worth they were called *alcaldes, regidores* or *capitanes de república* and they always found themselves outvoted by the royal officials, *corregidores* and *alcaldes mayores*, who were foreigners. Nevertheless, the differences between the Indian community and the Spanish *ayuntamiento* are not found, as is often supposed, in the greater prestige or in the greater or lesser amount of power exercised by one or the other. There are differences, but not of degree; rather, there are fundamental and significant cultural differences. The social worlds of the Spanish colonist and the besieged Indian are not only different but contradictory; they are worlds in opposition.

Today substantive differences persist in the communities which represent the extremities of the contradiction. But in the others, which underwent forceful acculturation and integration, the extremes were fused to the point where, sociologically speaking, the native communities stopped being Indian even when they legally retained the ancient statute. As Dobyns notes, for a long time many Indian communities in Peru have not been considered to contain Indians.[7] Hernández de Alba (1963) describes a similar situation in certain communities of the Cauca Valley and Tierra Adentro in Colombia. In Mexico, many legally registered Indian communities stopped being such in the years of violence when the revolution shook the old structure. In any Mestizo American country one can find Indian communities which have been integrated into the national society. Communities of specialized artisans—the highland Tarascans in Mexico, the Otavaleños of Ecuador, the peoples of the Mantaro Valley in Peru—are examples of regions of refuge which, having lost their original structure, allow the contemporary observer to study objectively the process of integration (Kaplan 1953; Buitrón 1964; Arguedas 1957).

Of course, this process has not been entirely comprehensive nor has the rate of its development been similar in all countries. In each, one can find communities that have undergone very few changes or where preponderantly colonial forms of organization persist. Elsewhere we have pointed out the extent to which the Indian republics conserved cultural features from the most remote Indian antiquity (Beltrán 1953). Not long ago Pedro Carrasco definitely answered those who assert the Spanish character of the Indian community; he again emphasized the importance of its Indian content.[8] We insist upon the fact that despite the continued persecution of pre-Columbian forms of government by European colonialism—with the same tenacity shown in decapitating the high American cultures—this destruction did not achieve total extinction; however great the deculturation, it never reached absolute proportions. In Mestizo America the indigenous agrarian culture persisted and still does so, along with the political forms that characterize it. Imposition of a political complex such as the Spanish *comuna* was not carried out upon a tabula rasa. The subordinate Indians maintained and defended their traditional political concepts. As a result, the Indian communities today represent different points in the process which fused political forms and concepts of conflicting cultures. Despite centuries of continued contact these cultures have still not achieved the complete and total resolution of their original contradictions.

One of the undoubtable advantages of the ethnohistorical focus comparing historical data with present day facts, is that ethnographic materials gathered from surviving communities shed light upon the interpretation of historical data. Reciprocally, historical data illuminate behavior patterns found in present day institutions, the precise meaning of which is difficult to comprehend without such clarification. Both cultural history and structural ethnography have great difficulty in deciphering, in isolation from one another, the thought underlying the formal aspects of the present day Indian community.

THE TERRITORIAL BASE. The surviving Indian communities can be placed in two separate categories. In the first are the so-called communities of origin, which are called communities in name only, since they maintain a formal political autonomy and thus become small independent republics or minor political cells within the structure of the national state. In the second category are the hacienda communities, characterized by their location in a territorial base no longer belonging to them. The hacienda owner or his representative holds the highest office in the power structure. In the hacienda community the Indians have recognized rights to the land and the hacienda owner has recognized obligations toward the Indians (Urquidi 1962). Obviously the hacienda owner is a substitute for the *cacique* or *curaca* (head man) in his relations with the *acasillados, huasipungueros* or *yanapas*, tenants forming the subject community. In those Mestizo American countries that have experienced effective agrarian redistribution, the hacienda communities have reverted to communities of origin because of restitution to the people of the lands usurped by the hacienda and liberation from servitude.

Early on, the Indian *comuna* was granted a territorial base which generally coincided with the area occupied by the ethnic group at the time of the conquest. Geographical descriptions from the sixteenth century provide information about the jurisdictions of the older Indian dominions and show how those areas served as territorial outlines for the *alcaldías mayores* or *corregimientos* of the colonial era, which in turn became the *municipios* or parishes of the Independence period. In his study of Mesoamerican *municipios*, Sol Tax (1965) points out that they are social and cultural units with a definite type of political organization, which undoubtedly correspond to basic ethnic divisions. Municipal groups may have the same or different languages. In the former case each ethnic group has a dialectical variation; the length of time that the groups have been independent social units or segregated political groups may be determined by the number and quality of important language changes. In addition, the particular mode of dress of each municipal group is one of the most visible symbols of ethnic separation (Drucker 1963).

Ownership of the territory forming the community's material base was given to its members through a grant by the colonial government. Some communities, particularly the more isolated ones or those in regions with extremely hostile geography, have managed to retain ownership of the lands from the time they were granted until the present, but not all were so fortunate. Most lands were invaded by Spanish or criollo settlers who took portions of forests, pastures, waters, or areas appropriate for raising wheat, and thereby reduced the community's resources so much that it was actually pushed to the limits of subsistence. At other times the settlers stripped communities of origin of all their land and reduced them to hacienda communities. In the latter case the *comuneros* retained certain rights to the land, which tied them to it, in exchange for a variety of services, some of which offended the dignity of the individual. Having survived into an era which holds the rights of man in high esteem, these communities and their members have been dramatized and distorted in literary works (Menton 1965).

The community's territory is not uniform, particularly in the mountainous habitat; it extends through various levels with differing resources, which help to maintain its autonomy. For example, the communities surrounding Lake Titicaca use the waters at its shores, where they exploit aquatic flora and fauna, agricultural lands of the nearby plain, and pastures in the mountainous *puna*. The Andean communities' vertical territory is reproduced on a smaller scale in the mountainous Mesoamerican communities; in different parts of their territory these communities can raise the crops of cold and temperate, or temperate and hot lands. In addition to this territorial diversity there are different qualities of soil and varieties of irrigation and water conservation—as when a community's lands form part of river marshes—or there may be an absence of water sources not provided by rain. As might be supposed, the *comuneros'* rights to use of water, land, forest, and pasture vary according to the nature of those resources. Some are used in common and others individually by each family group; consequently they are subject to different political arrangements.

Murra (1959) notes that use of the term *ownership* in reference to the legal condition of Indian communities often leads to a mistaken conception of the relationship of the corporate body to the land. European norms tend to see community members as co-owners of a territorial corporation; this co-ownership entails systematic participation in common political and religious business and each *comunero* appears as the private owner of a piece of cultivated land. Despite the long period of colonial control, the ethnic groups who retained their identity did not conceive of their relationship to the land in Western terms. It was conceived rather as a mystical relationship in which the *comunero* and the land, personalized as supernatural, maintained ties of mutual reciprocity which bound them in an institutionalized series of loyalties, rights, and obligations. Rather than co-owners, members of the corporate community considered themselves holders of rights in common. As coparticipants in a chain of reciprocities they made up the corporate community, partly bound by kinship relationships and partly by their coparticipation in rights and obligations to the land; they formed a territorial clan (Wolf 1955:457).

The area of a *municipio* in Mesoamerica constitutes the material base of an ethnic group forming a corporate community. In the Andean countries, where historical development was different from that of Mesoamerica, the ethnic group was not organized into communities based on the *municipio* or its South American counterpart, the parish or district (Nuñez del Prado 1962). It was fragmented into small communities which consisted of the territory and inhabitants of an *ayllu*, (the equivalent of the Mesoamerican *calpulli*), and which took the name *anejo* or *parcialidad*. Despite this fragmentation, for administrative purposes the parish or district is the unit of republican political organization in the same way as is the *municipio* in Mesoamerica. Districts such as those of Pisac or Chincheros in Peru are composed of a city whose jurisdiction includes a varying number of *ayllu* communities which together form the *llacta* community or pueblo (Ortiz del Prado 1965:113). This latter is what really constitutes the social and cultural unit that defines the ethnic group.

Of course, the consolidation of *anejos, parcialidades* or *parajes* does not take place arbitrarily. It occurs through the principle which Van Zantwijk (1965:195) calls competitive duality, which divides *ayllus* or *calpullis* into two halves or moieties, in institutionalized rivalry. Siverts (1960) calls these *fratrías* in his study of Oxchuc and Rubio Orbe (1956: 302-4), in his monograph on Punyaro, reports the form which that rivalry takes. The moiety containing Punyaro begins a flower war with its opposite, the object of which is possession of a church dedicated to San Juan. The use of offensive arms, except for fists, is not permitted in the fighting, but nonetheless serious injuries are frequently sustained and occasionally cause deaths. Institutionalized rivalry between the two moieties of the *llacta* community lasts only one day, after which there is a return to normal relations between the two opposing *ayllus*.

Ayllus or *calpullis* do not always constitute a compact establishment. Usually they are formed by the union of a varying number of hamlets or lineages, which in turn consist of the congregation of domestic groups or extended families. These domestic groups are the smallest socioeconomic units of the community and consequently the ones which truly possess rights and obligations relating to land, woods, pastures, and water. As may be imagined, those rights and obligations differ for different resources and, in regard to a single resource they also differ according to its nature. Pastures, woods, lake products, and land for swidden agriculture all entail rights and obligations for community members, while irrigated lands, wet lands which are cultivated only occasionally, groves of fruit trees, and cattail or reed swamps may be used by the extended family. There are limitations and conditions imposed on those rights and obligations, including the prohibition against selling land to nonmembers of the community; these hinder the formation of the concept of ownership in terms of Western thought.

COMPLEMENTARY DUALITY. The *geronte* is the eldest or most prominent member of the domestic group and the person representing the group to the outside. He is the one who makes decisions concerning relations with other domestic groups, whether these are related by marriage or simply neighbors. Authority and institutionalized power reside in him. Decisions about the internal governing of the domestic group are made by the eldest and most experienced woman. She is the internal authority, exercising power which operates within the group itself. The hamlet and community follow this pattern, with one body of internal and another of external authorities. In them the offices with greatest responsibility are held by *gerontes* who are married couples and commonly called *principales*.

The complementary duality of internal and external functionaries gives rise to a dual government whose form varies according to regions and countries (Van Zantwijk 1965: 195). In compact communities or ceremonial centers where the ethnic group has managed to persist without admitting foreign enclaves—*mistis*, Ladinos, *cholos* or *revestidos*—there is an internal governing body with a traditional pattern dating from the colonial period. This body has charge of matters arising from relations among community members and also between them and the supernatural world. It relies on general sanction and consensus and its members enjoy the greatest authority, honor, and esteem. The exercise of power in this body confers charisma—a mystic strength or sacred quality which increases with age and the wielding of authority. *Gerontes* who attain the highest offices in the power hierarchy awaken in the community the same ambivalent feelings of loving respect and obsequious fear inspired by supernatural beings. Their power is sometimes so great that it becomes dangerous and forces the community to sacrifice them. Many murders of witches that are reported and punished by national laws are simply the annihilation of *gerontes* whose powers exceed the common man's capacity for obedience and conformity (Siverts 1960).

In these communities external authority resides in the constitutional governing body, as sanctioned by the national society. It links the community formally with the departmental government and thus with the democratic institutions of the republic. This external government is the only one legally recognized and entrusted with relations between the community and outsiders. In general, external offices do not confer worth or prestige. Those who hold them are often thought to be the highest authorities of the ethnic group, but in reality they are subordinate to the *gerontes* in the internal government. The external government is made up of young men beginning their careers in the political hierarchy. Adequate performance of their jobs opens the doors for them to the internal governing body.

In compact communities where one part of the town is occupied by Indians and the other by non-Indians, the constitutional government is commonly in the hands of the latter. The Indians retain the internal governing body sub rosa, and have one of their own members among the external authorities in the constitutional government, usually holding a minor cargo such as *alcalde segundo* or *regidor*. The fact that this representation exists at all means that the person who holds it has sufficient powers to make decisions affecting the ethnic group. This role, it may be surmised, is one of the most difficult and thankless, since on the one hand its holder must transmit to the internal government of the community decisions of the national government which must be carried out, and on the other hand he must come forward and contradict those decisions when they affect community interests (Wisdom 1961:267). In ceremonial centers with a Ladino, *misti* or *cholo* enclave, when there is an Indian representative in the constitutional government he constitutes the external government of the community. The internal government functions separately in the ceremonial center proper or is scattered through the *parajes, anejos* or *parcialidades*. Whatever the situation—it goes without saying that they are many and varied—there is always a complementary duality of governments. This consists of the internal body, respected without question, and the external, with little prestige or authority, which is in contact with the Ladino society. Despite the obvious weakness of the external government, which is explained by its liaison function, it persists when the community becomes disorganized. That disorganization signifies a rearrangement of political relations with the national society and in the process the external authority is of greatest importance. An index of the underlying tendency to defy the *gerontes* is the seizure of power by young men during reorganizations of Indian communities undergoing the impact of messianic or revolutionary movements.

Another complementary duality which is important in the Indian political organization juxtaposes civil and ceremonial functions. This duality, unlike the above, is not native in origin, but appears rather to have its roots in the Greek dichotomy separating the body from the soul, the natural from the preternatural, that which is Caesar's from that which is God's. The community or republic was conceived by Spanish colonialism as an institution to deal with secular means of exploiting the Indians. The Spaniards soon had to accept that this institution was tied to another organism, partly derived from the religious brotherhoods or *cofradías*, whose goal was dealing with the supernatural (Menciás 1962:67). The Indians tolerated this complementary duality; in their world view the secular and sacred spheres overlapped without any dividing line. The secular governing body fulfills ceremonial functions and in turn the religious governing body exercises civil functions. On occasions it is difficult to determine whether a *geronte* is holding a civil or a religious cargo. For the most part it is the investigator who places the functionary in one or another category, using as evidence the functionary's title or the preponderant nature of his functions.

Furthermore, during the course of his political career the office holder passes from a preponderantly religious cargo to one that is mainly civil, both within the prestige scale of the formally dual hierarchy. In reality, it is the sacred cargos which bestow prestige and authority in accordance with the enormous effort in goods and services required by them. Civic cargos would appear to function as pauses or rests for the *comunero* on his way to the acquisition of power because of the low cost and effort required for them. The relative importance of the two governing bodies can be measured by observing them at the critical point of the community's disorganization prior to its reintegration into the national society. It is the religious body which then persists with unexpected tenacity, obstinately resisting absorption into the national church.

THE HIERARCHICAL SCALE. When sketching the model of the Indian community's political structure, we should not lose sight of the fact that it represents only an ideal construction which does not entirely apply to a concrete community. Numerous factors, such as the presence of Ladino or *cholo* enclaves, demographic density, technological levels, the amount and kinds of specializations, the relative economic importance of the market sphere with respect to the subsistence and prestige spheres, and the degree and extent to which domination mechanisms operate to maintain segregation, among others, all introduce considerable variation. Consequently the model can include only the significant features which are found most frequently.

Members of an Indian community organize their public life around a series of cargos on a scale which forms the power hierarchy. Upon attaining adulthood, at marriage, all community members acquire the right and obligation to take their place in the power hierarchy. Only the physically or mentally incapacitated, outsiders living in the community, and members who migrate to the plantations to obtain a salary, are excluded from participation. This comprehensive inclusion is one of the most constant features of the political structure of the Indian community. Nash (1956) considers it so significant that, as we have pointed out already, he assigns it the cardinal importance which kinship relations or the system of social classes have in other human groups.

Viewed by members of the community, the hierarchy is the instrument by which the individual, representing a nuclear or extended family, a lineage or fratria, is obliged to lend his services to the community and to redistribute the surplus capital goods he may have accumulated during the active years of his life. Each *comunero*, without exception, fills a cargo which is remunerative not in profits but in honor and esteem. This means that for the services he renders the community, the cargo holder is not compensated in cash or money but rather in the respect and esteem that rebound to him and to the members of his family, lineage, or barrio.

The newly married man enters the hierarchy at an early age and begins his apprenticeship with the more modest roles, those lowest in the civil or ceremonial government and least important in the internal and external governing bodies. After a year he becomes eligible for election to the next highest cargo; this election actually occurs after a varying period of rest and renovation of strength. Thus, through the years he climbs higher and higher in the power scale, alternating religious and secular functions, dealing with his own people and with outsiders. By fulfilling a cargo, the person who holds it becomes a *pasado* and as such he retains all the prestige and power of the position he achieved. Holding the highest positions bestows the rank of principal, elder, or *geronte*, and with it the power and charisma that accompany the exercise of authority.

The number of cargos and their position on the hierarchical scale is occasionally reduced to only a few, but at other times it expands, forming voluminous bodies of functionaries. These appear excessive for the small amount of public business if measured by the economizing criteria of industrial culture. Cargos are differentiated between small and large, the former situated at the lower rungs of the scale and the latter at higher ones. In some communities these levels are paralleled or replaced by a system of age grades. Each age group, level or ranking has definite functions in civil and ceremonial life and each occupies separate seats in town meetings or at the ceremonies of the brotherhoods.[9]

Cargos in the power hierarchy are held at a certain cost. Minor posts, which include the performance of tasks with little prestige such as carrying messages, cleaning the church or municipal building, and maintaining order as the town's police force, entail small expenditures for the cargo holder and his family. Sometimes the costs are merely the simple maintenance of the aspiring *geronte* during the year of his sojourn in the ceremonial center. On the other hand, such cargos as *prioste, mayordomo, pasón*, and *fiscal* impose the expenditure of large sums of goods and services, requiring the family to go into debt or to patiently accumulate food, drink, and money for redistribution in the ceremonial festivities. The ecclesiastic fees charged by the priest for celebrating the mass or blessing the oath of office or assumption of a cargo, the cost of candles and candlesticks, flowers and decorations, hiring musicians, firecrackers and rockets, and the price of the banquet and ceremonial drinking all increase in proportion to the rank assumed. Therefore, not all *comuneros* can reach the highest ranks and there is great reluctance to accept cargos which demand enormous sacrifices by the domestic group. Only social pressure and the compensation in honor and power make it possible for some persons to aspire to and hold the highest rungs of the ladder.

The significant features of the political structure of the Indian community make it different from the national society. The attainment of a rank, especially of a high rank, gives magico-religious knowledge, charisma, and power to the holder, to be used in the service and protection of the community. In the world view of the Indian, supernatural power is power by title, the source from which other forms of power emanate. The idea of the cargo, literally, as a burden or weight rather than a sinecure that can be used for personal profit and protection, is congruent with the ideology of the community. The cargo a person holds is an unmistakable index of the power available to him; the authority which he acquires and augments is derived from the demonstration of that power. Through adequately discharging his role the cargo holder has made patent the power invested in him; this is demonstrated by the prosperous and felicitous protection he has given the community in fulfilling his responsibilities.

The *geronte* possesses a mystic force which cannot be revoked once bestowed. It is not conferred with the rank because it is independent of the cargo. Thus the *geronte* is immune to jealousy, evil, and witchcraft; only his physical death, violent or natural, is capable of destroying the essence of the power. Keeping in mind the Indian's concept of power, there is no doubt that the social world in which he lives and of which he forms an inseparable part is fundamentally different from that in which the Ladino and *cholo* live. It is easily seen that the divergence is not a question of degree in the exercise of power, but of significant differences in the power itself.

The Indian community is a moral universe limited by the small number of its members and the boundaries of its territory. The features of the power structure in such circumstances enable the political hierarchy to be the only structure able to organize relationships among the community members themselves, between them and outsiders and between them and supernatural beings, native as well as foreign. Both the power itself and those who hold it are very charismatic; this is rarely seen among Ladinos and *cholos*. The Indian government is essentially sacred and, as such, offers no room for differing opinions and judgments. Those holding a cargo rely on absolute acceptance by the lineage, barrio, and town; they symbolize the unity and general consensus of all members of the corporate group.

Oriented this way, the Indian community's essence and form contrast with those of the national society. In the latter, the social structure of classes leads inescapably to conflict; consequently, the divergent opinions and judgments, confrontations, and disagreements among pressure groups in their struggle for power form the very marrow of the system. In the Indian community, on the contrary, consensus is the particular attribute which determines the nature of political relations. In addition, it is the only one permitted; the sacred nature of power would lose all meaning if threatened by dissension. However, the fact that harmony, unity of thought and of feeling constitute the social attitude of the Indian community in its internal affairs does not mean that consensus rules its relations with the caste structured regional society—and through it with the national society. When we analyze the external ties of the regional equation we shall clearly see that the Indo-Ladino situation is ruled by continuous conflict constantly fed by the process of domination.

The lack of discrepancies in the functioning of the Indian hierarchy could be interpreted romantically as expressing conformity and voluntary acceptance of the traditional forms of behavior without recourse to physical or moral coercion. We would thus be led to idealize the community in the same way as did the social reformers in Mestizo America who pioneered in the formulation of a revolutionary Indian policy. The discrepancies are not visible because consensus occurs as a process in which the feelings and opinions of the majority concur in handling social problems. In the Indian community the hierarchy acts as a single political party in which members argue among themselves over the rules which the group should follow as a unit (in the community as in a party, members include all adults of the parochial or national society, respectively). When all views are heard, the resulting consensus is general, unvarying, and firm, that is, sacred.

Furthermore, the political structure of the community is not a gerontocracy, as is often thought. Although the concept of authority parallels age in the cargo system as in that of kinship, those who hold power do not achieve and keep it by virtue of age but because of the knowledge and experience acquired in service to the community, and through contact with outsiders and supernatural beings. Young people should respect their elders but they are not excluded from the hierarchy. They form an integral part of it, participate in its important functions, and are heard and taken into account in the assemblies called to make decisions affecting the group. In truth, the *gerontes* rarely make administrative or ceremonial decisions without consulting the community. As stated, abuse of their power puts them in danger of their lives.

If we follow Lipset[10] and understand democracy to be a political system which provides institutionalized opportunities for change of governmental leaders as well as a social mechanism permitting the majority of the population to influence the most important decisions through elections of candidates for political office, the Indian community should be classified as a democracy in terms of its internal government. However, to do so would ascribe to it a character which it does not have. The concept of democracy has features that are foreign to the parochial communities with agrarian cultures and subsistence economies, where kinship relations are essential and the religious view of the world prevails over the rational. An examination of the functions of government and its ties with the national society will permit us to discover differences, sometimes subtle ones, that prevent the indiscriminate application of Western concepts to the regions of refuge.

NOTES

1. Nash (1957:826) states: "That part of the population which carries the national variety of culture is in fact the national society; it is scattered throughout the national territory; it is the link between the nation and other nations in the world and is the segment of the population in whom political control is vested and within which political control is contested. It is also that part of the population whose economic decisions have national repercussions."

2. Tax proposed the term non-national state but he specifically differentiated it from the multinational state (1946:338). Nash (1956), continuing with the term multiple society, implies the existence of a multinationed society. In Blanksten's commentary on Nash's presentation in the Seminar, this is how he understands it when he says: "In essence, Guatemala is, as the author has said, a non-national or multinational state" (1956:156).

3. Ovando, taking the position of the Bolivian Communist Party, states: "A scientific division of the Bolivian population into nations, nationalities, tribes, and ethnographic groups, is essential in order to outline a solution for the national-colonial problem in our country. . . . From the study of the Bolivian population we have made in this chapter, it can be concluded that we have a special demographic structure, with an intricate human problem, that Bolivia is not a national state using the historico-economic concept of nation after all. Rather it is a complex state with, from the national point of view, a variegated population, a state composed of ethnographic groups, tribes, nationalities and a nation. In sum, a state composed of nationalities, or, more appropriately, a multi-national state" (1961:25).

4. Adams (1962:409) asserts: "In the political sociology of Latin America there has developed over the past fifty years a myth about the community. Although it appears in various guises, it can be identified by a few salient features. The community, says the myth, is a natural grouping that has special characteristics leading to its perpetuation in the face of threats from the outside. This integral unity lies in the social relationships of which the community is composed. Most classically the indigenous community of Latin America is posed as the typical community of this kind. The relationships here are seen to be direct descendants of pre-Colombian relationships. Because it has survived so long, the indigenous community is said to be eternal. The myth peeks out of this argument when it is added that great steps must be taken to preserve these communities. Why, we ask, should the preservation of the eternal be so serious a problem?"

5. García (1948:269) adds: "The community is not really a way of ordering the work of society, nor a system for using the community's energies, but a regime of negative defenses. Economically, it impedes the loss of communal land; fiscally, the payment of ordinary taxes; demographically, the dispersion of related families; and culturally, the disappearance of

the languages, of certain traditions and legends given their expressive value by these languages, and of certain medico-sanitary practices."

6. Wolf states with fairness: "Nobles who remained in the villages, on the other hand, were reduced by loss of wealth and standing to the position of their Indian fellow citizens. Because his person was still suffused with the magic of past power, a former priest or local chieftain here and there assumed a post in a local community, but he soon lost the ability to command tribute or labor-power to which his ancestors had been accustomed. The new Indian communities were communities of the poor, too overburdened to sustain a class that had lost its function" (1959:213).

7. Dobyns (1964:97) concludes his magnificent research on Peruvian communities with the following paragraph: "Much that has previously been written about Indigenous Communities in Peru has been romantic rather than scientific, in its idealization of Community life. Much that has been written reflects deduction from political ideology rather than synthesis of observations of real Community behavior. Even scientific studies of particular Indigenous Communities have had to bear too heavy a burden of extrapolation for lack of systematic knowledge of the whole universe of Communities."

8. Carrasco (1961:485) says: "The purpose of this paper is to discuss the pre-Spanish background of this ladder system, and to outline its later development as a consequence of the Spanish conquest. The positions in the modern civil-religious hierarchy are part both of the municipal system of town government introduced in the early colonial period and of the local organization of the folk Catholic cult. Yearly terms of office were also part of the Spanish regulations and there are many other similarities between the modern Indian village organization and the Spanish municipal system (Font 1952). Consequently it could be assumed that the modern civil-religious hierarchy was basically of Spanish origin. Without denying the undoubtable Spanish contribution to its development, it is the point of this paper to stress its pre-Spanish antecedents and to show how they shaped the introduction of the Spanish municipal organization under the conditions of Colonial rule."

9. Weitlander & Hoogshagen (1960:209) consider the system of age grades to be: "an archaic form of social organization, as indicated by its existence among primitive groups from the northern and southern parts of the continent, and from other parts of the world."

10. Lipset (1963:25) declares: "Democracy may be defined as a complex society with a political system which provides regular constitutional opportunities for the change of governmental leaders and a social mechanism which permits the largest possible part of the population to influence the most important decisions by means of election among contenders for political office."

Chapter 10

POLITICAL FUNCTIONS AND CONNECTIONS

The Functions of Power

THE SYSTEM of cargos which creates the power structure in indigenous communities is essential to the existence and continuity of the traditional culture. Without it the segregation that keeps Indian and Ladino societies apart disappears. This is due to the fact that the power hierarchy performs functions which are highly integrative and which, directly or indirectly, tend to maintain the cohesion of the group and to protect it from outside contacts and their disorganizing effects.

The functions of power in indigenous governments are varied. Some provide the *comuneros* with membership or the *carta de naturaleza* that identifies them as Indians and binds them to traditional ideas and behavior patterns in their daily lives. Others offer them participation in the use of resources and arrange the reciprocal labor patterns and redistribution of surpluses to which they are obligated, so that social equilibrium will lessen the serious inequalities that generate envy and conflict. Still other functions include serving as intermediaries between the group and outsiders—the dominant Ladinos—or between the group and imperceptible supernatural beings. Most of the latter are benevolent but others rigorously punish those people who stray from the established norms. One last function, equally important, is social control, including moral and physical coercion to make the Indians conform to the patterns of behavior that have prevailed in the community since ancient times.

We shall examine these functions in detail. However, in isolating them to analyze and understand them better we must not lose sight of the fact that they never act as entities or independent mechanisms. Rather, they act together as inextricably interwoven elements, all of which join to further the community's social integration.

(1) DEFINITION OF MEMBERSHIP. It has already been pointed out that one of the most important features of the politico-religious structure of the community is its comprehensive character. All the adult members of the town or group, as active participants or *pasados* are an integral part of the power hierarchy. Consequently, a person is a *comunero* only to the extent that he has the right to participate and actually does participate in the government of the group. Residence is not enough; the groups of Ladinos or *mistis* who settle permanently in the municipal center are considered foreign enclaves. Nor is marriage with a group member sufficient if the familial relationship does not lead to the offer and acceptance of a cargo in the hierarchy. This rarely happens since the community tends to be strictly endogamous.

The real or potential possession of a cargo entails the obligation to uphold the symbols and values uniting the ethnic group. The community member, by the mere fact of forming part of the power hierarchy, is bound to practice and strengthen traditional ideas and action patterns. Anyone who refuses to assume cargos incurs the disdain of his relatives and friends. He is the butt of ridicule because a man is not a real man until he holds a *cargo*.[1] Those who persistently decline are expelled from the town or continue to reside in it as marginal men without recognized citizenship, as outcasts who prefer Ladino ways of life to their own. When they abandon participation in their group of origin, these outcasts become *revestidos* or *cholos*. Their number increases with the increase in anomie of the community. As has been mentioned, the political structure functions as an integrating force giving cohesion to the group, defining the boundaries of the community and membership within it.

(2) ALLOCATION OF RESOURCES. The indigenous community, composed of people and land, is in a constant process of regeneration. Some of its members die; others replace them when at marriage they reach adulthood and acquire rights over man, the

land, and its resources. For the most part these resources are neither unlimited nor of equal quantity and quality throughout the habitat at the group's disposal. Lands under cultivation must rest, irrigation waters require effective use, pasture lands must be rotated, and the endless variety of other products supplied by the environment require orderly exploitation so that each and every one of the community members may participate equally.

The allocation of these resources to heads of nuclear or extended families is a principal job of the hierarchy. Every year the *curaca* in some cases, the internal governing body and its *gerontes* in others, takes charge of the reallocation of resources–in particular of land, the resource par excellence–among group members. Young men replacing older members as well as the older members take part in the institutionalized distribution of cultivated lands, pastures and water, because contrary to what is often assumed, reallocation is not made arbitrarily. The *cacique* or the *gerontes*, who act as the responsible parties for the distribution, find themselves limited in their decisions by the norms transmitted by tradition and by the social pressures of the moment.

The reallocation of lands carries much symbolism and is egalitarian only in theory. The cultivated lands traditionally exploited by families and the rights which those families hold over permanent resources are confirmed year after year for the possessors and their heirs so that, for practical purposes, they become private property.[2] (Matos March 1965). On the other hand, vacant or resting lands, suitable for swidden or any other kind of seasonal agriculture, are distributed effectively among the young men beginning membership in the community. These are the lands called *tlacolol* in Mesoamerica because they are located on mountain slopes. The use of the most primitive methods of cultivation are of decisive influence in the classification of a resource as qualifying for annual reallocation (Lewis 1949).

In some Andean towns near Cuzco, the reallocation of resources retains strong ancient characteristics, pre-Columbian as well as colonial. Núñez del Prado informs us that in such towns, on one day every year, the *curaca*, the *comuneros*, and a large, festive group of people accompanying them make a ceremonial tour through the fields. The owners of parcels then take possession of the land by performing actions and making statements with a medieval ring; they peruse the boundaries, call out, throw rocks, and shoo everyone away. The ceremony of possession is accompanied, like all important Indian events, by the excessive output of food, liquor, and other goods. But the important fact is that possession takes place formally, despite the fact that the *comunero* and his family are already in possession of the parcel, and despite the fact that the land, in those towns, is regarded as merchandise, and therefore may be sold to outsiders (Núñez del Prado 1949).[2] As noted, the introduction of new concepts regarding property has not hindered the community from strongly guarding its function of resource allocation.

(3) ORGANIZATION OF RECIPROCAL LABOR The community government is the center through which its members are bound in a single social structure. The hierarchy not only knows the size and boundaries of the cultivated lands of each family, extended family or lineage, of each neighborhood, and of the community as a whole; it also maintains a minutely detailed register of work on the lands. For the Indian, land is not conceived of separately from the work which it requires. That work is based on a carefully arranged network of reciprocal labor patterns among members of the extended family, and the organization of such reciprocities is the duty of the *gerontes*.

The hierarchy's responsibility in this respect is greater when the work is performed on lands exploited communally, such as the school parcel, and when its products are intended for the general welfare, as with goods from the *mayordomías'* fields. Reciprocal work, or *mano vuelta*, characteristic at the family level, becomes cooperative work, in *tequio*, or *minga*, at the level of the neighborhood or town.[3] Every community member reserves a varying, but always high, number of working days to donate to the community for the collective good; he bestows this contribution, tribute or task in return for the services he receives. Instead of contributing money, which is scarce in a subsistence economy, he gives time and labor.

The construction of a road, a bridge, or a school, the cleaning, decorating and repairing of the church, the transportation of materials and other works and municipal services are done by community members through the *tequio* or *minga*. The *gerontes* take charge of planning, organizing and implementing communal work. All families are classified by the ages of their members, in accordance with the rank they have attained in the power scale, and in conformance with the prestige, esteem and experience acquired through services lent to the community. In fulfillment of duties imposed by group membership the *comuneros* answer the *gerontes'* call to participate in the *minga*.

Cooperative work, as a form of reciprocal work, has the characteristics of a social event where waste is fully visible. The *tequio* or minga is invariably accompanied by the eating of ceremonial foods, the abundant flow of chicha or other distilled or fermented drink, the *coqueo* in the Peruvian Highlands, enlivened with popular melodies. Refusal to participate in the *minga*—caused by factionalism within the community or by the abuse of community consensus by development programs operating in good or bad faith—brings with it loss of prestige, physical punishment, and in extreme cases, expulsion of the rebels from the communal territory. (Bernal Villa 1954). Through such procedures the internal government of the community reinforces its role as organizer of reciprocal labor, and makes the members of the group conform to the traditional norms that give it cohesion, balance, and equality.

(4) REDISTRIBUTION OF SURPLUSES. The community has three principal means of fulfilling ceremonial and administrative needs: (1) through exploitation of lands and resources set aside for the collective benefit; (2) through the imposition of a head tax which compels each member of the group to make a contribution in goods or money; and (3) through an offer by the potential cargo holder of his own family goods when he becomes the holder of the cargo in question (Carrasco 1961). This last procedure was important during the colonial period and is more so today.[4] The sums obtained by the hierarchy through head taxes or through the cooperative exploitation of resources are never comparable with the astonishingly large quantities of goods and services which the cargo holders—backbone of the community—contribute to the maintenance and continuance of the group's civic and religious life. Without that contribution the community could not subsist as a separate entity.

In studying the economic structure of the indigenous community we have been able to demonstrate the importance of the integrating principles of reciprocity and redistribution, as mechanisms that contribute significantly to it. Those principles regulate the functions of reciprocity and redistribution of indigenous governments, and differentiate the latter from modern forms of political organization. Of the two principles, redistribution is the one which is most explicitly different from those to which we are accustomed, and which best defines the character of the indigenous government and its corresponding ideology. Contrary to what happens at the national level, power is acquired in ways which tend to equalize the difference in possession of capital goods.

In effect, we have already pointed out that the obligation to form part of the power hierarchy includes each and every member of the group proper. Such participation is not free; it entails a price that increases as one advances to more important offices in the ceremonial life of the community, which means in the last analysis that a community member must have sufficient capital goods to fulfill the duties of the cargos. A self-contained community with a subsistence economy, located in a hostile geographical area, depending on traditional technology which makes exclusive use of biological energy in exploiting and transporting its resources, necessarily has very low productivity and few possibilities for raising cash harvests that might allow it a capacity for profit (Wolf 1951). The quantity of goods that the person can buy in the exterior and that the community consumes is very limited. In spite of the obvious limitations, the ceremonial calendar shows a growing number of fixed and movable dates allotted for conspicuous consumption and institutionalized waste.

The community, of course, is not a tabula rasa in which all extended families have equal incomes at their disposal. In conformity with the prevailing standards of the community there are the rich and the poor; in the Lake Titicaca area the former are called *camiris*. Raúl Galdo informs us that the term is applied to those who possess two or three hectares of agricultural land, two or three pair of oxen, and more ewes than the average owned in the community. It is noted that the economic distance separating rich families from poor ones, although not great, is enough to permit some of them to ascend the steps of the hierarchy more rapidly and reach the higher and more burdensome ranks. The *camiris* reach the rank of *gerontes* at an early age, while the poor advance slowly and become *gerontes* only when they are old men. To have resources, acquired by inheritance or by one's own efforts, is an advantage in the struggle for prestige and power. Nonetheless it is not wealth which determines social position but rather the consumption and institutionalized waste of such wealth. Families with more than the average amount of lands and livestock reach the rank of fame of *camiris*, but if family members avoid redistribution of their surpluses they are badly thought of and their prestige and social positions are low. In fact, as Cancian notes, it is precisely when it is squandering its wealth that a family makes its riches obvious through the adequate fulfillment of an office (Galdo 1962).[5] Economic rank is different and less important than social rank because the community structure places an unusual value on levels of status. The assumption of a cargo reflects the economic capacity of the *comunero*, but does not determine his economic rank.

In the hierarchical system created by the indigenous community, prestige and power are acquired by conspicuous consumption and institutionalized waste. To acquire prestige and power the indigenous family binds itself throughout life to a constant and laborious accumulation of surpluses beyond the bare necessities of subsistence, in order to distribute those surpluses through the holding of cargos. During the accumulation process, the family and its members do not limit themselves to exploiting their material resources, but also exploit their own human resources. They take advantage of the opportunities for contact offered by the money economy of the Ladino world with which they are in touch. Men rent their labor to the plantations and their wives go to work in the central city, trying thus to acquire the amount of hard cash necessary to assume a cargo. The community has conditioned in its members a compulsive attitude toward the saving of goods that will be utilized, certainly not in the formation of capital, but in conspicuous consumption. In this way the *merchandising libido* of some Indians can be explained; it makes them appear, incorrectly, to be individualists and penny capitalists (Cancian 1965:Chapter XII).

Scholars who have taken special interest in the analysis of the ceremonial aspects of indigenous cultures have estimated the cost involved in the fulfillment of a cargo in some communities, the amount of goods consumed during the ceremonial calendar, and the sources on which the *cargueros* draw to pay their obligations. The figures offered are truly enormous, and inexplicable in a subsistence economy. Hector Martínez, in analyzing the most important *mayordomías* in Vicos, a hacienda community, was able to discover that the principle source of income comes from livestock, which for the cargo holder often means doing without work animals. Sale of agricultural products, money-lending among families and work on the coastal haciendas as *enganchados* (debt laborers) are other methods of making money to which Vicosinos turn (Tax 1964).[6] The effort made is so great, the expenses to which they are obligated so disproportionate to average earnings, and the debts contracted so much greater than the capacity to pay, that the assumption of a cargo not only exhausts family surpluses but also ties up future surpluses so that *pasados* can no longer continue in the competition for prestige and power. The pauses or periods of rest between cargos increase and many people die before reaching the highest steps in the hierarchy. Only a few families are capable of staying in the race until the end.

The arguments presented up to now seem to demonstrate conclusively the operation of the redistributive principle in Indian economies which forms the axis of the prestige sphere. As part of the political structure the redistributive function acts as a mechanism for converting economic surplus into social position. It constitutes an institutionalized method of controlling family incomes, stipulates the rules by which the family may improve its public image, impedes the accumulation of goods to be used in conformity with capitalist models, and thus prevents the formation of interest groups and social classes (Martínez 1959; Vázquez 1965:414).

The redistributive function acts as a leveling mechanism by channeling the use of surpluses according to socially controlled patterns of ostentation. It forces families to consume their resources and incomes in ceremonial acts that benefit the collectivity and in doing so it removes any possibility a family might have to accumulate money or property for capital formation. Wealth, whether inherited or acquired, should be transformed into prestige through redistribution. The families who squander the most, who most generously give away whatever they possess, thereby demonstrate their moral worth and are recognized as estimable. They are greeted deferentially, given distinguished treatment, their valuable advice is sought, and they are accorded the endless series of considerations that make up the privileges of honor. The redistributive function, according to Nash, is an effective instrument for maintaining a socially homogeneous community and marks precisely and clearly the approved routes and methods for acquiring respect and political wisdom. The consumption of large quantities of goods and services in the cargo system, especially by rich people or *camiris*, considerably reduces the envy arising from unequal possession of resources. The cargo system effectively soothes this envy, allowing and even demanding that the rich contribute more in exchange for prestige and social esteem (Nash 1956).

The redistributive function, in the same way as the system of reciprocities, is an integrating force in the community. Cancian notes that the families which spend the enormous sums required to assume cargos must feel sure before doing so that their generous spending will receive an adequate compensation in respect, consideration, and honor. As the torment of social pressure upon them increases and is more continuous, it serves to gauge the recognition that will be accorded them by the community. Once the first investment is made, the debts contracted in money or reciprocal labor and the family's own work and goods consumed in the task are important factors in supporting the norms of extravagance that characterize the community. Not to support them would undermine the family's own investment, and to enter the Ladino world would mean losing them altogether.[7]

(5) SOCIAL RECREATION. In indigenous communities with an agrarian culture and incipient technology, the specialization of functions and institutions is far from achieving the sharpness and depth that it has in the context of modern civilization. In these communities there is no system of ideas and action patterns directed precisely at promoting recreation, pleasure, or esthetic emotions for their own sake. Recreation is implicit in a fiesta, in music, in dance, in the relaxation of eating and getting drunk together; it is secondary to the specific functions of the magico-religious or profane ceremonies.

The assumption of a cargo, the oath sworn upon assuming it, the discharge and exercise of authority, the transfer of its charismatic essence to the hands of new functionaries, are always accompanied by ostentatious displays dramatizing the institutionalization of power. These displays make their point through the exhibition of sumptuous garments, masks and jewels, a poem or myth told in oratory or flowery language, the dance that tirelessly repeats traditional movements and melodies, the explosion of fireworks, and many more activities of amusement and pleasure.

In such communities the recreational function of the governmental body is often the only one that gives recreation and amusement to the people and in doing so, provides them with effective psychological mechanisms for resolving the tensions arising from the competition for power. Also, fiestas and ceremonies attract to the civic-ceremonial center, the seat of authority, a large and enthusiastic group of families who live near each other or are related by marriage. They are gathered together repeatedly by the ritual calendar and put into contact and close communication; thus the scattered population is brought together from their hamlets and homesteads. They are bound by their general participation in doing things together, talking together and eating and drinking together to maintain the group's cohesion and the continuity of its behavioral patterns.

(6) RELATIONS WITH THE OUTSIDE WORLD. Eric Wolf (1951) calls the Mesoamerican indigenous community a closed community because it constitutes an endogamous human group, culturally, economically, and socially closed in its relations with the outside world. To avoid contact with the exterior the community creates a body of intermediaries, elected from among its younger members, on whose shoulders it has put the responsibility of severely restricting communication with outsiders. National and regional agents and institutions with which the community is in contact are considered outsiders, as are local agents and institutions that govern the life of neighboring communities also subject to the disintegrating action of the process of domination (Cancian 1965).

Formally, members of the indigenous community enjoy the general rights and obligations of citizens; in fact, they enter into direct correspondence with the sources of regional or national power infrequently. Orders, requests, and demands imposed by outside authorities arrive through a body of intermediaries. This body acts as a shock absorber which shields the Indians from contact with supralocal powers and structures. Crimes involving national sanctions are rarely made known to the judicial bodies with general jurisdiction and, excepting homicides and excesses endangering the public security, the community avoids as far as possible having its members judged and punished according to norms and procedures that are not its own.

Through such means, that part of the government that we call the external body becomes a liaison between local and outside institutions with which community members must deal. The role played by this body is functionally ambivalent. On the one hand, it facilitates contact between the local and national society. Measures imparted by the latter are accepted or rejected by the entire body of the local group. The external body transmits to the internal governing body the requirements placed on the community by the supralocal authority and it is this internal body that evaluates the appropriateness of accepting or refusing those demands and, consequently, which acts.

When the national political parties—in particular official parties—need to mobilize political support in favor of their candidates, the liaison afforded them by the external body lets them avoid burdensome intercourse with and propagandizing of populations that speak only a native language, are illiterate, and have no party organization. A discussion of the problem with the external body of the hierarchy is sufficient for the community—operating as a pressure group—to proceed as a single man and for its members to turn out unanimously, men, women, and children, at the election polls, in political demonstrations, and at meetings. In hacienda communities the *gamonal* substitutes for the external government and acts as intermediary between the Indian serfs and the nation. In such situations the *hacendado* is the person who directs the community's vote and its unanimous political participation in the way desired by the pressure group, of which he is part (Wolf 1951, 1966).

The intermediary role, on the other hand, has a contradictory aspect. It hinders the nation and its institutions from dealing individually with the Indians because it discourages the building of bonds between the latter and the national parties. Contact, as noted, facilitates the community's inclusion in the electoral lists and makes it possible for the official party to count on a unanimous vote in its favor. But at the same time it prevents the effective political integration of the Indians, since the nature and orientation of power as consensus obstructs the formation of factions which eventually could affiliate with competing political parties. When the nation is in a position to put aside the intermediating hierarchy and enter into direct contact with members of the ethnic group, the latter will no longer constitute a native community, sociologically speaking, and will become truly integrated into national society and political life.

(7) CONTACT WITH THE SPIRITUAL WORLD. The community's relations with spirits take place through its internal government; the religious functionaries of that government, besides dispensing justice, preside on ceremonial occasions as a sacerdotal body. They care for the church with its Catholic saints and for the other places—scattered in caves, lakes, and mountains—traditionally considered sacred because of the power of native spirits which has been manifested in them. They support and preside at the cults of the ritual calendar; they organize the saints' fiestas and particularly the one dedicated to the town's patron saint, ruler of their world, and protector of the community.

The ritual function of this body is important because it dramatizes the basic values that influence the decision-making process.[8] It is accepted as a proven fact, needing no demonstration, that the older and more experienced religious functionaries—the *gerontes*—are the only men who truly know the rites and the appropriate times when they should be performed, as well as the amount and kind of offerings with which the gods should be propitiated, in payment or reciprocal labor, for the goods which they must apportion to the community. They are the ones who decide the dates when the fields are plowed, sown and harvested, the kind of crop rotation required by the soil, and the magico-religious formulas and procedures which must be practiced for the harvest to render the desired fruit.

When a disaster threatens the life of the group the governmental body formed by the *gerontes* takes charge of protecting the town. The community trusts in the potency of the sacred power given to the functionaries by the spirits with whom they are in communication. In reality the religious government has the most influence and authority in the indigenous community but it does not constitute a theocracy, as is sometimes claimed. The *gerontes* do not come from a caste within the ethnic group. They are heads of extended families, lineages or neighborhoods, who leave their ordinary tasks for a specified time to dedicate their experience and power to the good of the community.

Religion is not a private business nor the exclusive concern of one lineage or caste; neither is it a direct relationship between the worshiper and the god. It is a matter concerning the collectivity, and the *gerontes*—governmental functionaries specializing in dealing with the spirits—are the only men gifted with the necessary charisma to maintain a constant conversation with the sacred elements. The nonindividual character of worship in indigenous religions, for Nash, arises from the fact that it is the *gerontes* and not the people of the community whose function it is to maintain and uphold religious worship (Siverts 1960). In the indigenous community the power structure acts as an intermediary between gods and men. It joins the latter with the spirits, but at the same time it removes them from the dangers involved in contact with the sacred.

The ritual role of the *gerontes*, in accordance with their other features, has been a powerful brake on the ecumenical tendencies of the Protestant and Catholic churches. National as well as regional ecclesiastical authorities and those in ceremonial centers or in the small towns which are community capitals have no direct or personal contact with the community members; contact is made through the hierarchy. It is the religious functionaries who, on taking a cargo, celebrating a ritual, or preparing a fiesta for the patron saint, initiate conversations with the church representative and cover the ecclesiastical costs in kind or money, but the parish priest or the protestant minister relates with difficulty to the Indians as persons or as individual entities.

The hierarchy stands as intermediary between the world view of the indigenous community—which syncretizes pre-Columbian religious concepts and practices with Christian-colonial ideas and action patterns—and that held by Catholic or Protestant dogma. The parish priest hears the oath of office of *priostes, alféreces, mayordomos, pasiones* and other functionaries of the civic-religious hierarchy; in some Andean countries apparently it is he who chooses, names, and directs them according to his own fancy and will. In reality—perhaps without full consciousness of the fact—he is obliged to use them as intermediaries between his parishioners and the deity. The *mayordomías, priostazgos, cofradías* and other brotherhoods of the Indian communities translate and reinterpret religious mandates according to traditional meanings.

The religious hierarchy, as noted by Nash (1956), both joins and separates the community and the church. It gives local significance to the symbols of the faith, and the organisms and functionaries that make up the body of *gerontes* are the true center of the sacred organization, rather than the priest and his church. Church and state in Mestizo-American countries confront a very similar dilemma. To be a truly national church or state they must include the indigenous population within their respective structures, and they cannot achieve this as long as they need to use the hierarchy as an intermediary. Only when they are capable of establishing direct political or religious ties with the community members will the latter be effectively integrated into the church or the nation.

(8) SOCIAL CONTROL. Preservation of law and public order is the responsibility of the internal governing body, and to this end it has the right and privilege of exercising coercion against those who turn away from the norms established by tradition or who rebel against them. In general, the local government lacks a bureaucratically organized apparatus to try offenders, but it can always set up a court, presided over by *gerontes*, or name one of them to fulfill the role of judge. Next to the municipal building is a jail which is usually empty because the subordinate status of the community prevents it from formally hearing offenses or important crimes. If these take place, the local government must transfer the matter to the national authorities and it is they who apply sanctions involving loss of liberty or of life.

No authority could maintain itself for long by depending exclusively on the use of physical coercion to maintain social order, and the indigenous community is no exception. Its stability is based on the operation of integrating mechanisms which give coherence to the ethnic group and which shape individual conduct within patterns made valid by tradition. The most powerful of those mechanisms is the process of enculturation which causes internalization from an early age of the social and cultural guides that give the group its particular character, and obliges members to follow those guides without question; the people simply consider them good and stick to them. Other mechanisms may be mentioned, among them the economic ones whose principles we have already analyzed. It is sufficient to note their importance here.

We should nevertheless refer to the psychological mechanisms which operate with such surprising success in the indigenous agrarian communities. They are expressed in various ways, all effective: through envy, and through the use of ridicule, witchcraft, or the simple threat of the latter. Regarding the conservation of the Indian's traditional customs in the Chiapas Highlands, Villa Rojas (1947) notes the importance of beliefs based on the concept of the *nagual*, involving the transformation of the native shaman into a dangerous animal. The religious functionaries, gifted with an unfailing power of transformation, know the thoughts and actions of community members through conversations with the spirits, who are always ready to intervene, punishing with illness or accident anyone who violates the mores of the community. Punishment consists of harm administered by one of the *gerontes* changed into a *nagual*, and it is considered a manifestation of the guilt of whomever it is inflicted upon.

Illness, as noted, is not considered the result of a conflict of natural forces but the reflection of a social conflict, in that the injured person is considered to be a social offender. In the religious sphere this is tantamount to violation of religious duties and loyalties. Since illness is invested with social meaning, the anxiety which it produces in the patient and his relatives is very great. Because of this, once the relationship between sickness and social behavior is established, the presence of an actual illness is not necessary for the *gerontes* to act as agents of social control. The simple threat of their exercising the functions imposed by their role is sufficient to influence strongly the regulation of group conduct and the maintenance and preservation of the traditional order.

Both the function of purposeful social control and those previously analyzed have integrative effects insofar as they reinforce the life styles of the ethnic group and discourage or restrict conduct that diverges from traditional norms. Phenomena that could lead to disorganization, such as the abuse of power, the accumulation of money for capitalist goals, or the spending of it according to outside patterns, are reduced to a minimum. In this way, all the group members are kept in constant equilibrium and social equality. The integrative functions of government include what Carrasco calls survival value; its subtle operation is responsible for the persistence and continuity of community culture (Carrasco 1961).

POLITICAL TIES. Up to now we have analyzed the indigenous community as if it were an independent world. Of course we noted the link it has with national and ecclesiastic authorities through the civic-religious hierarchy, but we have never emphasized the extreme dependency to which it is subjected by *mistis* or Ladinos by virtue of its position at the very lowest levels of the vertical social organization. In the caste system of the regions of refuge the indigenous community suffers the consequences of its subordinate position. Willingly or by force it accepts the processes of domination that hinder its development toward equitable forms of coexistence.

Subjugation is expressed objectively through the presence, within the heart of the community government, of a series of outside functionaries representing the regional oligarchy. The most conspicuous agents of domination are, of course, the political lieutenant or his Mesoamerican equivalent, the municipal secretary in civil business, and the parish priest in religious matters. The community does not participate either directly or indirectly in the selection and naming of these outsiders; it simply tolerates them as unavoidable impositions. Their power is a reflection of the supralocal authority and forces the community to obey their orders and resolutions within the institutional channels of domination. It also forces the community to cover the costs of dependency through a multitude of services and money tributes. In order to facilitate the mission of these outside agents the community names native counterparts, called *escribanos* or *sacristanes* respectively. These counterparts enjoy a special status in the native government because their functions are permanent, specialized, and to some extent compensated.

The sources of power from which agents of domination derive their authority are located in the metropolis, *chef-lieu* of the region of refuge. The fact that the national administrative structure equates Indian and non-Indian municipalities does not hold sway in these regions because the action arm of the central government does not effectively reach them. The isolation, poverty, and hostility of the physical environment, the ethnic and cultural heterogeneity of the inhabitants, and other features defining the Indian reserves, make integration of the regions into the national society extremely difficult and costly. The effort required by the national society to break the obsolete structure is beyond the regular workings of the administrative machinery. It requires action which is specifically focused to overcome the challenge of the persistence of that structure in the heart of a modern society. Such a program is not easy to implement and maintain in developing countries.

In the regional metropolis the political organization is dominated by a small elite which forms the tip of the social pyramid. Its most outstanding members occupy key positions in the city government, the positions of greatest authority and remuneration. In Ladino society positions in the government hierarchy are not considered as cargos but as sinecures which the incumbents may use for their own benefit. In fact this is regarded with ambivalence; it is hoped that the functionary will sacrifice himself for the good of the community and at the same time that he will exploit his position of power to increase his own goods and privileges. Corruption is fomented and believed in, while simultaneously, honesty and competency are demanded.

The governing elite is generally composed of a few extended families which have exercised power for generations. At any given moment one of these families may occupy the apex of the political pyramid. Sometimes a coup d'etat or a true revolutionary movement overthrows the governing group and for some years the directing family remains in obscurity; inevitably power is recovered by sons or nephews. Families in the metropolis maintain ties of affinity with the powers governing the department or nation; such links enable them to hold the positions they have acquired. Furthermore, those same families lend support and protection to other families in secondary cities or in the central towns of Indian communities. They construct an intricate network of *compadrazgo* (fictive kinship) ties which sometimes extend to *revestidos* or *cholos*.

Not infrequently the head of one of these families acquires political predominance as a derivation of his economic power, and sets himself up as *caudillo* or strong man of the region of refuge. He temporarily occupies the most important office in the city government; however more often he stays apart from the formal exercise of authority, but not from real power. He uses his influence for the nomination of his allies to key posts and also controls the naming of Ladino representatives in the community government. From the purely legal point of view the Indian governments name their employees. What actually happens is that the *caudillo* or, in his stead the urban elite, designates these agents of domination who, free from the social pressures of the city, become exploiters of the community.

The justification for the city's domination of the Indian is based on what Sjoberg calls the invocation of absolutes, that is, on power legitimized by forces which are independent of human action.[9] *Mistis* or Ladinos consider themselves inherently superior to the Indians, not because of specifically acquired skills but because of divine disposition, by virtue of having been born into a family, lineage, or caste which had long before usurped the highest position in a vertically structured social order. The ideology of ethnic superiority maintains the caste system operative in regions of refuge. It rationalizes the meddling by urban governments in the communities of their hinterland and the demand that these communities accept incontrovertible and indisputable domination as a natural right.

It is not our intent to make an analysis of the political structure of the Ladino city, the metropolis of the region of refuge; that task falls within the competence of specialists in political science. We only wish to make note of the importance in this structure of the ecclesiastic organization headed by the bishop and canons of the cathedral who are related to the governing families, as well as the great influence of the student body when a university or college is located in the metropolis, as is frequently the case. The eminently aristocratic nature of both organisms helps to maintain the domination of the city over the Indian communities.

Before concluding these arguments, the political relations among the subordinate peoples merit some comment. Each Indian community is a closed corporation of persons sharing a common affiliation, who distinguish themselves from neighboring communities with total ethnocentrism, considering themselves the chosen people. Their differences are expressed in the worship of a different patron saint, in speaking a particular language or dialect, and in the use of clothing which quickly identifies the wearer as belonging to a specific ethnic group.

Relations between two neighboring Indian communities are organized horizontally. One Indian community does not dominate another but neither is it tied to the other by any political unity which might transcend the narrow dimensions of parochial nucleus, even when both share a similar language and culture. The Indians of both communities know, of course, that they belong to a single social world, which classifies them as Indians and segregates them from the Ladino world. But within that single world relations between the communities are hostile and are conducted through intermediaries who are the control agents of the Ladino city or who belong to the social group *revestidos* or *cholos* residing within the communities in conflict.

The *cholo* or *revestido* is an Indian who for economic reasons–lack of land or demographic pressure–has lost his affiliation as a member of a corporate community and has adopted the aspirations and value system of the Ladino society (Mangin 1965). He is a completely marginal man, rejected by both Indians and *mistis*, but necessary to both as an intermediary or culture broker. As an individual the *cholo* belongs nowhere; as a member of a social group he is an intercaste in the social structure of the region of refuge. A person's inclusion in this stratum implies at least minimal participation in the national culture and consciousness, and the possibility of actively operating in the political relations of the closed communities.

NOTES

1. Santiana (1948-9:265) and Costales (1966:208) say: "No Indian would ever consent to leave this world without having taken the staff of office. Not only for the social prestige, but also because he feels that heaven will not open for him if he has never carried the staff. At the moment of death, he who held the staff does not turn to the Christian priest, but simply asks that his people place the staff on his chest." Rubio Orbe (1956:285) adds: "To hold a religious office is a type of indispensable prerequisite for acquiring significance and value among the members of the social group. In the whole valley of Otavalo and in the country, *Mana cargu yallishca* (he who does not hold office), along with being an insult, signifies a position of inferiority, of marginality to the community."

2. Julio de la Fuente, in a report presented at UNESCO in 1948, states: "Among the many ceremonies ascribed to the authority role, that of *mañanakuy* should be mentioned. Not only is it practiced in Chinchero, but appears to be general to the whole area. By this ceremony a person is given possession of the lands assigned to him by the village. That is, they confirm his rights over the land by means of this ceremony, which takes place in February; the local *curaca* confirms his rights. The person who holds a piece of communal land sets out accompanied by his wife, the *curaca*, and others. He walks around the plot, throws his hat into the air, throws himself upon the ground, and says something to the effect of 'This is my piece of land.' and other things. His wife throws her cap into the air and then sits on the ground. Then the 'owner' of the plot gives everyone coca leaves and invites them to eat and drink. The *curaca* and his followers continue to the next plot. This ceremony apparently is dying out because the number of communal plots is diminishing, however slowly. The *curaca* is also the person who gives land rights to those recently widowed."

Miskin (1964:144) adds: "The present system of land tenure in Kauri is that of private property, which consists of a house, a garden, and plots for farming. Farm plots are inherited in individual parcels, and the district governor confirms their boundaries annually. There is also saint's land and land belonging to the District Council. The former is in the nominal possession of the Indian *mayordomo* of the saint for one year. Moreover, this land is cultivated collectively, and the whole collectivity receives the benefits of the harvest during the fiesta. The land of the District Council, which appears to have originally been in the hands of the *curaca* or *cacique* of the district at the beginning of the Republic, has passed into the hands of the governing body of the district capital. This land is rented to Indians from the same Kauri and the harvest serves to pay the expenses of the district administration. There is no true *ejido* or communal land, no communal pastures, and cultivated lands lying fallow serve as pastures, garbage dumps, or resting places."

3. See Guevara (1957) for distinct types of *minga* or *minca* .

4. When the Spanish colonial regime established itself firmly in America, the Indians

of the governing elite who had managed to survive the catastrophe of conquest were eagerly sought as the basis for an indirect government that would permit easy management of native manual labor. The native lords were recognized by the *macehuales*, the pueblo community, and were the only body of authority suitable for utilization by colonial interests. The native lords swore obedience to the Spanish Crown, which duly conceded them the rank and condition of nobility.

We have noted that this appointment entailed the mechanical transfer of the privileges and obligations of the noble state in the European courts. The colonial governors were astonished when a significant number of native lords refused the advantages and offices of the new rank, so graciously offered, stating that they did not possess sufficient goods to fulfill the responsibility. The revenues and taxes accruing to the *cacique* and the services rendered to him, so obviously attractive to the Western mentality, were not sufficient to entice the native lords. They considered, as do the *macehuales* today, that the duties of government are literally burdens and not privileges.

Delfina López Sarrelangue (1965: Chapter V) has meticulously documented the series of privileges in terms of rank and financial profit accorded to the lords when they were recognized as noble. Many of these privileges appear to be of little value if measured according to economizing criteria, but there is no doubt that in their own context they carried great weight in determining an individual's position in the colonial social scale, divided as it was by the caste barrier. Appointment to the nobility meant that one was included with his descendants in the dominant caste. Rejection of such rank and position by the native lords was inexplicable in terms of contemporary western thought. Let us look at those privileges and judge for ourselves the cost of renouncing them. First among the privileges of rank was courtesy of title. The nobleman enjoyed the right to put don before his name and its use was obligatory in addressing or invoking him. Nonetheless, the title did not have the charismatic connotation of the title *tzin* that accompanied the name of leaders of the old Aztec society. The privilege of luxury reinforced that of title. The nobleman could wear silk, lace, ornaments, gold jewelry, precious stones, and clothing of Peninsular design; he could live in a well-built house made of masonry with a tile roof; he could eat beef and drink Castilian wine, both prohibited to *macehuales*. At conquest, use of the ancient, showy paraphernalia of masks and feathers was abolished. Other privileges of rank gave the nobleman the right to use arms for defense and decoration, to ride a horse, which made him a caballero, and to occupy a prominent seat in all public ceremonies.

In addition, the nobleman was not subject to the ordinary justice; he could only be judged by his peers or betters. He had the prerogative to address the king personally and directly when necessary. He was exempt from paying tribute and if he so desired or was interested, he could participate in the deliberations of the town hall and vote on public business. Finally, as the culmination of these great privileges of rank, he was granted the privilege of governing. The highest offices of the Indian republic were reserved for him, among them those of *cacique* or *gobernador*, of *alcalde* and *regidor*. However, under colonial domination community government was certainly no privilege. Providing manual labor for *repartimientos* and *mitas*, setting and collecting tribute and other taxes imposed on the conquered, all entailed responsibilities that could not be adequately recompensed.

The monetary privileges of nobility involved economic retribution. The nobleman enjoyed a revenue from the royal treasuries, and shared in the tributes and services to which ordinary men were obligated. He had rights to tenancy of lands and waters granted him by the crown. These could be in the form of patrimony—goods of which he could dispose freely—as well as of goods tied to the *cacicazgo* neither alienable nor divisible. Land tenancy entailed the additional concession of sufficient manual labor to produce profits. The lessees assigned to the *cacicazgo* were responsible for crops and also had to serve the *cacique* in his house. Forms of feudal servitude were transported to the colony as the monetary privileges of the Indian nobility. In exchange for those privileges, which were fewer for functionaries of lower rank, the governors were obligated to certain responsibilities which, in accordance with native tradition, were too heavy for those carrying them. Let us say once again that this burden was represented by the redistributive function that obligated the Indian authority to squander his goods.

Colonial documents inform us that it was the norm for *caciques* to be generous with visitors, whether they were important or poor, and they also report that when the lords did not fulfill their duties of hospitality the natives neither respected nor served them. Recent ethnographic research allows greater insight. The *caciques* and important functionaries were obliged to redistribute among members of their own group the production surpluses they had accumulated or could accumulate during their active years, whether these surpluses came from rents, taxation or their own efforts. Were they not to do so, they would lose the cargo, the authority they had achieved and their hard won prestige.

5. Vázquez (1955) says: "The principal index of wealth . . . consists of the number of animals a family possesses."

6. Wolf (1959:224) in criticizing Tax, states: "But the Indian is not merely quantitatively different in his economic involvements from other members of the society. He differs qualitatively from the poor non-Indian Mexican or Guatemalan because he is culturally different from them. Superficially, he may resemble the individual economic agent of classical economics, unrestrictedly exchanging goods in a capitalist market. But he is not a capitalist, nor free of restrictions. His economic goal is not capital accumulation but subsistence and participation in the religio-political system of his community. He handles money; but he does not use money to build capital. It is for him merely one way of reckoning equivalences, of appraising the value of goods in exchange. The Indian works first so that he may eat. When he feels that he has accomplished this goal, he labors to build a surplus so that he can sponsor a ceremony and gain prestige in the eyes of his fellow Indians. In the course of his sponsorship, he redistributes or destroys his surplus by providing displays of fireworks or dressing the saint's image in a new cloak. Clearly, the quality of his involvement in the national economy differs from that of the commercial farmer, industrial worker, or entrepreneur."

7. This leads us to reconsider historical data with insight from ethnographic materials. The Indian nobles who refused colonial offices with the excuse that they lacked sufficient goods to fulfill the responsibility expressed their decisions in terms of Indian values. In accordance with the integrative principles of redistribution, the revenues and tax returns that went with the concession of nobility were not really personal income for the nobleman. The money, goods, and services they received for fulfilling the cargo had to be redistributed among members of the community by means of patronage of ceremonies, hospitality and assistance to needy families. The *cacique* or *curaca* might hold patrimonial goods or receive rents and services, but he was prohibited from capitalist accumulation in the style of European nobles and functionaries.

We can also evaluate the role played by the Catholic hierarchy during the colonial period and in our own days in regard to religious consumption as a derivation of the fulfillment of religious cargos. The hierarchy has often been accused of encouraging ceremonial waste in order to obtain profits from it. Jorge Mencías carried out research in Ecuador that produced significant figures. Only five percent of the total cost of the fiesta of San Augustin, celebrated in the communities researched in Riobamba, was absorbed by parish costs. The remaining ninety-five percent went to cover such expenses as chicha, *aguardiente* and food purchases. "To abolish drink is to abolish the major expense" (Mencías 1962:133).

8. Lambert (1963:209) states: "While in advanced societies the middle and proletarian classes that begin to acquire education, include millions of individuals who wish to participate in the political life, in archaic societies the nobles, and they alone, participate personally in the political life, and there are only a few thousand of them. Nevertheless, through the play of universal suffrage, personal clientage permits the rural nobility to assure itself of majorities at the local level and to constitute important minorities at the national level."

9. Sjoberg states: "The appeal to absolutes is, in essence, a claim to legitimization by forces independent of human action. Thus the rule of the sovereign and the existing normative structure are justified on the grounds that they are in conformance with the will of God, or the gods, and/or 'natural law.' Such a state of affairs is held to have existed from the beginning of time and can not be modified; indeed the average man in the traditional city or the peasant community can conceive of no other situation" (1960:225).

Chapter 11

IDEOLOGICAL STRUCTURE

Social Determination

OUR ANALYSIS of the features found in the regions of refuge has enabled us to discover significant differences in the social behavior of the human groups inhabiting them. We have been able to verify the existence of a symbiosis of populations which biologically, socially, economically, and culturally form two distinct worlds. These are separated by an ethnic barrier over which the Indian and Ladino confront each other. Our analysis has also shown quantitative and qualitative differences between the global or inclusive society of the national state and the regional societies which tie the Indian and Ladino to each other. As part of the dominant group in the regional equation, the Ladino shows dissident features in his ideas and action patterns that prevent his complete inclusion in the tableau of attitudes, feelings, and concepts of which the national character is composed.

Initially the Indo-Ladino confrontation was a conflict between biologically dissimilar human groups. Long centuries of contact and the situation in which it took place largely erased the racial distance. A considerable amount of Indian genes were introduced into the Ladino genetic pool and at the same time the biological composition of the Indian population was profoundly changed by the addition of an unusually large portion of foreign genes. In the countries of nuclear America, mixing is such an obvious phenomenon that there can be no objection to calling the people Mestizo. In many of them the term Mestizo connotes preference and favor, which is at odds with the pejorative connotation it previously held. In spite of this mixing, in the regions of refuge of those Mestizo-American countries, racial differences between dominant and dominated groups are still observable, sometimes with great clarity. At least in the people's thought, the conviction that those differences exist and that they are substantial lives on. What is the basis of such a belief? Why are people persuaded by their interests to abandon biological and adhere to social criteria?

Indians and Ladinos have created different responses to the resources of a single habitat. With few exceptions the former live in *caseríos, parajes* or *parcialidades* forming small, corporate, homogeneous populations that are shaped in great part by the hostile geography. The requirements of self-sufficiency are filled by occupying various environments in mountainous territory; the Indian's adaptation to the habitat is vertical. The Ladino, on the other hand, lives in cities, either the regional city or in secondary urban centers. His adaptation to the environment depends to a greater or lesser degree on the symbiosis established with the former; it is an indirect adaptation effected through exploitation of the Indian. The results of the mechanisms of domination are most important: the Ladino's use of the habitat's resources are confined to the narrowness and obsolescence of his local interest, in sharp contrast to the national society, whose world-wide interests allow enjoyment of the products and innovations of distant peoples. Why is there such attachment to backward forms of adaptation that subject the individual to the tyranny of a geographic determinism that has already been conquered?

We have shown that the techniques used by the Indian in cultivating the land, in pasturage, in exploiting forests and lakes, or in subsistence artisanship, depend on muscular energy, which affords very low productivity. Technological poverty entails an economic penury that blocks Indian communities from making the investments necessary for change. Seen from a wide temporal perspective, Indian technology is consistent, stable, and inefficient. All this is in opposition to the national society whose modern technology, constantly in the process of renovation, uses increasingly powerful and productive energy sources. Ladino society is, at least formally, part of the modern world, but the technology and organization employed in exploiting natural and human resources are inadequate and unprofitable. Why do the Indian and Ladino prefer the stability of poverty to the expectations of improvement promised by technological change?

We have already explained the differences in basic orientation of the Indian and Ladino economies. In the former the principles of reciprocity and redistribution regulate the subsistence and prestige spheres and channel production and consumption so that an equal amount of capital goods is held by all members of the community. On the other hand, the Mestizo-American countries move within the ambit of industrial society, which is guided by the comprehensive market principle, conducive to the accumulation of goods for capital formation, and which favors the creation of interest groups, inequality of income, and the class struggle. However, neither Ladino society nor, more understandably, Indian society, is modern or capitalist, even when they form part of a modern capitalist society. Why do they remain underdeveloped in the midst of the economic evolution experienced by developing countries?

The Indians' language and culture differ from those of the Ladinos. Differences in customs and practices are objectified in dress, manners, rituals, and the endless and complex ideas and values that identify each as belonging to societies with opposing life styles. In the social structure of the region of refuge the Ladino is in a superior position and the Indian in a subordinate one. There is no formal barrier to an Indian changing his status to Ladino. It is often asserted that an Indian has only to change the symbols identifying him as such—particularly his language and clothing—in order to be accepted with good will in the Ladino world. It is not mentioned that before being fully admitted, the Indian must pass through the undefined state of the marginal man, the *cholo* or *revestido*, for one or perhaps several generations. Regardless of the advantages of participation in an advanced culture and in a caste considered to be superior, the Indian's acculturation and integration into the national culture and society are desperately slow processes. Why does the Indian not respond to the stimuli which make membership in the modern society and culture desirable?

These questions and others of the same tenor that have been implicit in the course of this discussion have been resolved by the sociology of knowledge. We turn to its premises to explain the confusions arising when we analyze ideas and behavior patterns that are believed to be irrational or inconsistent. In the first place we must clarify the differences in the conceptual schemes of Indians and Ladinos. Secondly, we must clarify the contradictions emerging from the introduction of group interests into conceptions which crystalize as ideologies and which are expressed in the interethnic relationships of a caste structure.

IMAGO MUNDI. From the very moment of his birth, man is part of an organized group with ideas, feelings, and values that are structured into a body of doctrine which serves as a mental framework for action. He is never born into a world without meaning, not even in the most primitive of ethnic groups. There is always a cultural reserve enabling him to place himself in the universe and to interpret it. In contrast to animals, limited to the specific possibilities of their instinctual impulses, man makes use of instruments provided by his culture for contending with the habitat. Human behavior, as differentiated from instinctive behavior, is learned; it is socially conditioned through a prolonged process of enculturation. The initial phases of enculturation internalize in the child's subconscious the combined responses created by the organized group to resolve easily and coherently the problems of adaptation to the physical and social surroundings.

Psychologically, man must live in a comprehensible world, in a world conceived and imagined in terms that are congruent with his social life. The culture and structure of human relations are not identical throughout the inhabited world. Forms of adaptation to varying habitats are necessarily different and even the responses to the challenges of a single habitat are many. One of the constants of human experience is precisely its exuberant diversity. The existence of different social structures and cultures implies an infinity of ways in which the world image may be generated. Indeed, every ethnic group has a particular world view. No society, however extensive and advanced its cultural instruments, can embrace all of reality simultaneously and from all possible angles. Each group chooses a concrete point of observation and contemplates the limitless stretches of existence from it. Each group has its own image of reality, its particular view of the world as seen and interpreted from its own perspective.[1]

German sociologists give the name *Weltanschauung* to the body of ideas and values, forming a concept of the world and of things created by a particular society; North American anthropologists call it the *world view*; and philosophers faithful to good Latin usage call it *imago mundi*. In the regions of refuge, human groups with different cultures interact in the same habitat. Each of them has chosen a different point of observation for interpreting reality, corresponding to the different structure of its social life. In such regions it is possible to observe the confrontation of two ethnic groups, each with a different *Weltanschauung*. Robert Redfield (1962:269) was the scholar who showed perhaps the greatest concern for discovering the contradictory factors of each group's *imago mundis,* when he analyzed the world view of primitive civilizations.[2]

The American Indian's conception of the world has been called personal because he views phenomena of the universe as resulting from the workings of personal agents conceived as supernatural beings or entities. His relations with nature, taken in their entirety or in their constitutive parts, take place under the assumption that cosmic forces are capable of perception and sensitivity, as if they were persons gifted with consciousness and passion. Consequently the facts of nature are not interpreted like so-called scientific concepts containing empirical references. The Indian believes himself the axis of the universe and judges the group of which he is a part to be the only really human and true one. Accepting as an axiom that nature is governed by personal agents who think and feel, and allowing that everything that happens does so with reference to man as represented by himself, the Indian supposes that he can influence nature to act in his favor. As a consequence, the purpose of his rituals, aside from expressing feelings of gratitude, respect, and solemnity, is to manipulate signs and symbols that are instruments for achieving his goals (Honigmann 1959). Lévy-Bruhl, exaggerating its distinctive features, called such thought prelogical. In truth the primitive world view of the Indian is penetrated by empirical elements in sufficient quantity and quality to counteract the strong effects of magico-religious beliefs (Lévy-Bruhl 1928, 1930, 1935, 1938, 1945, 1947).

According to Lévy-Bruhl, primitive societies show an understanding of the world, of the self, of others, and of the collective group which is essentially different from that of modern society. The laws of formal logic are replaced by mystic participation based on the affective nature of the supernatural. Consciousness of time and space, causality, the concept of the outside world and of society, and data regarding immediate experience, are all different. The world view of primitive man is stable because of the mystic nature impregnating it, but it is also little differentiated; it corresponds to the concrete social structure of scarcely specialized ethnic groups (Gurvitch 1963:107). In studying the world view of a highly acculturated Mesoamerican community, Sol Tax (1941) was able to demonstrate the personal character of its collective symbols, but these coincided with impersonal social relations.[3] As stated previously, variations of the norms are always possible but they do not alter the general tendency, noted by Lévy- Bruhl, of a close correspondence between the social structure and the world view.

The Indian's personal conception of the world does not differ in general terms from that held by the part of humanity called primitive, archaic, or inferior. The Indian is so deeply immersed in nature that all natural phenomena have a symbolic meaning for him. He compares those meanings with reality and obtains specific concepts of causality, space, and time that establish an intimate and reciprocal dependency between man and natural phenomena. Nature and man, cosmic events and human events, are intermixed so that primitive experience is immediate and personal (Gutkind 1956). This conception of the world held by the Indian implies a confusion between the ego and what the ego confronts; a person tends to see himself in unity with nature rather than as a separate entity. He does not seek to dominate or change it; he simply conforms to it in order to form an integrated system of man-in-nature (Wallace 1961:124).

The world view of modern societies is the exact opposite of the primitive, at least ideally speaking. Nature is impersonal. Gods, lesser supernatural beings, and other anthropomorphic entities created by man to explain the organization and functioning of the universe are not part of it. Signs and symbols in rites and ceremonies are not manipulated in order to produce phenomena without empirical bases or to reify the ideal, but rather to achieve certain goals—such as the strengthening of social solidarity—in which the connection between the process and the final product may be shown. Rites are fundamentally expressive, not vehicles of mystic participation. Although this description is largely ideal, the dominant cognitive orientation is true beyond doubt. It forms the body of doctrine considered to belong to man in today's industrial culture.

The scientific world view characteristic of the modern world, in other words the rationally oriented, impersonal world view, appears to have been born in the West at the time when the Hebrews separated God from nature or when the Greeks sacrilegiously explained the cosmos on the basis of what they called natural laws.[4] The impersonal world view matured in Europe during the Rennaissance, giving nourishment and strength to scientific thought. Diffusion of this throughout the world was propitious for technical progress, economic development, and the formation of modern nation states. The fact that the latter are part of the industrial world and that the general orientation of their ideology is directed through channels ruled by judgment and rationality does not mean that all the citizens of modern countries hold a scientific world view. The old manner of thinking, seeing, and interpreting reality still constitutes part of the modern cultural heritage and possibly will never be completely displaced.

FALSE CONSCIOUSNESS. Confrontations between primitive and modern world views allow a better penetration of the essence of Indian thought as well as of its counterpart, scientific thought, which theoretically rule social activities in Mestizo-American countries. The comparison, however, does not reveal differences between the Indian and Ladino concepts of the world and of the things in it because, as we have noted, the Ladinos form part of the national society and therefore participate in its *Weltanschauung*. This statement is true to some extent but it contains only parts of the truth. Every inclusive society—especially those uniting opposing communities in the process of national formation—is a heterogeneous society made up of different classes, castes, or life styles.

In Mestizo-American societies Ladinos or *mistis* are the sector of the population which is consciously situated apart from the majority of citizens as a regional elite. They hold a world view which challenges scientific assumptions and interpretations. They construct their own mental framework and from it contemplate the limited field of their universe, according to their own fancy and satisfaction. Their world view lacks authenticity and is in opposition to democratic hypotheses and the orthodox interpretations of national consciousness, but it does not therefore fail to constitute a basis for action. It doubtless originated because false interests perverted the moral purposes of scientifically based social thought; it should be studied to discover the false premises on which it is based.

When one sector of the national population, the Ladinos, proclaims that exploitation of the Indians is natural or desirable, we are in the presence of persons holding scientifically untenable beliefs. The Social Darwinism which justifies subjugation of the weak by the strong is a distortion of rational thought that does not stand up under critical analysis. Nevertheless it forms part of the conceptual scheme of the dominant group in the regions of refuge. Ideological influences vitiate thought and are never as dangerous as when they appeal to rationalizations, that is to apparently scientific explanations. The Ladino lives in symbiosis with the Indian and his entire economy revolves around exploitation of the native work force. If he were to lose that, his system of security would fall apart.

Some inhabitants of Ladino metropolises openly assert that exploitation of the Indians is indispensable for the Ladinos' very survival; elite interests demonstrate this. However, cynical or blatant expression of rascist or ethnocentric beliefs is certainly the exception. In most cases people sincerely believe in their own superiority and the inferiority of others. Thus class or caste interests resort to physical coercion only in extreme situations. Generally they use far more effective and subtle mechanisms which become self-perpetuating as part of the group's super ego. We easily believe that what we want is true: with a prayer in Latin, nothing is more desired as the truth than our own interests. There is nothing to prevent the firm internalization of those interests in the subconscious through enculturation and their later emergence at the conscious level as established truths that need no demonstration. In this way the superiority of the Ladino over the Indian becomes a moral postulate.

That all thought is inspired and dominated by interests is unquestionable. The world views of both primitive and modern man are determined in the last analysis by a basic social interest, the need to live in a comprehensible universe. We know, however, that when a person or group holds ideas originating to an important extent in some personal or group interest, that thought is not genuine because it is the expression of problematical mental states, the end result of an ideology. Dialectical materialism uses the term ideology to designate the conscious mental process that ignores the forces determining it and leading it to the formulation of a false consciousness (Moore 1964:47). Those forces remain hidden in the subconscious; they are the class or caste interests that determine false thought. There is the same distance between a world view and an ideology as between genuine social interests and spurious ones.

Paradoxically, in the intercultural situation of the regions of refuge the ideology of the dominant caste emerges from the same world view that is based on genuine interests. The mental framework of the world view or *Weltanschauung* is an institutionalized form of thought determined by the historical development of the national society. Those belonging to it easily understand what is said and done within the system of meanings that lie within their conceptual scheme; all the members have been conditioned precisely for this (Stark 1969:18). On the other hand, as an inevitable consequence of cultural conditioning, it is only with difficulty that they understand what is done and said within different conceptual schemes, within societies such as the Indian, which are so distant from industrial civilization.

Ethnocentrism is an integrating force in every society. It aggravates this problematical situation by abetting the conversion of incomprehension into hostility toward the thought processes of peoples considered inferior. Language that is not understood, economic behavior which appears irrational, the structuring of kinship relationships, the power hierarchy, and religious practices are classified as inefficient, inscrutable, and superstitious. Werner Stark (1964:19) makes it explicit that all this is due to the fact that thought is not only determined by social life but also bound to it. The Ladino is bound to the same degree as the Indian, emotionally and intellectually, to his culture. In other words, each is prejudiced against the ideas and values of others. As noted, passage from genuine consciousness to a false one is easy for the group in the dominant position.

In every *Weltanschauung* there are problems of knowledge and will. Problems of knowledge comprise the sum total of interpretations of the world and of life in it; of will, it is the totality of values according to which one lives (Sombart 1964:13). A balance is maintained between cognitive and normative interests, the composition of which varies from culture to culture. In some, as in modern industrial culture, primacy is given to cognitive or rational aspects. In other cultures, such as primitive ones, priority of values or emotions prevails. When the equilibrium is broken the world view loses its legitimacy and becomes an ideology (Redfield 1963:109). The world view held by modern countries is a scientific *Weltanschauung* in which rational interests predominate. The introduction into that view of normative interests arising from situations of domination destroys the balance achieved and gives birth to an ideology (Parsons 1951:348).

In the regions of refuge of Mestizo-American countries, the priority given by caste interests to their value system, operating in a global society with a scientific *Weltanschauung*, distorts the thought of the people participating in the national consciousness and forces them to live in the unreality of an ideology. The mere presence of such an ideology in the heart of a country that is formally democratic creates several dilemmas. Perhaps the most important is that which allows the survival of a false consciousness in a heterogeneous society that postulates the rights of man in its constitution as well as in its political orientation. Ladino ideology exists today not simply as a distortion of rational thought but also as anachronistic, residual, and retrograde thought. It is a remnant of the colonial situation, which has never progressively evolved in the same way as the social thought of the rest of the nation.

Another dilemma, no less important, is that concerning the question of whether Ladino ideology forms and configures the exploitative system of the regions of refuge or whether, on the contrary, the economic and social structure established by colonial exploitation has given rise to ideological thought. Sombart maintains that *spirit*, as expressed in the *Weltanschauung* of the era, gives form to a culture and therefore to the economic system of that culture.[5] Sombart's postulate derives directly from the idealism of Max Weber and his conviction that the Protestant ethic engendered the capitalist system (Tawney 1959). Because they are false consciousnesses, all ideologies, including the Ladino, are merely echoes or reflections of class or caste interests. Their annihilation entails a total change of the economic and social structure in which those interests originate. It is not the ethnic but the material conditions which are essential in the situation.

THE FUNCTION OF IDEOLOGY. Without overlooking the fundamental importance of economics in determining the social and cultural forms of human aggregates, it is also impossible to deny that the genius and unique nature of a community's or society's life style is not always derived from economic relationships. In order to point out the most salient and visible characteristics of the Indian culture, it is best to analyze its political structure, as in our study of the functions of the power hierarchy. In all of Mestizo-America the particular features of such functions also best reveal the very essence of the life style. In order to put into relief the most singular aspect of Ladino society it is necessary to consider its ideology.

We shall consider the features of the ideology as it operates in the regions of refuge from the Ladino viewpoint, for purposes of analysis and interpretation. Thus we view the subjugated Indian from the Ladino's side of the wall that has been erected by the caste system. By so doing we are able to investigate the ideological situation with empathy, putting ourselves in the Ladino's place; only in this way can we fully understand the most basic reasons for actions that are incompatible with the morality of our times. What Ladinos say and do is significant in so far as it reveals the total ideological structure and the common assumptions of public opinion. However, we shall not describe the current stereotypes one by one, nor the individual acts performed with very weak justification. When appropriate, several of these may be given as support or simple illustration (de la Fuente 1965). In the discussion of ethnic minorities we gave an account of the various control mechanisms resorted to by the dominant caste or class to maintain itself in a position of superiority.

(1) *Provide Identity*. An ideology that justifies the subjugation and exploitation of the Indian compels the Ladino to form a false image of himself. The true image produced by disinterested contemplation is too sombre to serve as a model. It is composed of prejudices and ethnic preconceptions which do not stand up under rational analysis. In this undesirable situation the Ladino resorts to an indirect solution: he builds his self-image through comparison with a contrasting one, that of the Indian, to which he attributes stigma, blemishes, and dirt. The prolonged contact of two ethnic groups, who for centuries have remained separate in a conflict situation of superiority and subordination, is reflected in the concepts and opinions which each group has of the other. Both conceive of themselves in terms of contrast: all the defects, vices, and weaknesses imputed to the other have counterparts in the perfections, virtues, and talents they attribute to themselves.

The Ladino's image of the Indian, rather than that which the latter has of the former, is pervasive in the caste structure, since it justifies the inferior position and low social status in which aboriginal peoples are kept. During the early years of colonization, racial differences provided the basis for beliefs about Indian irrationality. Despite the fact that since then ecclesiastical authorities have declared the preconception false, its implications have been so deeply instilled in the thought of the masses that they still exercise an incontestable influence. Ladinos call themselves reasonable people to express the contrasting opinion they have of Indians, whom they label native, primitive or savage, giving those qualities a pejorative connotation.

Dress is too obvious a status symbol to be overlooked. During the nineteenth century the Ladinos of Ciudad Las Casas made their racial background evident by retaining the *coleta* or pigtail even after it had gone out of fashion; for this reason they were called *coletos*. The *chupas* of Riobamba owe their nickname of *rabones* to the clothing that indicated their social position (Costales 1957:235). The Indian dresses in a manner that emanates as much from the aboriginal as from the Spanish colonial style. In some cases, as in the communities of Alto Peru, masculine dress is almost entirely European; in others, as in certain Mesoamerican *municipios*, it is preponderantly American. But in both, the beauty of the garments is unquestionable. The variety and richness of color, the patient and elegant work seen in the feminine clothing of the different ethnic groups, is so well known as to be scarcely worthwhile mentioning. Nonetheless, the Ladino interprets these as examples of bad taste, carelessness, and dirtiness as contrasted with his own clothing, considered by him to be elegant, well-fitting, and conservative.

The Indian's home is generally an adequate response to a hostile habitat. Even in the poorest Indian communities, nutrition is obtained through a balanced diet which fills protein needs by ingestion of insects such as the

Nahua *ahuauhtli* or the Aymara *chichi*, both of high nutritional value (Gaddo 1962:98). In preparing foodstuffs, simple but effective techniques are used, such as the souring of *pozol* or crushing of *chuño* to increase their assimilative properties or retard spoilage. In contrast, the Ladino's house is of tile or stucco, whitewashed adobe or bricks of baked mud, but it has no effective means for heating in mountainous climates or for suitable ventilation in hot areas. His food is rich in meat and milk products; he prefers cereals such as wheat and other European grains. The Ladino disdains the Indian diet and finds it repugnant. Even though he may enjoy the delicacies of Indian cooking within the privacy of his family, he never confesses this preference in front of another Ladino. In the same way he will never live in a *putuco* or straw house, both of which are censured by public consensus as pigsties (Martínez 1962:76).

The contrast is even greater in terms of the occupations of the two peoples. The Indians are kept tied to primary occupations: cultivation of the land, tending flocks, fishing, and gathering. For them manual labor is one of the values that give great "distinction" in the community. Ladinos never perform the work of preparing the land for farming or other low callings associated with day laborers. They consider manufacturing, professional, or commercial activities as suitable. The ideal of disinterested culture leads them to place a high value on leisure, artistic skill, and intellectual speculation (Lambert 1963:124). Although *mistis* of the oldest families may, in fact, perform manual labor, they commonly deny it, especially if such activities have the characteristics of Indian work. The Ladino who takes up a broom to sweep or the *misti* who carries merchandise from the market is severely sanctioned with ridicule and contempt for performing work belonging to the Indian rustic or *pongo*.

Thus, on the basis of contrasts, of conceptual opposites to use Copeland's expression (1964:204), the Ladino constructs his image, idealizes the model, and makes it operate as a mechanism for furnishing identity. In such circumstances, membership in the superior caste is acquired through negative identification with the opposite image, through affirmation of what is non-Indian, which generally means through self-negation. Persons who have recently become Ladinos or *mistis* and more especially the *revestidos* or *cholos* who seek a place in the social hierarchy have the greatest need to proclaim their false identity, negating the color of their skin, the physical features that reveal their native ancestry, their Indian tastes and preferences, and above all, rejecting the occupational roles in which the economic structure places the Indian. The Mestizo-American maxim, that the greatest exploiter of the Indian is the Indian disguised as a white, exposes the false consciousness of Ladino ideology.

(2) *Legitimize Superiority*. Beliefs about the Indian form a perspective and orientation that express the Ladino's awareness of caste in an obvious way. These beliefs are integral elements of an ideology whose main theme is the divine nature of Ladino superiority and the immutability of the established order. His system of beliefs gives the Ladino rationalizations that legitimize the superior position he occupies in the structure of interethnic relations. Once these beliefs are institutionalized they form part of a body of juridical ordinances that maintain domination and this domination persists even long after the legislation is changed by pressures from outside the region of refuge. The Ladino ideology is no longer a legal code but it continues to be a credo, part of the morality and religion of the people.

(3) *Obstruct Integration*. The patterns of ideas constituting the ideological structure of the regions of refuge have a double and contradictory function. On the one hand they put into play mechanisms that enhance group cohesion. They give the group a self-image with which members can proudly identify and they offer satisfactory rationalizations that legitimize domination. On the other hand they distinguish Ladinos from Indians, creating sociological races that are separate and conflicting, and thus the integration of different populations is hindered. The image the Ladino forms of the Indian leads him to despise and fear him. The Indian is foreign and hostile and has no right to seek membership in the Ladino group. His integration becomes a repugnant process for the receiving society because he has been represented as morally and religiously impure.

Verbal or physical aggression, segregation and other ideological control mechanisms which impede integration are not confined to the Indian as a sociological race; they extend to the Indian as a person as well. Their inclusion in the inferior caste means that all Indians are measured by the same severe yardstick. There is no distinction made between the common Indian who has not yet earned a position of respect in the community, and the *geronte* with his charisma, mystic experience, and wisdom, who is *primus inter pares* in his hamlet or community. The image of both is the same and the treatment given them similar. For the Ladino all Indians are called José or Mariá and all are peons. The category of Indian does not allow internal stratification; it is a caste in which all are considered inferiors.

Because of ideology, the Indians of different ethnic groups are categorized equally; for purpose of maintaining the status quo and avoiding integration, all Indians are cut from the same cloth. The ideology does not accept the existence of substantive variations between the itinerant Indian who lives in the tropical marsh using tuber agriculture and the Andean Indian who constructs irrigated terraces and lives in concentrated settlements. Both belong to a single category, Indian, which is juxtaposed with Ladino, also conceived as a single category. Passage from one category to another is formally possible; one can always find the case of an Indian who made the leap from the depths of a tribal situation to the highest levels of national society. Nevertheless, when the phenomenon is evaluated statistically it is unquestionable that as a mechanism hindering integration and buttressing the caste structure, ideology is very effective.

(4) *Consolidate the Economic Structure*. One of the most persistent patterns of belief in Ladino thought is an inheritence from the colonial regime. The social relations established at that time totally disappeared in the culturally and economically more advanced regions. On the other hand, they remained alive in the regions of refuge, primarily in areas with a hacienda economy based on the hacienda-serf relationship (Ponce de Léon 1964:204). In these domination situations the system of relationships is a symbiosis tying the Indian and Ladino to a common destiny. The latter cannot live without the former because the entire economic order of the city, the regional center, revolves around exploitation of the Indian work force and of its resources.

In order to maintain this situation, the beliefs internalized by public opinion are aimed at keeping the Indian in the countryside, bound to a technically inefficient agriculture, to primitive herding on the heights of the wild puna, to fishing in the little used lakes of the altiplano, to precarious hunting and to collecting grasses, fruits, and insects that are increasingly scarce. Migration of the Indian to the city–especially to industrializing cities–is unauthorized. It is asserted that the Indian is irresponsible, that he does not adapt to the rhythm of systematic work, that he cannot tolerate city ways, and that his place is on the land, in the hacienda where he is guided in his work, helped in his tribulations, and where he can borrow cash for his prestige economy. (Vargas 1945: 141).

According to regional ideology, the Indian depends on Ladino support. He is like a child, a minor who must be governed by the firm but paternal hand of the *hacendado*. These beliefs and preconceptions are obviously aimed at preventing the liberation of the subjugated Indian, at hindering his passage from the caste to the class structure. For this purpose the Ladino idealizes the past and the patriarchal relationships of the old colonial regime. He foments great alarm in the public mind when the attraction exercised by centers of economic development robs him of his plentiful manual labor. The countryside will be without workers! Agriculture will suffer serious losses! As noted, the prime function of the ideology is to maintain and conserve an economic system specifically structured to exploit the Indian.

If one reveals the archaic, impoverished, and disarticulated character of the economic system based on latifundia and on feudal forms of exploiting the land and man's labor; if one shows the low productivity of the pre-Columbian and colonial techniques used by Indians and Ladinos; and if one remarks on the underdevelopment of the regions of refuge, ideology always has on hand rationalizations that allow it to attribute, or blame such disturbing facts on the Indians (MacIver and Page 1960: 432). They are a burden to the nation and ballast for the country's progress. Thus ideology unloads its own responsibility upon the inferior caste and aborts any means, such as an agrarian reform, for modifying the traditional state of things. Its mission is to defend the obsolete economic system.

In summation, the very diverse characteristics outlined so far of the regions of refuge and of the situations of their inhabitants are the unavoidable results of the domination process which sometimes resorts to physical coercion but which generally makes use of other much more farsighted methods, methods which avoid violent reactions and messianic movements. One of those mechanisms, perhaps the shrewdest, is the sustained and reinforced promulgation of an ideology that states as given the innate superiority of the Ladino over the Indian and which is generally accepted by both. The cultural patterns of the Indian, his artistic productions, his different conception of the world, of time and of progress, in fine, everything considered or categorized as Indian is held to be despicable. The mental climate thus established makes ethnic segregation inevitable, blocks social mobility, hinders cultural evolution and keeps the regions of refuge in a permanent state of underdevelopment.

NOTES

1. Stark adds: "The thesis of the sociology of knowledge is that the election of the point of observation from which the *ens universale* is contemplated, depends in every society, seen concretely, on the human relations that make that society what it is" (Stark 1964:6).

2. Redfield's interest and constancy can be appreciated by reading the correspondence he carried on with Calixta Guiteras (1965:283). See also Tax's comments in the epilogue of the book.

3. Tax (1941:37) states: "It appears justifiable to say that the world view typical of preliterate peoples is different from that typical in our Western urban society. In the first place the primitive view is quantitatively smaller and more restricted in its range; we know about them and they do not know about us; we have some acquaintance with the whole world, they of a very small portion; we are said to be more sophisticated than they. In the second place the two views differ in content." To document the last proposition, he relies on Boas (1964: Chapters XI and XII).

4. Farrington (1951:27) informs us: "The epicures were the most consistent heroes of materialism and the most resolute enemies of the supernatural in antiquity. They contributed, more than any others, to keeping alive the conviction of the possibility of a true science of nature. They were the ones who did most to conserve the understanding of the discoveries man had made thanks to his conquest of nature and to his understanding that his civilization should be understood as a human experiment."

5. Sombart (1964:II. 15) expressing agreement: "Today we are convinced that the so-called materialist or economic interpretation of history is erroneous as a cultural generalization. We know that it is always the spirit, as expressed in the *Weltanschauung* of the era, that gives form to a culture, and therefore to an economic system."

Chapter 12

INDIANIST ACTION

THE SOCIAL changes that have taken place in Mestizo America acquired in some countries the rhythm of revolutionary movements that violently transform traditional structures. The Mexican Revolution of 1910 was of course the first great upheaval of the present century. Although it did not reach the high degree of radicalization of those that followed, from the first the need was asserted that in order to achieve economic modernization it would be necessary to terminate the latifundia and distribute land to the peasants. The urgent need for basic changes in the situation of domination in the countryside and especially in the caste structure of the regions of refuge was quickly recognized. Thus the revolution sought to integrate the socially and culturally segregated ethnic groups, generally designated as Indians, into the national society. It put into operation two systems of action which since then have gone hand in hand: agrarianism and Indianism.

The latter, which concerns us now, was born in Mexico and other Mestizo American countries as a natural consequence of a nationalism whose basis in things Indian was largely a reaction against European colonialism. In those countries ethnic heterogeneity offered the solution to a dilemma arising from the existence of population groups segregated by caste barriers. A true nation can be formed only with equal and rational participation by all the citizenry of the entire society. The superordinate Ladino caste, with its false consciousness inherited from colonial domination, could not act as a nucleus around which the Indians and intercastes of *revestidos*, *cholos* and Mestizos could congregate. That caste's thoughts and emotions were centered beyond the country's borders, enraptured by the old European metropolises.

As a result nationalist ideology turned to the American past. It reevaluated the pre-Columbian Indian and took his image as a paradigm. This process explains the paradoxical coexistence in Mestizo America of two contrasting images of the Indian: the dirty image created by Ladino ideology that persists unchanged in the regions of refuge, and the idealized image that forms part of the official ideology and is a point of departure for a policy of national unity and homogeneity.[1] Revolutionary movements carry their policies to extremes; the Mexican movement caused a tremor throughout the continent that was aimed at erasing the evolutionary distance between Indian and Ladino.

A statement of the social problems arising from the backward state in which Indian and tribal populations have been kept was made in the First Interamerican Indianist Congress of 1940. Representatives of the most advanced Indian groups and of progressive sectors of national populations agreed on a series of resolutions aimed at inducing cultural change and promoting community development. The congress helped to achieve this result by its activity on behalf of the assembled social scientists during the deliberations as well as by formulating conclusions; the responsibility for establishing the principles, methods and techniques of Indianist policies fell upon the shoulders of the social scientists present.

In order to apply the proposed measures, it was considered indispensable to create specialized organisms in each country to deal with the underdeveloped ethnic groups. These organisms were called National Indian Institutes, and were affiliated with a permanent committee of the congress, the Interamerican Indian Institute, founded cooperatively by the various American nations.

THE DILEMMA OF SPECIALIZATION. The edict of the congress was by no means easy to fulfill. One of the most characteristic features of modern life is the specialization of knowledge and technology that forces the scientist and technician to work in ever narrower aspects of a given discipline. This reinforced in the organisms responsible for regional planning and community development in the regions of refuge a much discussed dilemma, the need to accentuate the importance of general action without reducing specialized action.

Of course this conflict is not limited to community development but embraces all aspects of public administration. A concomitant dilemma is whether it is more useful and appropriate to provide services and fulfill needs through specialized or generalized institutions. In reality, by observing the way in which public administration is constituted and what its significant functions are, it is easy to show a distinct tendency towards specialization. This tendency has enabled and continues to encourage the appearance of a growing number of organisms and decentralized agencies, in addition to ministries and departments of state, that are responsible for carrying out very specific activities.

But we go even farther. In the characteristic and traditional offices of the executive branch of the government, the tendency toward specialization has provoked and continues to generate a diffusion of previously concentrated activities, thus giving rise to specialized divisions and subdivisions. This specialization has the enormous advantage of putting research and technical application into the hands of persons who are suitably trained or equipped in a particular branch of knowledge, but at the same time it facilitates the disarticulation of organically structured activities.

In the large cities and their suburbs, the extreme division of labor required by the industrial economy demands specialization for providing services and fulfilling needs. A modern and elaborately complicated society such as ours could not prosper otherwise. Because of this, highly industrialized and consequently highly developed countries are organized on the basis of progressive and accelerated specialization.

The situation in developing countries is different. The tendency toward specialization works profitably in the modern sectors but not in the marginal regions where the population's life styles are backward and rustic, with very low specialization and little division of labor. Those marginal regions include the regions of refuge inhabited by Indians with languages and cultures differing from the national one. As an inevitable result of their historical development, these Indians have been exploited by culturally more advanced groups. They have been kept cloistered in their regions of refuge, living a life of mere subsistence and holding firmly to their old values and behavior patterns by virtue of a tenacious conservation which creates motivations and attitudes opposed to change and transformation.

These intercultural regions have an ecology, technology, dual economy, and social, political, and ideological structures whose features are incompatible with modern industrial life. The specialized functions of ministries, departments, and decentralized organisms are carried out through ordinary administrative channels but are not used by the inhabitants. Their isolation, dispersion, primitive technology, the primary production activities into which they have been forced, the intermeshed relationships, and semifeudal control binding them, and the ideology of conformity or fatalism created by those conditions, all hinder the inhabitants from taking advantage of the benefits of specialized governmental action.

Because of this, in these regions—and to a large degree in rural communities sharing the national culture—specialized governmental programs have had to seek new techniques for implementation. One of these was to complement the specialized action of each governmental agency with additional outside activities usually located, in urban life, in other offices. With these additions, action takes on a generalized or integral hue which has been able to adapt well to rural situations. In Mexico, the Secretariat of Agriculture implemented integral development at Teotihuacán, and the Secretary of Education created cultural missions and *casas del pueblo*. These two agencies were the first to understand that action in Indian and rural communities must be multilateral to be effective, even though the work might go beyond the strict limits of the specific function in their charge. Subsequently, when the Secretariat of Health founded rural public health centers, it felt obliged to follow the same route. Other agencies are also doing so, among them the Agrarian Department in its attempts at a thoroughgoing agrarian reform.

Another method was aimed at achieving a rational and integral approach to the problems of the indigenous regions of refuge. This consisted of the creation of an organism specializing precisely in the development of Indian communities. Some years before the Congress of Pátzcuaro, Mexico had seriously considered the need for an agency that would present to the federal executive the problems afflicting the Indian populations and which would implement a coordinated effort of governmental action aimed at them. It was obvious that the government's general program, composed of different agencies of public administration, was not effective in improving the harsh conditions of life which the Indians encountered. The lack of coordinated efforts, their short duration, and the neglect in which the less favored regions remained for lack of an appropriate understanding of their needs, appeared to be the causal factors. (Caso 1955:13).

The new organism, called the Autonomous Department of Indian Affairs, was to define and keep a close watch on governmental action in order to give it congruence and continuity as well as to insure its success. It was to call attention to the deplorable situation of tribal peoples and ensure that the largest possible amount of the state's economic resources be invested in them. Thus conceived, the department was a mere agency of procurement and coordination, lacking the authority to impose its decisions on individuals and on the offices whose coordination it had to establish and maintain.

It seems obvious that coordinated work is a form of collaboration that appears easy at first but which presents many difficulties in execution. Coordination entails limitations on one's own independence on behalf of a common effort as well as tolerance of the entry by those implementing coordinated action in areas of activity considered to be private. Jealousies over jurisdiction, competence or credit must be overcome and the collectivities' well being must take precedence over the particular interests of the participating organisms. (United Nations 1963). The Department of Indian Affairs did not know how to, or could not, overcome the obstacles presented by coordination; ten years after its founding it disappeared as an autonomous department. Some of its functions went to the Secretariat of Education, which now fulfills them through the General Directorate of Indian Affairs. When this department was created the alternative presented in its constitution was examined and rejected; this would have set up an organism through which the Government of the Republic would effect the various aspects of its economic, social, educational, and governmental work on behalf of the Indian population. It was objected that "this would represent a concentration of the work of the Secretaries of State and of the Administrative Departments vis-à-vis the rest of the country; such work with respect to the Indians should be the responsibility of a single office" (Comas 1953:103).[2] This alternative—direct realization of Indian action—and its opposite—solicitation and coordination of said action—were reconsidered when the National Indian Institute was created to rectify the absence of the abolished specialized agency. specialized agency.

Similar problems were encountered by other Mestizo-American countries in organizing Indianist action agencies. In South America the International Labor Organization contributed powerfully to the formation of such organs as the Andine Mission in Ecuador, the National Plan for the Integration of the Aboriginal Population in Peru, and Bolivia's Plan for Rural Development.[3] Initially the programs were the complete responsibility of the international organism which worked through *action bases* conceived as agencies of integral action. Later they were transferred to Ministries of State and remained henceforth under national control and administration. This transfer immediately created the need to coordinate the multiple activities of the bases with the particular ones of the different ministries. In Peru the dilemma led to the recent creation of *united action zones* that place the activities of specialized directorates and ministries under a single director. We shall not give special attention to the inspiring history of South American efforts, among which the Indianist center in Warisata and the programs of integration of land parcels in Puno are examples.[4] Instead we shall focus on Mexico, both because this country has been among those showing greatest concern for formulating Indianist theory and practice and because it is the one with whose experiences we are best acquainted.

The law which created the National Indian Institute in Mexico stipulated that its duties would include research, planning, promotion, assessment, diffusion, and direct implementation of development projects for the Indian communities. In addition it was given the power to coordinate and direct governmental action in relation to those communities. An advisory council for the Institute was created, with representatives from the various secretariats and departments of state concerned with Indianist action so as to better implement coordinated projects. An important position was given to the General Directorate of Indian

Affairs both in the council and in the work of coordination.[5]

The country attained maturity in its administrative organization and in an increasingly clear understanding of the mechanisms of development and acculturation as well as their opposites, enculturation and domination. These factors made it possible to initiate solidly based centers for community development, called Coordinating Centers in the indigenous regions of refuge. These agencies were to work with not only the groups of subjugated Indians, but with the entire underdeveloped population. It will be seen presently that the operations put into practice by these centers represent only one aspect of government action—neither its totality nor its only form. The continuation and completion of these operations require that the regular offices of public administration continue functioning simultaneously in their normal operations.

COORDINATING CENTERS. Coordinating Centers are governmental organizations created by presidential decree and entrusted with implementation of programs of integral action in the intercultural regions of refuge. To do this, they coordinate the activities of the various offices of the government in their area or work directly in community development projects when the administrative channels do not reach Indian communities.

In practice the centers reach a compromise between the two alternatives, based on a balance between the functions of coordination and direct implementation. Through accomodations with the organs of national, state, and municipal administrations the distribution of duties is arranged. These reinforce those already in operation or initiate others that are necessary within the radiuses of action and sectors of jurisdiction determined by the agreements.

Despite the fact that they are governmental agencies, the Coordinating Centers do not have the use of force among their powers. The right cum privilege to exercise coercion, to allow some acts and prohibit others, to define and redefine relationships between community members in cases of conflict, are all located in the leaders of the population groups, with whom the centers work and upon whose cooperation they must rely in all cases. The job of the centers is inducement of change, not its forced acceptance.

In addition, the intercultural situation in which their action evolves compels them to not limit their work to indigenous population groups. Although it is true that the emphasis and greater part of their actions are directed at resolving the serious problems of the Indian communities, those of the Ladino city are not forgotten. It is necessary to change the latter's economic structure and backward ideology in order to achieve long lasting results. Integral action entails a chain of specific actions not only directed at the many aspects of one culture, but at the totality of interacting cultures.

MATERIAL BASE. In accordance with the above, the site of the Coordinating Center is in the Ladino city, the metropolis of the region of refuge. It is located there in order to take advantage of the fact that the guidelines for all types of relations between the urban center and its hinterland originate in the Ladino city. The principle installations—the central offices, training school, legal attorney's office, health clinic, agricultural demonstration posts, the demonstration animal farm, laboratories and workshops, employees' houses—are located there, in direct contact and communication with the agencies and institutions of the city.

The center's action flows from the heart of the city through an inhabited area, the size of which is determined by the size of the region of refuge. Proximity or distance, difficulty or ease of access, and the warmth of the welcome between the city and Indian populations determine the areas where work will be carried on and at what levels of intensity.

The first area, called the demonstration area, is that in which physical and social conditions allow such vigorous action that direct, constant, and firsthand contact can be maintained with the population. In the demonstration area educational and sanitary services are installed as well as medical posts and agricultural and other stations and their use is stimulated. The most important innovations, however, are economic development projects that demonstrate modern methods for exploiting the resources of the habitat, resources such as soils, pasturage, forests, rivers, and lakes.

The second area is called the area of diffusion. The Coordinating Center does not implement direct action in these areas either because it lacks the necessary funds to finance installations or because it has encountered barriers of resistance in the Indian settlements which it has been unable to overcome. Sanitary campaigns, legal advisers, and recreation activities do reach the area of diffusion indirectly, but there is more dependence here on the demonstration effects produced by work in the first areas than on deliberately implemented action. When levels of aspiration are raised in the population directly affected by demonstration projects, the desire for emulation is awakened elsewhere; the effects are difficult to evaluate but nonetheless real.

The third area, that of migration, includes the places outside the region of refuge where Indians sell their labor as salaried workers. The Coordinating Center's action in such areas—usually sugar cane, coffee, or henequen plantations—consists in simple vigilence of the treatment of the Indian worker. To do this it has recourse to assistance from the labor organizations with which it works. When migration is directed to the large cities or centers of industrial development, the center turns over responsibility for working with the Indians to the governmental agencies already active in those places.

Finally, there is the mobilization area, which relates to high population density of the regions of refuge and the need to mobilize the surplus underemployed toward places where unoccupied land still exists. When such transfer is planned and carried out, the Coordinating Center is one of several governmental agencies which cooperate in coping with a program planned at the national level.

AGRARIAN FUNCTIONS. Many Latin American countries that entered the atomic era maintaining the old dual structure fundamentally unchanged have grasped that a previous and necessary condition of the march towards progress is the reform of agrarian institutions. This reform should substantially change man-land relationships and put the land into the hands of those who work it. The equitable and rational redistribution of resources previously monopolized by a few elite families is the most expeditious way to crack the pillars supporting the traditional order. In this way the landowning latifundista loses the instruments of control for subjugating the farmer, keeping him in permanent servitude and underdevelopment. Agrarian reform awakens in the campesino a sense of possession of the parcel he cultivates and gives him economic security, guaranteed independence, and dignified status in a new order that generates powerful incentives for sociocultural change. Through increased productivity and a just distribution of income, this new order aims at the achievement of higher standards of living and better forms of community life. (United Nations 1963).

In countries such as Mexico and some others that have implemented an agrarian reform, community development programs can rely on firm support for the execution of programs of integral action and the achievement of significant and continuing results. But even in those countries land redistribution is not equally effective everywhere. Inadequate technical and administrative resources mean that marginal regions of refuge receive few of the benefits of agrarian action. Those regions are the ones most in need of help, yet resistance to the reform there often shows signs of turning into violent opposition. The local oligarchy, which is the dominant group and at the same time the sector directly affected by redistribution, feels its very existence threatened. It resorts to physical force or compulsion, put at its disposal by the Ladino hierarchy, to continue the Indian communities' rejection—induced by ignorance or fear—of the rights conceded to them.[6]

When national political action reaches the regions of refuge through development programs a hidden battle immediately commences between the local hierarchy and the interests of the program. The dispute may be resolved in favor of the Indian communities if the governmental organism specifically entrusted with executing the reform is willing to invest a vigorous and sustained effort, capable of overcoming stubborn opposition. The duty of the Coordinating Center is to inspire that willingness and to help the agrarian agency in its mission of redistribution. This is done in a variety of ways. For example, the Coordinating Center may help a community develop and substantiate petitions for title to communal lands, the formation or expansion of an ejido, or the establishment of a population center, which could then qualify for ejido status. The Coordinating Center may act as attorney in defense of a community's claims. Or it may survey land claims in order to help the agrarian authorities execute decisions already handed down.

AGRICULTURAL FUNCTION. Secure land tenancy contributes greatly to the creation of the conditions necessary for the population's active participation in development programs and particularly in completing the work of the agrarian reform. An agrarian reform does not end with the equitable redistribution of land. In order to be effective it includes a total agricultural reform with two essential and complementary actions: (1) improvement in the knowledge and technology at the community's disposal for contending with the habitat, and (2) a change in the motivations and attitudes of the community itself so that the new knowledge and technology are accepted and assimilated. These two are the fundamental tasks entrusted to the agricultural program.

In communities with a modern culture, open to change and oriented toward the constant and sustained progress of agricultural knowledge and techniques, the work of an agricultural extension program is generally limited to providing new knowledge and techniques after these have been sifted through research, experimentation, and demonstration. Diffusion of improved seeds with higher yields, new methods for cultivation, fighting diseases, adequate use of fertilizers, rational exploitation of livestock and forests, and other innovations which increase productivity year after year, find wide acceptance among the progressive farmers who keep abreast of scientific advances. In this case agricultural extension is a simple process of the continuous transmission of new technology.

In the indigenous populations with primitive cultures and closed to change, implementation of agricultural extension work requires the establishment of prior conditions so that innovations proposed from without by agents who are foreign to the group may be adopted and become part of the community structure. Such conditions involve changing the integrative mechanisms that maintain the stability of Indian cultures and keep them separate and identifiable. In these cases it is not sufficient to show the advantages and benefits of new knowledge and techniques in increasing agricultural, livestock, and forest productivity for them to be accepted and used. Externally induced innovation brings subsequent repercussions that go beyond simple scientific or technological change. Its acceptance entails basic alterations in traditionally established values and in the norms of behavior that give meaning and reason to community life.

Agrarian reform is one of the prior conditions of technological change but there are others—internally generated by the Indian communities or induced by development programs—that create favorable attitudes toward change.[7] Among them are secularization and individualization of institutions, weakening of the power of the consanguineous hierarchy, increase in geographic and social mobility, exacerbation of demographic pressure, and improvement of interethnic relations. Yet another condition is ending the regions' isolation through construction of roads and an educational system to combat the population's illiteracy and monolingualism; in sum, through the implementation of an integral action plan attending to the harmonic development of all aspects of the group's culture.

Until the foregoing conditions are met, agricultural extension, defined as the total process of dissemination of a new technology, has to proceed with caution and constraint in achieving its goals. Any attempt to modify primitive technology, for example, must keep in mind that there is a reason for its existence. Considered from the framework of industrial culture, primitive technology is anachronistic and as such it is one of the many factors retarding progress. But examined within its own context it is a living and functional element of the culture. Its survival and retention is based sometimes on the poor quality of the soil, at others on the inclemency of the climate, on the abrupt gradients of the typography or on any of the other features forming the hostile profile of the regions of refuge. The mechanical transplant and imposition of modern technology into those regions often provokes irreparable destruction of the old which the new is incapable of replacing.[8]

In the Coordinating Centers the agricultural, livestock, and forestry extensions include the usual installations such as laboratories, posts for experimentation, demonstration and propagation, an animal farm, and tanks for breeding fish. It develops diffusion activities as well through common, generally applied methods. But it acts without precipitation, always seeking to accomodate itself to the situations, problems, and requirements of the community cultures; the fundamental goal is always to remove the obstacles in the way of the impulse toward progress, which is inherent in human nature and which in the Indian communities appears to have lost its force and vigor through continuous frustrations (Dey 1961). Its actions are simple, significant for the common person, and uncomplex. They do not go far beyond primitive technical horizons, with meticulous attention to the emotional reactions of the Indian and to the will he shows in undertaking the adventure of his own development. In performing his work the extensionist always relies upon the valuable help of the agricultural promoter—for the most part an Indian community leader—who knows profoundly the culture and psychology of the group from which he comes.

ECONOMIC FUNCTION. It is not the job of the Coordinating Centers to implement economic development in the regions of refuge. That work is the concern of the sum total of specialized governmental agencies acting on the national level. The centers' tasks are more modest but nonetheless important. They are to establish the prerequisites that are indispensable so that once administrative channels reach the regions of refuge, the latter can be integrated into plans for the country as a whole. The prior conditions to which we have referred consist basically of the construction of four principle types of infrastructure: transportation, credit, health, and education.

The characteristics particular to the regions of refuge have been noted repeatedly. They force the Coordinating Centers to accept a task that otherwise would fall to the governmental agency specifically responsible for road construction. In these regions, in the short-run roads are not used sufficiently to necessarily justify the monetary investment. Necessary roads begin as opening breaches in the isolation of the communities, tying them more directly to the central city. For the most part these roads will be used by staffs of the development programs to carry education, health, and other services that comprise integral action to the communities rapidly and expeditiously. Community participation in construction of the road network is limited to contributing to or helping with the small local roads directly affecting them (Caso et al. 1964).

When these initial roads acquire economic importance and become entry and exit routes for products and persons—breaking the self-sufficiency and geographic immobility of the regions of refuge—the Coordinating Centers stop implementing direct action and turn to specialized federal and state agencies, which take charge of expansion, repair, and maintenance of the dirt roads, which continue to help in the expansion of the market and in the money economy. Continuous coordination with specialized agencies from the initial phases enables Indian action agents to participate in planning the network of regional roads deliberately or accidentally affecting their work area and thus to coordinate the interests of the community development program with those of national integration. When the opening breaches are planned and constructed the possibility is always kept in mind that sooner or later they may be transformed into feeder roads for more major routes whose construction is anticipated.

Creation of a credit infrastructure to undermine the bases of the inefficient and anachronistic dual economy of the Ladino city and its Indian hinterland is another goal of the Coordinating Centers. Community development programs must attack the practice of extending credit with interest for the purpose of conspicuous consumption in anticipation of the wages that the Indian will earn as a laborer on the coffee, sugar cane, cotton, or banana plantations. Other factors to be attacked include the excessive profit margins at the expense of volume sales that keep the Indian's needs for manufactured articles unfulfilled, the small size of the internal market as a consequence of low per capita income, sparse capital formation, its unproductive administration, and other consequences of the domination process. Step by step the preconditions must be built that will make it possible for the regular administrative channels to take charge of modernizing the obsolete economy (Marroquín 1956).

As a general rule, neither the Indian nor the Ladino in the regions of refuge is a good credit risk in terms of the rules and regulations of the public or private national banking system. The characteristics of land tenancy, the types and amounts of crops raised, low productivity, the lack of transportation, storehouses and business organization, all discourage credit operations. It is the task of the Coordinating Centers to extend bridges between underdeveloped communities and the institutions in charge of supplying credit, so that they may serve Indians and Ladinos.

The mechanisms available to Indianist action for achieving its objectives are varied. They are always limited to a few goals that are simple and modest in scope. The principle goal has been to advise the ejidos and communities in the rational use of their forestry, agricultural, and livestock resources, both in terms of organizing cooperative business and, once formed, administering them. This advice is consciously aimed at strengthening associations for communal work, in accordance with modern economic norms but oriented toward social service rather than primarily toward obtaining a profit or surplus.

The Indian communities' agricultural surpluses are generally small and are sold at harvest time or before at prices far below their market value. The Ladino merchants, who give high interest loans, corner products in order to sell them in times of scarcity at high prices to the very same Indians. In order to partly remedy the instability of agricultural export prices, the Coordinating Centers cooperate with the decentralized governmental agencies entrusted with the purchase of these products. This cooperation is necessary in order for the agencies to carry out their regulative tasks, based on guaranteed prices (Torres Ordóñez 1958).

It cannot be doubted that the effective operation of the domination process in regions of refuge is largely determined by the low levels of schooling. The rates of illiteracy are so high that in practice only Ladinos in the region's main city obtain the benefits of education. Neither Ladinos in the secondary nucleuses nor the Indians dispersed throughout the hinterland do so. A high percentage of the latter speak only their mother tongue (Aguirre Beltrán 1953 b).

Another function of the Coordinating Center is to supervise building the educational infrastructure to provide a solid foundation for development. The training of qualified workers, formation of subtechnical and subprofessional teams needed for modernization and of highly capable staffs for directing and administering promotion of land, livestock, forests, and industry are all predicated on the prior literacy of the population. Thus the first step to be taken is to teach the monolingual Indians to read their native tongue. Concurrently they must be taught Spanish so that they can easily manage the official language, the means by which all Mexicans relate to one another.

This first step is the responsibility of the Coordinating Center. With a specific purpose, the Center limits directly implemented educational action to a single step in the formative process, namely literacy and Spanish. Once this is achieved the Coordinating Center turns to coordinated action and puts the education of the bilingual Indians into the hands of specialized agencies. Thus, in rural and urban schools, in primary boarding schools, secondary educational institutions, and in technical schools and universities, they can continue their preparation and extend their capabilities.

Coordinated action complements directly implemented action to establish the preconditions that are essential if the Indians are to benefit fully from the education offered by the State. In this way the uncertain procedure of erecting special schools for the Indians at the primary, secondary, and advanced levels is avoided. That procedure offers the attraction of a specific focus, but this is counteracted by the problem of segregating or giving apparently privileged status to the sector of the population most in need of integrative mechanisms to join it to the national society (De la Fuente 1965).

Construction of a public health infrastructure in the regions of refuge is the last of the tasks necessary for economic action to take force and be sustained. In planning any community development program one of the conditions on which modernization and economic increase must rest is the health of the inhabitants. The consequences of endemic and communicable diseases on productivity have been sufficiently demonstrated so that their mere mention justifies efforts to erradicate them (Martínez 1963). In the popular characterization of the campesino in the tropics as lazy and indolent, the illnesses that weaken and sap his efficiency play a greater part than is generally supposed.

Medical concepts and practices found in the regions of refuge, as well as other intercultural features, are obsolete. Among Indians as well as Ladinos, magico-religious explanations of diseases prevail, as do treatments consistent with such diagnoses. In the particular case of the Indian populations, curing acts not only as an instrument to dissolve the anxiety provoked by invalidism and death, but it is also a powerful tool for social cohesion, assuring cultural stability and continuity. Under these conditions, Indianist action is directed at achieving the rationalization and secularization of traditional medical concepts and practices and at simultaneously weakening the cohesive mechanisms rooted in magic and religion. With attainment of both goals, the public health work implemented directly by the Coordinating Center no longer has a reason for being and responsibility for maintaining the health of the people passes to a specialized agency. (Aguirre Beltrán 1955; Caso et al. 1962).

In addition to the activities outlined here, the Coordinating Centers directly implement or coordinate others that appear when the first set of goals has been attained. Among the latter, housing and urbanization programs that clearly transform the landscape of the Indian hinterland should be cited. Let us say, finally, that in the conception as well as execution of Indianist activity, research is invariably used as the most effective instrument for understanding and resolving problems. For completion of all those tasks the center relies on a university trained technical staff. It also relies on anthropologically oriented subprofessional and auxiliary staffs among which the cultural development agents originally appointed by the Coordinating Centers are outstanding.[9]

NOTES

1. Iwanska (1964:536) states: "Without any help from Mexican national ideology Mexico has achieved quite an outstanding degree of fusion between Spanish and Indian traditions, both in material culture and in certain customs. But the country has not achieved so far a unity on the level of consciousness, has not achieved ideological unity, and I doubt very much whether such a unity can ever be achieved without serious reformulation of the Mexican national ideology. The substitution of the image of the contemporary Indian peasant for the image of mythologized Neo-Indian seems to be the first necessary step in this reformulation."

2. Comas (1953) transcribes the exposition of the motives behind the law that created the Autonomous Department of Indian Affairs (Department Autónomo de Asuntos Indígenas), January 1, 1936.

3. Rens (1961:490) expounds the doctrine of integration, *piedra angular* of the Andine program, informing us that: "it is not directed only to Indians, who, thanks to their efforts and work, can lift themselves out of exploitation and serfdom. This doctrine calls equally upon the leading classes and all other sectors of the population of the Andine countries requesting them to open the doors of the nation to all disadvantaged citizens, so as to help in their general instruction and professional formation and to create the necessary conditions so that they can exercise, without obstacles and based on their own merits, all skills and professions. Therefore the doctrine of integration presents two aspects: on the one hand it constitutes a call to the Indian masses to learn, by their own efforts, to improve their conditions; on the other hand the document demonstrates to other sectors of the population that upon implementing equality for Indian citizens in the nation, these populations, once integrated, will enrich the nation by increasing its economic potential, social cohesion and cultural achievements."

After defining the bases of action, he states: "These bases are not adjusted to any rigid formula, which explains why if all have some characteristics in common, no two are identical. An action base consists of a team of national and international experts integrated by a chief, an agronomist, a doctor, an educational specialist, a veterinarian, a social worker, a nurse, a midwife, some instructors in professional and artesanry skills, etc. Every base is established in some place selected jointly by the government involved and the International Labor Organization, in consultation with the other participating organizations. In general this site is the center of a typically Indian region, from which the works can radiate outward among a rather large population."

4. Studies of the Indian nucleuses are few and inaccessible. Elizardo Pérez (1962) published an extensive work, largely biographical, relating the titanic labor of the founders of Warisata. Toribio Clauré (1949) tells of the birth of his rural school in Vacas. Rafael Reyeros (1937), in a very fine little book, tells of his visit, on the suggestion of Alfredo Guillén Pinto, to the nucleus of Caquiaviri. In Mexico, Velasco (1940) reported on the Indian experiment in Warisata. Regarding integration of land parcels, the PNIPA, Lima, published a mimeographed report by two agronomists, Guillermo Bendezú and Carlos Samaniego (1965). Previously, Hector Martínez (1964) had released an analysis of the attempt formulated by social agents and their organizer, Professor Luis Gallegos, "who explained to members of the Program's *jefatura* in conversations with them the possibility of the project and its form of implementation."

5. See Caso (1958:55) for a vivid explication of the initial work of the first Coordinating Center in Chiapas.

6. Canelas (1966) in Bolivia and Seoane (1963) and Malpica (1963) [sic] in Peru have all produced excellent studies on agrarian reform.

7. See Foster (1964) Chapter VIII.

8. See Spicer (1963) Part IV, "Conceptual Instruments for the Solution of Human Problems."

9. See de la Fuente (1964b) Chapter VIII, "A Program for the Preparation of *Promotores* in Mexico."

BIBLIOGRAPHY

ADAMS, R.N.

1953 A change from caste to class in a Peruvian sierra town. Social Forces 31:238-44.

1956 Ladinización en Guatemala. *In* Integracíon Social de Guatemala, J Arriola. ed, Guatemala: SISG.

1959 A Community in the Andes: Problems and Progress in Muquiyauyo. Seattle: University of Washington Press.

1962 The community in Latin America: a changing myth. The Centennial Review 6:409-34.

AGARWALA, A. N., and S. P. SINGH

1963 La Economía del Subdesarrollo. Madrid: Tecnos.

AGUILAR, L. F.

1922 Cuestiones Indígenas. Cuzco: Biblioteca El Comercio.

AGUIRRE BELTRAN, G.

1946 La Población Negra de México. México City: Fuente Cultural.

1952 Problemas de la Población Indigena de la Cuenca del Tepalcatepec. México City: INI.

1953a Formas de Gobierno Indigena. México City: Imprenta Universitaria.

1953b Teoría y práctica de la educación indígena. *In* Estudios Sociologicos. IV Congreso de Sociología. México City: UNAM.

1955 Programas de Salud en la Situación Intercultural. México:III.

1957 El Proceso de Aculturación. México City: UNAM.

1963 Medicina y Magia. El Proceso de Aculturación en la Estructura Colonial. México City: INI.

1965 La integración de la población negra a la sociedad nacional. Paper presented at the Conference on Race and Class in Latin America during the National Period. Cornell University, Ithaca, New York. Mimeo.

AGUIRRE BELTRAN, G., and R. POZAS ARCINIEGA

1954 Instituciones indigenas en el México actural. *In* Metados y Resultados de la Politica Indigenista en México, A. Caso, et al., eds. México City: INI.

ALLPORT, G. W.

1963 La Naturaleza del Prejuicio. Buenos Aires: Eudeba.

ARGUEDAS, J. M.

1957 Evolución de las comunidades indígenas: en valle del Mantaro y la ciudad de Huancayo. Un caso de fusión de culturas no comprometida por la acción de instituciones de origen colonial. Revista del Museo Nacional, Lima 26:78-151.

ARGUEDAS, J. M., ed.

1964 Estudios Sobre la Cultura Actual del Perú. Lima: UNMSM.

ARRIOLA, J. L., ed.

1956 Integración Social de Guatemala. Guatemala: SISG.

BALANDIER, G.

1963 Sociologie Actuelle de l'Afrique noire. Paris: PUF.

BARAN, P. A.

1964 La Economía Política del Crecimiento. México City: FCE.

BARBER, B.

1964 Estratificación Social. México City: FCE.

BARCLEY, G. W.

1955 Urban growth and population redistribution in the far East. Proceedings of the World Population Conference, Rome. United Nations 2:715-25.

BARNES, H. E., and H. BECKER

1938 Social Thought from Lore to Science. 2 Vols. Boston: Heath.

BARNETT, A.

1950 The Human Species: A Biology of Man. London: Norton.

BARNETT, H. G.

1953 Innovation: The Basis of Cultural Change. New York: McGraw-Hill.

BARRE, R.

1962 El Desarrollo Económico. Análisis y Política. México City: FCE.

BARTHOLOMEW, G. A., and J. BIRDSELL

1962 Ecology and the protohominides. *In* Culture and the Evolution of Man. A. Montague, ed. New York and London: Oxford University Press.

BARRE, R.

1962 El Desarrollo Económico. Análisis y Política. México City: FCE.

BASCOM, W. R.

1948 Ponapean prestige economy. Southwestern Journal of Anthropology 4:211-21.

BASCOM, W. R., and M. J. HERSKOVITS, eds.
1959 Continuity and Change in African Cultures. Chicago: Phoenix.

BATES, M.
1952 Where Winter Never Comes: A Study of Man and Nature in the Tropics. New York: Scribners.
1962 The Prevalence of People. New York: Scribners.

BAUER, P. T., and B. S. YAMEY
1965 Economía de los países subdesarrollados. Mexico City: Editorial Humanidades.

BEALS, R. L.
1951 Urbanism, urbanization and acculturation. American Anthropologist 53:1-10.
1954 Social stratification in Latin America. American Journal of Sociology 63:327-339.
1956 Commentarios a Richard N. Adams. *In* Integración Social de Guatemala, J.L. Ariola, ed. Guatemala, C.A.:SISG.
1965 Impact of modern economy on a traditional system of markets. Paper read at the Round Table. Universidad Benito Juarez, Oaxaca, México.

BECKER, H.
1942 Changing societies as family contexts. *In* Marriage and the Family, H. Becker and R. Hill, eds. Boston: Heath.
1950 Sacred and secular societies: considered with reference to Folk-state and similar classifications. Social Forces 28:361-76.

BECKER, H., and R. HILL, eds.
1942 Marriage and the Family. Boston: Heath.

BELSHAW, C. S.
1965 Traditional Exchange and Modern Markets. Englewood Cliffs, N. J.: Prentice-Hall.

BENDEZÚ, G., and C. SAMANIEGO
1965 La Familia Extensa y la Integración Parcelaria en el Altiplano de Puno, Peru. Lima: PNIPA. Mimeo.

BERELSON, B., ed.
1963 The Behavioral Sciences Today. New York: Harper.

BERNAL VILLA, S.
1954 Economía de los páez. Revista Colombiana de Antropologia 3:291-367.

BERZUNZA PINTO, R.
1941 Los Indigenas y la República Mexicana. La Política indigenista del Partido Comunista Mexicano. México.

BIRKET-SMITH, K.
1960 Primitive Man and His Ways. New York: Mentor.

BLACKER, C. P.
1947 Stages in population growth. Eugenics Review 39:88-102.

BLANKSTEIN, G. I.
1956 Comentario a Manning Nash. *In* Integracion Social de Guatemala, J. L. Arriola, ed. Guatemala C.G.: SISG.

BLANQUEL, E.
1963 El Pensamiento Político de Ricardo Flores Magón, Precursor de la Revolución Mexicana. Ph. D. Dissertation, Facultad de Filosofía y Letras, National University of México, México City.

BOAZ, F.
1946 Race and Democratic Society. New York: Agustin.
1964 Cuestiones Fundamentales de Antropologia Cultural (The Mind of Primitive Man). Buenos Aires: Solar-Hachette.

BOEKE, J. H.
1930 Dualistische Economie. Leiden: S. C. Van Doesburg.
1942 The Structure of the Netherlands Indian Economy. New York: Institute of Pacific Relations.
1953 Economics and Economic Policy of Dual Societies as Exemplified by Indonesia. New York: Institute of Pacific Relations.
1954 La developpment du capitalisme en Indonésie et en Ouganda. Bulletin International des Sciences Sociales 6:473-83.

BOGUE, D. J.
1964 Internal migration. *In* The Study of Population: An Inventory and Appraisal. Chicago: University of Chicago Press.

BOUVIER, M.
1965 Las Clases Scoales y el Marxismo. Buenos Aires: Platino.

BOWMAN, I.
1957 Settlement by the modern pioneer. *In* Geography in the Twentieth Century, G. Taylor, ed. London: Methuen.

BRYSON, L., ed.
1965 Cambios Sociales en América Latina. México City: Libreros Mexicanos Unidos.

BUITRÓN, A.
1964 Tata Imbabura. Quito: Misión Andina.

CANCIAN, F.
1965 Economics and Prestige in a Maya Community: The Religious Cargo System in Zinacantan. Stanford: Stanford University Press.

CANELAS, A.
1966 Mito y Realidad de la Reforma Agraria. La Paz: Los Amigos del Libro.

CARPENTER, C. R.
1958 Territoriality: a review of concepts and problems. *In* Behavior and Evolution, G. C. Simpson and A. Roe, eds. New Haven: Yale University Press.

CARRASCO, P.
1961 The civil-religious hierarchy in mesoamerican communities: pre-Spanish background and colonial development. American Anthropologist 63:483-97.

CARR-SAUNDERS, M.
1939 Población Mundial. México D.F.: FCE.

CASO, A.
1955 ¿Que es el INI? México D. F.: INI.
1958 Indigenismo. México D. F.: INI.

CASO, A., et al.
1954 Métodos y Resultados de la Política Indigenista en México. México City: INI.
1962 Los Centros Coordinadores. México D. F.: INI.
1964 Realidades y Proyectos: 16 Años de Trabajo. México City: INI.

CASTRO POZO, H.
1924 Nuestra Comunidad Indigena. Lima: E. L. Lucero.

CHAPPLE, E. D., and C. S. COON
1953 Principles of Anthropology. New York: Holt.

CIPOLLA, C. M.
1964 Historia Económica de la Población Mundial. Buenos Aires: Eudeba.

CLARK, C.
1951 The Conditions of Economic Progress. London: Macmillan.
1955 What constitutes rural over-population? Proceedings of the World Population Conference, Rome. United Nations 5:227-50.

CLAURÉ, T.
1949 Una Escula Rural en Vacas. La Paz: Empressa Editoria

COLBY, B. N., and P. L. VAN DER BERGHE
1961 Ethnic relations in southeastern Mexico. American Anthropologist 63:772-92.

COMAS, J.
1953 Ensayos Sobre Indigenismo. México, D. F.: III.
1957 Manual de Anthropologis Fisica. México, D. F.: FCE.
1964 La Antropología Social Aplicada en México. Trayectoria y Antologia. México, D. F.: III.

COON, C. S., and E. E. HUNT
1963 Anthropology A to Z. New York: Grosset's.

COONTZ, S. H.
1960 Teorías de la Población y su Interpretación Económica. México, D.F.: FCE.

COPELAND, L. C.
1964 Las funciones de una idealogía racial. *In* Historia y Elementos de la Sociología del Conocimiento. 2 Vols, I. L. Horowitz, ed. Buenos Aires: Eudeba.

COSER, L. A.
1961 Las Funciones del Conflicto Social. México, D. F.: FCE.

COSTALES, P., and A. COSTALES
1957 Katekil: Historia Cultural del Campesino del Chimborazo. Quito: Llacta
1966 El Quishihuar o el Arbol de Dios. Quito: IEAG.

COX, O. C.
1948 Caste, Class, and Race. Garden City: Doubleday.

CREVENNA, T. R.
1951 Materiales Para el Estudio de la Clase Media en la America Latina. Washington, D. C.: Union Panamericana.

DAHRENDORF, R.
1959 Class and Class Conflict in Industrial Society. Stanford: Stanford University Press.

DALTON, G.
1961 Economic theory and primitive society. American Anthropologist 63:1-25.

DANIELS, F.
1955 Population in relation to the development of solar engergy. Proceedings of the World Population Conference, Rome. United Nations 5:15-24.

DAVIS, K.
1955 Internal migration and urbanization in relation to economic development. Proceedings of the World Population Conference, Rome. United Nations 2:783-801.
1963 Social demography. *In* The Behavioral Sciences, B. Berelson, ed. New York: Harper.
1965 La Sociedad Humana. 2 Vols. Buenos Aires: Eudeba.

DE CASTRO, J.
1952 Geopolitique de la Faim. Paris: Les Editions Ouvrières.
1964 Geopolitica del Hambre. Essayos Sobre los Problemas Alimentarios y Demograficos del Mundo. Buenos Aires: Solar-Hachette.

DE LA FUENTE, J.
1952 Ethnic and communal relations. *In* Heritage of Conquest, S. Tax, ed. Glencoe: The Free Press.
1964a Relaciones étnicas en Mesoamérica. *In* La Antropología Social Aplicada en México. Trayectoria y Antologia, J. Comas, ed. México, D. F.: III.
1964b Educación, antropología y desarrolla de la Comunidad. México, D.F.: INI.
1965 Relaciones Interétnicas. México, D. F.: INI.

DE LAS CASAS, FRAY BARTOLOMÉ
1822 Obras Completas. Paris: En Casa de Rosa.

DEY, S.
1961 Extension and community development. Paper read at the Ninth International Training Center on Methods and Program Planning in Agriculture and Home Economics Extension, Wageningen, Netherlands. Mimeo.

DÍAZ BARRIGA, J., J. Q. OLASCOAGA, A. SCÁRPITA, and N. J. WHITTAKER
1965 Doctrina del Desarrollo de los Pueblos. Importancia Fundamental de la Nutricíon. México, D. F.: Junta Nacional para el Mejoramiento de la Alimentacion.

DICKINSON, R. E.
1961 Ciudad, Región y Regionalismo. Contribución Geográfica a la Ecología Humana. Barcelona: Omega.

DIEGUES, M., Jr.
1952 Introducción a la Sociología Regional. México, D. F.: UNAM.
DIEZ DE SAN MIGUEL, G.
1964 Visita Hecha la Provincia de Chucuito por . . . el Año 1567. Lima: Casa de la Cultura.
DOBYNS, H. F.
1951 Blunders with bolsas. Human Organization 10:25-32.
1964 The Social Matrix of Peruvial Indigenous Communities. Ithaca: Cornell University Press.
DOBZHANSKY, T.
1941 Genetics and the Origin of Species. New York: Columbia University Press.
DOLLARD, J.
1937 Caste and Class in a Southern Town. New Haven: Yale University Press.
DRUCKER, S.
1963 Cambios de Indumentaria. México, D. F.: INI.
DU BOIS, C.
1961 The People of Alor. 2 Vols. New York: Harper.
DUMONT, A.
1890 Dépopulation et Civilization. Paris: Lecrosnien et Babé.
DUMONT, L.
1960 Castes, racisme et stratification. Cahiers Internationaux de Sociologie 29:91-112.
DURÁN, FRAY DIEGO
1951 Historia de las Indias de Nueva España y Islas de Tierra Firme. 2 Vols. México, D. F.: Editora Nacional.
DURKHEIM, E.
1961 Sociologia. Cordoba: Assandri.
ERASMUS, C. J.
1965 The occurrence and disappearance of reciprocal farm labor in Latin America. *In* Contemporary Cultures and Societies of Latin America. D. B. Heath and R. A. Adams, eds. New York: Random House.
EVANS-PRITCHARD, E. E.
1962 Social Anthropology and Other Essays. Glencoe: The Free Press.
FARRINGTON, B.
1951 Demócrito, platón y epicura. *In* Filosofía del Futuro, R. W. Sellers, et al., eds. México, D. F.: Compania General de Ediciones.
FIRTH, R.
1954 La monnaie, le travail et l'évolution sociale dans les systèmes economiques de la région indo-pacifique. Bulletin International des Sciences Sociales 6:445-56.
1958 Human Types: An Introduction to Social Anthropology. New York: Mentor.
1963a Tipos Humanos: Una Introducción a la Antropologia Social. Buenos Aires: Eudeba.
1963b Elements of Social Organization. Boston: Beacon Press.
1964 A viewpoint of economic anthropology. *In* Capital, Saving and Credit in Peasant Societies, R. Firth and B. S. Yamey, eds. Chicago: Aldine.
FIRTH, R., and B. S. YAMEY, eds.
1964 Capital, Saving and Credit in Peasant Societies. Chicago: Aldine.
FLORES, E.
1962 Tratado de Economia Agrícola. México, D. F.: FCE.
FORDE, C. D.
1953 Habitat, Economy and Society: A Geographical Introduction To Ethnology. London: Methuen.
FORDE, C. D., and M. DOUGLAS
1960 Primitive economics. *In* Man, Culture and Society, H. L. Shapiro, ed. New York: Oxford University Press.
FORSYTH, W. D.
1942 The Myth of Open Spaces. Melbourne: Melbourne University Press.
FOSTER, G. M.
1942 A Primitive Mexican Economy. New York: Augustin.
1964 Las Culturas Tradicionales y los Cambios Técnicos. México, D. F.: FCE.
FRIEDE, J.
1944 El Indio en Lucha por la Tierra. Historia de los Resguardos del Macizo Central Colombiano. Bogota: Espiral.
FROMM, E.
1947 Man for Himself. New York: Rinehart.
1958 El Miedo a la Libertad. Buenos Aires: Paidós.
FURNIVALL, J. S.
1939 Netherlands India. Cambridge: Cambridge University Press.
FUSFELD, D. B.
1957 Economic theory misplaced: livelihood in primitive society. *In* Trade and Markets in the Early Empires, K. Polanyi, et al., eds. New York: The Free Press.
GALDO PAGAZA, R.
1962a El Indígena y el Mestizo de Vilquechico. Lima: Mtal. Mimeo.
1962b Economía de las Colectivades Indígenas Colindantes con el Lago Titacaca. Lima: Matai. Mimeo.
GAMIO, M.
1956 Estudios Antropológicos Publicados en Homenaje el Doctor Manuel Gamio. México, D.F.: Dirección General de Publicaciones.
GARCÍA, A.
1948 Regímenes indígenas de salariado. America Indigena 8:249-87.
GARCÍA, U.
1930 El Nuevo Indio. Ensayos Indianistas Sobre la Sierra Sur-Peruana. Cuzco: Editorial Rozas.
GILLAN, J.
1949 Mestizo America. *In* Most of the World, R. Linton, ed. New York: Columbia University Press.
1951 The Culture of Security in San Carlos. New Orleans: Tulane University Press.

GONNARD, R.
1945 Historia de las Doctrinas de la Población. México, D. F.: Editorial America.
GONZÁLEZ CASANOVA, P.
1965 La Democracia en México. México, D. F.: Ediciones Era.
GOULD, J., and W. L. KOLB, eds.
1964 A Dictionary of the Social Sciences. Glencoe: The Free Press.
GOUROU, P.
1953 Les Pays Tropicaux. Principes d'une Geographie Humaine et Economique. Paris: PUF.
GUEVARA, D.
1957 Las Mingas en el Ecuador. Quito: Editorial Universitaria.
GUITERAS HOLMES, C.
1965 Los Peligros del Alma. México, D. F.: FCE.
GURVITCH, G.
1960 El Concepto de Clases Sociales de Marx a nuestros días. Buenos Aires: Ediciones Galatea.
1963 Problemas de la sociologie de la connaissance. *In* El Concepto de Clases Sociales, G. Gurvitch, ed. Buenos Aires: Ediciones Galatea.
GURVITCH, G., ed.
1963 Traíte de Sociologie. 2 Vols. Paris: PUF.
GUTKIND, E. A.
1956 Our world from the air: conflict and adaptation. *In* Man's Role in Changing the Face of the Earth. W. Thomas, ed. Chicago: University of Chicago Press.
GUYOL, N. B.
1955 Population and energy resources. Proceedings of the World Population Conference, Rome. United Nations 5:25-46.
GERTH, H. H., and C. W. MILLS, eds.
1948 From Max Weber: Essays in Sociology. London: Routledge and Kegan Paul.
HALLOWELL, H. I.
1955 Culture and Experience. Philadelphia: University of Pennsylvania Press.
HAMMOND, P. B.
1959 Economic change and Mossi acculturation. *In* Continuity and Change in African Cultures, W. R. Bascom and M. J. Herskovits, eds. Chicago: Phoenix.
HAMMOND, P., ed.
1965 Culture and Social Anthropology: Selected Readings. New York: Macmillan.
HAUSER, P. M., ed.
1965 The Population Dilemma. Englewood Cliffs: Prentice-Hall.
HAUSER, P. M., and O. D. DUNCAN, eds.
1964 The Study of Population: An Inventory and Appraisal. Chicago: University of Chicago Press.
HAWLEY, A. M.
1962 Ecología Humana. Madrid: Tecnos.
HEATH, D. B., and R. N. ADAMS
1965 Contemporary Cultures and Societies of Latin America. New York: Random House.
HEIDIGER, H. P.
1961 The evolution of territorial behavior. *In* Social Life of Early Man, S. Washburn, ed. New York: Viking.
HEINTZ, P., ed.
1960 Sociología del Poder. Santiago: Andrés Bello.
HERMITTE, M. E.
1962 Social Mobility in a Chiapas Bicultural Town. Ph.D. Dissertation, University of Chicago, Chicago. Mimeo.
HERNÁNDEZ DE ALBA, G.
1963 The highland tribes of southern Colombia. *In* Native Peoples of South America, J. Steward and L. Faron, eds. New York: McGraw-Hill.
HERSKOVITS, M. J.
1926 The cattle complex in east Africa. American Anthropologist 28:230-72; 361-80; 494-528; 633-64.
1940 The Economic Life of Primitive Peoples. New York: Knopf.
1945 The processes of cultural change. *In* The Science of Man in the World Crisis, R. Linton, ed. New York: Columbia University Press.
1948 Man and His Works. New York: Knopf.
1954a Antropología Económica. Mexico, D. F.: FCE.
1954b Motivations et modèles culturels en periode de transformation technique. Bulletin International des Sciences Sociales 6:432-444.
HIGGINS, B.
1959 Economic Development: Principles, Problems and Policies. New York: Norton.
HIRSCHMAN, A. B.
1964 La Estragegia del Desarrollo Económico. México, D. F.: FCE.
HOEBEL, E. A.
1961 El Hombre en el Mundo Primitivo. Introducción a la Anthropología. Barcelona: Omega.
HOLMBERG, A. R.
1965 Actitudes y valores cambiantes de la communidad en Perú: estudio experimental de cambio dirigido. *In* Cambios Sociales en America Latina, L. Bryson, ed. México, D. F.: Libreros Mexicanos Unidos.
HONIGMANN, J. J.
1959 The World of Man. New York: Harper.
HOPKINS, T. K.
1957 Sociology and the substantive view of the economy. *In* Trade and Market in the Early Empires, R. Polanyi, et al., eds. New York: The Free Press.
HOROWITZ, I. L., ed.
1964 Historia y Elementos de la Sociología Del Conocimiento. 2 Vols. Buenos Aires: Eudeba.
HOSELITZ, B. F.
1962 Aspectos Sociológicos del Desarrollo Económico. Barcelona: Hispano Europea.
HOUTART, F.
1964 El Cambio Social en América Latina. Bruselas: FERES.

HOYT, E. E.
1955 El Trabajador Indígena en las Fincas Cafetaleras de Guatemala. Ciencias Sociales 6:258-68.
HUNTER, M.
1964 Reaction to Conquest: Effects of Contacts with Europeans on the Pondo of South Africa. London: Oxford University Press.
HUNTINGTON, E.
1962 Mainspring of Civilization. New York: Mentor.
HURTADO, A.
1951 El hombre en las grandes alturas habitadas. *In* Conferencia de Ciencias Antropológicas. Lima: UNMSM.
IWANSKA, A.
1964 The Mexican Indian image and identity. Journal of Inter-American Studies 6:529-36.
JACOBS, M., and B. J. STEEN
1959 General Anthropology. New York: Barnes and Noble.
KANT, E.
1965 Classification and problems of migrations. *In* Readings in Cultural Geography, P. Wagner and M. Mikesell, eds. Chicago: University of Chicago Press.
KAPLAN, B. A.
1953 Ethnic identification in an Indian Mestizo community. Phylon 14:179-90.
KEITH, SIR A.
1931 Ethics on The Problem of Peace Considered from a New Point of View. London: Kegan Paul.
KENNEDY, R.
1945 The Colonial crisis and the future. *In* The Science of Man in the World Crisis, R. Linton, ed. New York: Columbia University Press.
KOENIG, S.
1961 Sociology. New York: Barnes & Noble.
KRADER, L., and A. PALERM, eds.
1958 Estudios de Ecología Humana. Washington, D. C.: Unión Panamericana.
KROEBER, A. L.
1948 Anthropology. New York: Harcourt.
KUZNETS, S.
1955 Underdeveloped countries and the preindustrial phase in the advanced countries: an attempt at comparison. Preceedings of the World Population Conference, Rome. United Nations 5:947-69.
1964 Aspectos Cuantitativos del Desarrollo Económico. México, D. F.: CEML.
LAMBERT, J.
1963 Amerique Latine. Structures Sociales et Institutions Politiques. Paris: PUF.
LANDIS, P. H.
1943 Population Problems: A Cultural Interpretation. New York: American Book Company.
LEE, A. M.
1964 Principles of Sociology. New York: Barnes & Noble.
LEIBENSTEIN, H.
1963 Economic Backwardness and Economic Growth. New York: Wiley.
LEÓN-PORTILLA, M.
1962 Indians in the Hemisphere Today. Guide to the Indian Population. México, D.F.: III.
LÉVI-STRAUSS, C.
1958 Anthropologie Structurale. Paris: Plon.
LEVY, C.
1961 Les critères du sous-developpement. Tiers-Monde 39:137-48. Paris: PUF.
LEVY-BRUHL, L.
1928 L'Ame Primitive. Paris: Alcan.
1930 Le Surnaturel et la Nature dans la Mentalité Primitive. Paris: Alcan.
1935 La Mythologie Primitive. Paris: Alcan.
1938 L'Experience Mystique et les Symboles Chez les Primitifs. Paris: Alcan.
1945 La Mentalidad Primitiva. Buenos Aires: Lautaro.
1947 Las Funciones Mentales en las Sociedades Inferiores. Buenos Aires: Lautaro.
LEWIS, A.
1954 Economic development with unlimited supplies of labour. The Manchester School of Economic and Social Studies 147:139-191.
LEWIS, O.
1949 Plow culture and hoe culture:: a study in contrasts. Rural Sociology 14:116-27.
LINTON, R.
1943 Nativistic movement. American Anthropologist 45:230-40.
1944 Estudio del Hombre. México, D. F.: FCE.
LINTON, R., ed.
1945 The Science of Man in the World Crisis. New York: Columbia University Press.
1949 Most of the World. New York: Columbia University Press.
LIPSCHUTZ, A.
1956 La Comunidad Indígena en América y en Chile. Santiago: Editorial Universitaria.
LIPSET, S. M.
1963 El Hombre Politico. Buenos Aires: Eudeba.
LÓPEZ SARRELANGUE, D. E.
1965 La Nobleza Indígena de Pátzcuaro en la Época Virreinal. México, D. F.: UNAM.
LORIMER, F.
1954 Culture and Human Fertility. Paris: UNESCO.
LOYO, G.
1943 La Presíon Demográfica. México, D.F.: El Colegio de México.
1960 La Población de México. Estado Actual y Tendencias. 1960-1980. México, D.F.: IMRNR.
LUELMO, J. (M. OLMEDO)
1965 El Desarrollo de la Sociedad. 2 Vols. México, D. F.: FCE.
MACIVER, R. M., and C. H. PAGE
1960 Sociología. Madrid: Tecnos.

MAINE, H. S.
1963 Ancient Law. Boston: Beacon Press.
MAIR, L.
1962 Primitive Government. Baltimore: Penguin.
MALINOWSKI, B.
1944 A Scientific Theory of Culture and Other Essays. Chapel Hill: University of North Carolina Press.
1945 The Dynamics of Culture Change. New Haven: Yale University Press.
1961 Argonauts of the Western Pacific. New York: Dutton.
MALINOWSKI, B., and J. DE LA FUENTE
1957 La Economía de un Sistema de Mercados en México. México, D.F.: Acta Antropologica.
MALPICA, C. Q.
1963 Guerra a Muerte al Latifundio. Lima: Ediciones Voz Rebelde.
MANGIN, W. P.
1955 Estratificación social en el Callejón de Huaylas. Revista del Museo Nacional, Lima 24:174-89.
MARIÁTEGUI, J. C.
1928 Siete Ensayos de Interpretación de la Realidad Peruana. Lima: Biblioteca Amauta.
MARROQUÍN, A. D.
1955 Introducción al mercado indígena Méxicano, Saenah, Mexico. Mimeo.
1956 Problemas económicos de las comunidades indígenas de México. Saenah, Mexico. Mimeo.
1957 La Ciudad Mercado. México, D. F.: Imprenta Universitaria.
1958 Características de la economía indigena Mexicana. Accíon Indigenista 56.
MARTÍNEZ, H.
1959 Vicos: las fiestas en la integración y desintegración cultural. Revista del Museo Nacional, Lima 28:189-247.
1961 Las Migraciones Altiplánicas y la Colonización del Tambopata. Lima: PNIPA.
1962 El Indigena y el Mestizo de Taraco. Lima: MTA. MIMEO.
MARTÍNEZ, P. D.
1963 Planeación de la salud pública como factor de desarrollo nacional. Salud Pública de México 621-26.
MATOS MAR, J.
1965 Algunas caracterizaciones generals de las comunidades indigenas del área andina. Cuadernos de Antropologiá, Lima 3:1-12.
MCCLELLAN, D. C.
1961 The Achieving Society. Princeton: Van Nostrand.
MCKINNEY, J. C., and C. P. LOOMIS
1963 The application of gemeinschaft and gesellschaft as related to other typologies. *In* Community and Society, F. Toennies, ed. New York: Harper.
MEGGERS, B. J.
1958 Ambiente y cultura en la cuenca amazónica: un examen de la teória del determinismo ambiental. Krader y Palerm 71-90.
MENCÍAS, J.
1962 Riobamba, Ecuador. Estudio de Elevación Socio-Cultural del Indio. Friburgo: Feres.
MENDIETA Y NUÑEZ, L.
1938 La Economia Del Indio. México, D. F.: INI.
MENTON, S.
1965 The changing view of the Indian in the Latin American novel. Conference on Race and Class in Latin America During the National Period. Cornell University, Ithaca, New York. Mimeo.
MISHKIN, B.
1964 Posesión de la tierra en la comunidad de Kauri, Quispicanchis, Cuzco. *In* Estudios Sobre la Cultura Actual del Perú, J. M. Arguedas, ed. Lima: UNMSM.
MONGE MEDRANO, C.
1962 Aclimatación en los Andes. Lima: PNIPA.
MONTAGU, A., ed.
1962 Culture and the Evolution of Man. New York: Oxford University Press.
MOORE, S.
1964 Ideología y alienación. *In* Historia y Elementos de la Sociologia del Conocimiento, I. Horowitz, ed. Buenos Aires: Eudeba.
MOORE, W. E.
1951 Industrialization and Labor. Ithaca: Cornell University Press.
MORLEY, S. G.
1947 La Civilización Maya. México, D.F.: FCE.
MUMFORD, L.
1938 The Culture of Cities. New York: Harcourt.
MURRA, J. V.
1959 Land Tenures in the Inca State. Paper read at the Symposium on Land Tenures in the High Civilizations of Americas, Annual Meetings of the American Anthropological Association, Mexico 1959.
MYINT, H.
1965 Economía de los Países en Desarrollo. Madrid: Ediciones RIALP.
MYRDAL, G.
1964 Teoría Económica y Regiones Subdesarrolladas. México, D.F.: FCE.
NACIONES UNIDAS
1963 Informa del grupo especial de expertos en desarrollo de la comunidad. Consejo Económico Social, 63-05386. Mimeo.
NADEL, S. F.
1962 The Theory of Social Structure. London: Cohen.
NASH, M.
1956 Relaciones políticas en Guatemala. *In* Integración Social de Guatemala, J. L. Arriola, ed. Guatemala: SISG.
1957 The multiple society in economic development: Mexico and Guatemala. American Anthropologist 59:825-33.

1964 The Indian economics of middle America. *In* Actas y Memorias del XXXV Congreso Internacional de Americanistas 3:299-311.
NAVARRETE, A., and I. NAVARRETTE
1963 El subempleo en los países subdesarrollados. *In* La economía del Subdesarrollo, A. N. Agarwala and S. P. Singh, eds. Madrid: Tecnos.
NEALE, W. C.
1965 Reciprocity and redistribution. *In* Cultural and Social Anthropology: Selected Readings, P. Hammond, ed. New York: Macmillan.
NESTURJ, M. F.
1965 Las Razas Humanas. Moscú: Editoral Progreso.
NIDA, E. A.
1954 Customs and Cultures: Anthropology for Christian Missions. New York: Harper.
NUÑEZ DEL PRADO, O.
1949 Chinchero, un pueblo andino del sur. Revista Universitaria 38:177-230.
1962 Sicuani, un Pueblo Grande. Reacción Social Para la Colonización de Maldonado. Lima: PNIPA.
1964 El hombre y la familia: su matrimonio y organización politica social en Q'ero. *In* Estudios Sobre la Cultura Actual del Perú, J. M. Arguedas, ed. Lima: UNMSM.
1965 Aspects of Andean native life. *In* Contemporary Cultures and Societies of Latin America, D. B. Heath and R. N. Adams, eds. New York: Random House.
NURKSE, R.
1963 Problemas de Formación de Capital en los Países Insuficientemente desarrollados. México, D. F.: FCE.

OLIVEIRA, R. C. DE
1964 Ó Indio e o Mundo dos Brancos: A Situaçao dos Tukúna do Alto Solimoes. Sao Paulo: Difusão Européia do Livro.
ORTIZ, V. P.
1962 Organización social en la Pampa de Llave, Puno. Lima: Mtai. Mimeo.
1965 Las Sub-Culturas Peruanas. Lima: PNIPA.
OVANDO, J.
1961 Sobre el Problema Nacional y Colonial de Bolivia. Cochabamba: Editorial Canelas.

PALERM, Á.
1952 Notas sobre la clase media en México. Comentario a un Estudio ne N. L. Wheten. Ciencias Sociales 3:18-27; 129-35.
PARSONS, T.
1951 The Social System. Glencoe: The Free Press.
1954 Essays in Sociological Theory. Glencoe: The Free Press.
PELZER, K. J.
1957 Geography and the tropics. *In* Geography in the Twentieth Century, G. Taylor, ed. London: Methuen.
PÉREZ, ELIZARDO
1962 Warisata: La Escuela-Ayllu. La Paz.
PIDDINGTON, R.
1957 An Introduction to Social Anthropology. 2 Vols. London: Oiver.
PITT-RIVERS, J. A., and N. A. MCQUOWN
1964 Social, Cultural and Linguistic Change in the Highlands of Chiapas. Department of Anthropology, University of Chicago. Rototype.
POLANYI, K.
1944 The Great Transformation. New York: Rinehart.
1957a Aristotle discovers the economy. *In* Trade and Market in the Early Empires, K. Polanyi, C. M. Arensberg, and H. W. Pearson, eds. New York: The Free Press.
1957b The economy as instituted process. *In* Trade and Market in the Early Empires, K. Polanyi, C. M. Arensberg, and H. W. Pearson, eds. New York: The Free Press.
POLANYI, K., C. M. ARENSBERG, and H. W. PEARSON, eds.
1957 Trade and Market in the Early Empires. New York: The Free Press.
PONCE DE LEÓN, F.
1946 Al Servicio de los Aborígenes Peruanos. Cuzco: Miranda.
POZAS, R.
1945 El fraccionamiento de la tierra por el mecanismo de la herencia en Chamula. Revista Mexicana de Estudios Antropologicos 7:187-97.
1959 Chamula Un Pueblo Indio de los Altos de Chiapas. México, D. F.: INI.
PRESSAT, R.
1961 Caractéristiques démographiques des pays sous-développés: mortalité. Le Tiers-Monde, Cahier 39:175-88.
PULGAR VIDAL, J.
1939 Las Ocho Regiones Naturales del Perú. Lima: UNMSM

QUINTERO, R.
1964 Antropologiá de las Ciudades Latino Americanas. Caracas: Universidad Central de Venezuela.

REDFIELD, R.
1942 La sociedad folk. Revista Mexicana de sociologia 4(3).
1944 Yucatán. Una Cultura en Transición. México, D. F.: FCE.
1962 The primitive world view. *In* Human Nature and the Study of Society. The Papers of Robert Redfield, Margaret P. Redfield, ed. 2 Vols. Chicago: University of Chicago Press.
1963 El Mundo Primitivo y sus Transformaciones. México, D. F.: FCE.
REDFIELD, R., and A. VILLA ROJAS
1962 Chan Kom: A Maya Village. Chicago: University of Chicago Press.
REICHEL-DOLMATOFF, G.
1956 Casta, clase y aculturación en una población de Colombia. *In* Estudios Antropoló-

gicos Publicados en Homenaje al Doctor Manuel Gamio, M. Gamio, ed. México, D. F.: Direccion General de Publicaciones.
REICHEL-DOLMATOFF, G., and A. REICHEL-DOLMATOFF
1961 The People of Aritama. Chicago: University of Chicago Press.
RENS, J.
1961 El programa Andino. Revista Internacional del Trabajo 64:485-531.
1963 Evolución y perspectiva del programa andino. Revista Internacional del Trabajo 68:1-19.
REYEROS, R. A.
1937 Caquiavira. La Paz: Empresa Ed.
RIBEIRO, D.
1957 Culturas e linguas indigenas do brasil. Educação e Ciencias Sociais. Rio de Janeiro. 2:5-102.
RODRÍQUEZ SONDOVAL, L.
1949 Vida Económico Social del Indio Libre de la Sierra Equatoriana. Washington, D. C.: The Catholic University of America Press.
RUBIO OBRE, G.
1956 Punyara. Estudia de Antropología Social y Cultural de una Comunidad Indígena y Mestiza. Quito: Casa de la Cultura Ecuatoriana.
SÁENZ, M.
1933 Sobre el Indio Peruano y su Incorporación al Medio Nacional. México, D. F.: SEP.
SAHLENS, M. D.
1964 Culture and environment. *In* Heritage of Conquest, S. Tax, ed. Glencoe: The Free Press.
SANTIANA, A.
1948 Los Indios mojanda. Ethnografía y folklore. Revista de Filosofia y Letras, Quito. 238-74.
SAUER, C. O.
1956 The agency of man on the earth. *In* Man's Role in Changing the Face of the Earth, W. Thomas, ed. Chicago: University of Chicago Press.
1963 Land and Life. Berkeley: University of California Press.
SAUVY, A.
1963 Theorie General de la Population. 2 Vols. Paris: PUF.
SCHADEL, R. P., et al.
1959 Los Recursos Humanos del Departamento de Puno. Lima: Plan Regional para el Desarrollo del Sur del Perú.
SCHUMACHER, E. F.
1955 Populations in relation to the development of energy from coal. Proceedings of the World Population Conference, Rome, United Nations 5:149-64.
SCOTT, R. E.
1959 Mexican Government in Transition. Urbana: The University of Illinois Press.
SELLERS, R. W., et al.
1951 Filosofía del Futuro. México, D. F.: Compañía General de Ediciones.
SEOANNE, E.
1963 Surcos de Paz. Lima: Empresa Editoria.
SHANNON, L. W.
1957 Underdeveloped Areas: A Book of Readings and Research. New York: Harper.
SHAPERA, I.
1951 The Khoisan Peoples of South Africa: Bushmen and Hottentots. London: Routledge.
SHAPIRO, H. L., ed.
1960 Man, Culture and Society. New York: Oxford University Press.
SILVA HERZOG, J.
1963 El Petróleo de México. México, D. F.: Secretaria del Patrimonio Nacional.
SILVERT, K. H.
1962 La Sociedad Problema. Reacción y Revolución en America Latina. Buenos Aires: Paidós.
SIMPSON, G. C., and A. ROE, eds.
1958 Behavior and Evolution. New Haven: Yale University Press.
SIVERTS, H.
1960 Political organization in a Tzeltal community in Chiapas, México. Alpha Kappa Deltan 30:14-28.
SJOBERG, G.
1960 The Preindustrial City. New York: The Free Press.
SOMBART, W.
1964 Weltanschauung, ciencia y economia. *In* Historia y Elementos de la Sociología del Conocimiento. 2 Vols. I. L. Horowitz, ed. Buenos Aires: Eudeba.
SPENGLER, J. J.
1964 Economics and demography. *In* The Study of Population: An Inventory and Appraisal, P. M. Hauser and O. D. Duncan, eds. Chicago: The University of Chicago Press.
SPICER, E. H.
1963 Problemas Humanos en el Cambio Tecnológico. México, D. F.: Editorial Letras.
SPOEHR, A.
1956 Cultural differences in the interpretation of natural resources. *In* Man's Role in Changing the Face of the Earth, W. Thomas, ed. Chicago: The University of Chicago Press.
STARK, W.
1964 Los antecedentes de la sociología del conocimiento. *In* Historia y Elementos de la Sociología del Conocimiento. 2 Vols. I. L. Horowitz, ed. Buenos Aires: Eudeba.
STAVENHAGEN, R.
1962 Estratificación y estructura de clases. Ciencias Politicas y Sociales 27.
1964 Essai comparitif sur les classes sociales rurales et la stratification dans quelques pays sous-developpes. Ph.D. Dissertation. Paris: Ecole Pratique des Hautes Etudes. Mimeo.

STEININGER, G. R., and P. VAN DE VELDE
1935 Three Dollars a Year. Being the Story of a San Pablo Cuatro Venados, a Typical Zapotecan Indian Village, That Hangs on a Slope of the Sierra in South-Western Mexico. New York: Delphic Studios.
STERN, B. J.
1951 Algunos aspectos del materialismo histórico. *In* Filosofía del Futuro, R. W. Sellers, et al., eds. México, D.F.: Compañia General de Ediciones.
TAEUBER, I. B.
1965 Population growth in underdeveloped areas. *In* The Study of Population: An inventory and an Appraisal, P. M. Hauser and O. D. Duncan, eds. Chicago: The University of Chicago Press.
TAWNEY, R. H.
1959 La Religión en el Origen del Capitalismo. Buenos Aires: Dedalo.
TAX, S.
1937 The municipios of the midwestern highlands of Guatemala. American Anthropologist 39:423-44.
1941 World view and social relations in Guatemala. American Anthropologist 43:27-42.
1946 The education of underpriviledged peoples in dependent and independent territories. The Journal of Negro Education 15:336-45.
1956 Los Indios en la economía de Guatemala. *In* Integración Social de Guatemala, J. L. Arriola, ed. Guatemala: SISG.
1964a El Capitalismo del Centavo. Una Economía Indígena de Guatemala. 2 Vols. Guatemala: SISG.
1964b Horizons of Anthropology. Chicago: Aldine.
1965 Los Municipios del Altiplano Meso-Occidental de Guatemala. Cuadernos del SISG, Number 9. Guatemala: SISG.
TAX, S., ed.
1952 Heritage of Conquest. Glencoe: The Free Press.
TAYLOR, G., ed.
1957 Geography in the Twentieth Century. London: Methuen.
THOMAS, B.
1964 International migration. *In* The Study of Population: An Inventory and Appraisal, P. M. Hauser and O. D. Duncan, eds. Chicago: The University of Chicago Press.
THOMAS, W.
1956 Man's Role in Changing the Face of the Earth. Chicago: The University of Chicago Press.
THOMPSON, J. E.
1937 Mexico Before Cortez. An Account of the Daily Life, Religion, and Ritual of the Aztecs and Kindred People. New York: Scribners.
TOENNIES, F.
1963 Community and Society. New York: Harper.
TORRES ORDÓÑEZ, L.
1958 El último recurso. Accion Indigenista 64.
TUMIN, M. M.
1952 Caste in a Peasant Society. Princeton: Princeton University Press.
1956 Cultura, casta y clase en Guatemala: una nueva evaluación. *In* Integracíon Social de Guatemala, J. L. Arriolo, ed. Guatemala: SISG.
UNITED NATIONS
1963 Draft Report on Co-ordination of Rural Development Activities. Administrative Committee on Co-Ordination. 63-36082, United Nations, New York. Mimeo.
URQUIDI, A.
1962 Plan Decenal y Proyecto de Emmiendas de la ley de Reforma Agraria. Cochabamba: Imprenta Universitaria.
VAN DEN BERGHE, P.
1958 The dynamics of racial prejudice: an ideal type dichotomy. Social Forces 37: 138-41.
VAN HECKE, M. T.
1951 Migratory Labor in American Agriculture. Report of the President's Commission on Migratory Labor. Washington, D. C.: GPO.
VAN ZANTWIJK, R. A. M.
1965 Lastdragers en Hoofden. De Sociale en Cultrele Eigenheid van eeen Turaskische Gemeenschap. Amsterdam. Rototype.
VARALLANOS, J.
1962 El Cholo y el Perú. Introducción el Estudio Sociológico de un Hombre y un Pueblo Mestizos y su Destino Cultural. Buenos Aires: Imprenta Lopez.
VARGAS, I.
1946 Apuntes Críticos Sobre Asuntos Indigenistas. Cuzco: Tip. Americana.
VAZQUEZ, M. C.
1955 Cambios en la estratificación social en una hacienda andina del Perú. Revista del Museo Nacional, Lima 24:190-209.
1961 Hacienda, Peonaje y Servidumbre en los Andes Peruanos. Lima: Editorial Estudios Andinos.
1965 Changes in the social stratification of an Andean hacienda. *In* Contemporary Cultures and Societies of Latin America, D. B. Heath and R. N. Adams, eds. New York: Random House.
VAVILOV, I.
1963 Phytogeographic basis of plant breeding. *In* Land and Sea, C. Sauer, ed. Berkeley: University of California Press.
VEBLEN, T.
1963 Teoría de la Clase Ociosa. México, D. F.: FCE.
VELASCO, A.
1940 El Escuela Indigenal de Warisata. México, D. F.: Departmento de Asuntos Indígenas.
VILLA ROJAS, A.
1947 Kinship and Nagualism in a Tzeltal community, Southeastern Mexico. American Anthropologist 49:578-87.

1955 Los Mazatecos y el Problema Indígena de la Cuenca del Papaloapan. México City: INI.

WAGLEY, C., and M. HARRIS
1958 Minorities in the New World. Six Cases Studies. New York: Columbia University Press.
1965 A typology of Latin American subcultures. *In* Contemporary Cultures and Societies of Latin America, D. B. Heath and R. N. Adams, eds. New York: Random House.

WAGNER, PHILIP L., and M. W. MIKESELL, eds.
1965 Readings in Cultural Geography. Chicago: The University of Chicago Press.

WALLACE, A. F. C.
1961 Cultura y Personalidad. Buenos Aires: Paidós.
1963 Culture and Personality. New York: Random House.

WASHBURN, S. L., ed.
1961 Social Life of Early Man. Viking Fund Publications in Anthropology, No. 31. New York: Wenner Gren.

WATSON, J. W.
1957 The Sociological aspects of geography. *In* Geography in the Twentieth Century, G. Taylor, ed. London: Methuen.

WARNER, W. L.
1960 Social Class in America. New York: Harper.

WEBER, M.
1960 Los tipos de dominación. *In* Sociologia del Poder, P. Heintz, ed. Santiago: Andrés Bello.

WEIDENREICH, F.
1946 Apes, Giants and Man. Chicago: The University of Chicago Press.

WEITLANER, R. J., and C. HOOGSHAGEN
1960 Grados de edad en Oaxaca. Revista Mexicana de Estudios Antropológicos 16:183-209.

WEST, R. C.
1948 Cultural geography of the modern Tarascan area. Smithsonian Institute of Social Anthropology. Publication 7, Washington, D.C.

WHITE, L. A.
1964 La Ciencia de la Cultura. Un Estudio Sobre el Hombre y la Civilización. Buenos Aires: Paidós.

WHITEFORD, A. H.
1963 Popayán y Querétaro. Bogotá: Universidad Nacional de Colombia.

WIRTH, L.
1945 The problem of minority groups. *In* The Science of Man in the World Crisis, R. Linton, ed. New York: Columbia University Press.

WISDOM, C.
1961 Los Chortis de Guatemala. Guatemala: SISB.

WOLF, R. C.
1951 Closed corporate peasant communities in Mesoamerica and central Java. SWJA 13:1-18.
1955 Types of Latin American peasantry: a preliminary discussion. American Anthropologist 57:452-71.
1956 Aspects of group relations in a complex society: Mexico. American Anthropologist 58: 1065-78.
1959 Sons of the Shaking Earth. Chicago: The University of Chicago Press.
1966 Peasants. Englewood Cliffs: Prentice-Hall.

WRONG, D. H.
1961 La Población. Buenos Aires: Paidós.

INDEX